Everyday Equalities

Everyday Equalities

Making Multicultures in Settler Colonial Cities

Ruth Fincher, Kurt Iveson,
Helga Leitner, and Valerie Preston

University of Minnesota Press
Minneapolis
London

The University of Minnesota Press gratefully acknowledges the financial assistance provided for the publication of this book by the Faculty of Liberal Arts and Professional Studies, York University, Toronto.

Portions of chapter 6 were previously published in Helga Leitner and Samuel Nowak, "Making Multi-racial Counter-publics: Toward Egalitarian Spaces in Urban Politics," in *The Routledge Handbook on Spaces of Urban Politics*, ed. A. Jonas, B. Miller, K. Ward, and D. Wilson, 451–64 (London: Routledge, 2018); and Kristin M. Sziarto and Helga Leitner, "Immigrants Riding for Justice: Space-time and Emotions in the Construction of a Counterpublic," *Political Geography* 29, no. 7 (2010): 381–91.

Copyright 2019 by the Regents of the University of Minnesota

All rights reserved. No part of this publication may be reproduced, stored in a retrieval system, or transmitted, in any form or by any means, electronic, mechanical, photocopying, recording, or otherwise, without the prior written permission of the publisher.

Published by the University of Minnesota Press
111 Third Avenue South, Suite 290
Minneapolis, MN 55401-2520
http://www.upress.umn.edu

Printed in the United States of America on acid-free paper

The University of Minnesota is an equal-opportunity educator and employer.

Library of Congress Cataloging-in-Publication Data
Names: Fincher, Ruth, author. | Iveson, Kurt, author. | Leitner, Helga, author. | Preston, Valerie, author.
Title: Everyday equalities : making multicultures in settler colonial cities / Ruth Fincher, Kurt Iveson, Helga Leitner, and Valerie Preston.
Description: Minneapolis : University of Minnesota Press, [2019] | Includes bibliographical references and index.
Identifiers: LCCN 2018058399| ISBN 978-0-8166-9463-1 (hc) | ISBN 978-0-8166-9464-8 (pb)
Subjects: LCSH: Multiculturalism—Case studies. | City planning—Case studies. | Ethnicity—Case studies. | Equality—Case studies. | Sociology, Urban—Case studies.
Classification: LCC HM1271 .F547 2019 | DDC 305.8—dc23
LC record available at https://lccn.loc.gov/2018058399

UMP BmB

Contents

Acknowledgments	vii
Introduction. Everyday Urban Multicultures: Encountering Difference, Enacting Equality	1
1 Encounters with Difference in the Urban Everyday: A Relational Approach	19
2 The Political Potential of Encounters: Being Together in Difference as Equals	33
3 Making a Home in Melbourne	53
4 Working for a Living in Toronto	93
5 Moving around the City in Sydney	133
6 Making Publics in Los Angeles	171
Conclusion: Toward a Praxis of Everyday Equalities	203
Notes	223
Bibliography	229
Index	251

Acknowledgments

THIS BOOK IS THE PRODUCT of half a decade of collaborative thinking and writing. It could not have been written without the assistance and support, both intellectual and practical, of many people: our past and present students (Sam Nowak, Kristin Sziarto, Chris Strunk, Iris Levin, Mariastella Pulvirenti, Kathryn Dennler, Silvia D'Addario, Ekaterina Morihovitis), colleagues (Eric Sheppard, Michael Webber, Kate Shaw, Michele Lobo, Steve Tufts, Brian Ray, Marshia Akbar, Mark Davidson), research collaborators (the Riders on the Immigrant Workers Freedom Ride, directors and staff of the worker centers, leaders and organizers in the Sydney Alliance), and last but not least, our partners (Nancy, Michael, Joe, and Eric). We wish to extend our deep gratitude to all of them.

The original book proposal was written when three of us (Helga Leitner, Valerie Preston, Ruth Fincher) were privileged to have a residency at the Rockefeller Center in Bellagio in late 2012. In a gorgeous and supportive setting, there was time for long discussions and periods of reading and contemplation, punctuated by calls to Australia to our (envious) fourth author, Kurt Iveson. Thus our thanks also go to the Rockefeller Foundation and the staff at the Bellagio Center for their generous gift of the intellectual space to develop our initial thinking. Multimedia artist and University of California, Berkeley, professor Allan deSouza was also a resident at the Bellagio Center, inviting us to join his explorations of migration, colonialism, and difference in visual art, performance, and writing. We are very grateful for permission to use a detail from his image *Borough Boogie Woogie* on the cover of this book (see talwargallery.com/allanalia-pr/).

While modern communications technologies were helpful in connecting us across the ocean as we embarked on the writing process, we soon recognized they are no substitute for face-to-face

{ vii }

viii   *Acknowledgments*

meetings. Thus we acknowledge with gratitude support for this purpose from the geography departments and universities where we work. The authors and publisher also acknowledge the support of the Faculty of Liberal Arts and Professional Studies, York University, Toronto.

We thank Jason Weidemann, our editor at the University of Minnesota Press, for his patience and unwavering encouragement, as well as the reviewers and readers of the book manuscript who provided useful suggestions on our work. We thank, as well, Haydie Gooder for her fine editing and indexing.

The book emerged from our common interest in highlighting the positive potential of encounters with difference in urban multicultures, and in identifying what it might take to realize this potential. To that end we make a special acknowledgment of urban residents who have worked toward realizing this potential by being together in difference as equals.

Los Angeles, Melbourne, Sydney, and Toronto
April 2019

{ Introduction }

Everyday Urban Multicultures

Encountering Difference, Enacting Equality

IN HIS WIDE-RANGING AND ENERGETIC characterizations of contemporary European societies, Paul Gilroy (2004, 2005) diagnoses a postimperial melancholia that is associated with racist violence and an inability to welcome immigrants from former colonies. Yet he also finds signs of a hopeful, lived culture in the everyday lives of these socially diverse societies that he terms *multiculture*. For Gilroy (2004, 158), multiculture is a form of culture, emerging in fits and starts, particularly in Europe's "congested metropolitan spaces." It is characterized by (largely) convivial and unpredictable social interactions between newcomers and the long-term residents of places and societies. It is also evolving rapidly in response to growing concerns about racialized religious difference engendered by contemporary fears regarding terrorism and its presumed threat to personal security (Triandafyllidou et al. 2012).

Gilroy's identification of progressive multiculture amidst the inequality and intolerance of imperial cities like London offers a starting point for our book. His reflections on London's multiculture constitute a response to one of the defining questions of urban life: if city life is by definition a "being together of strangers" (Young 1990), what forms of "being together" should we encourage and strive for in cities of diversity? In his work, Stuart Hall termed this the "multicultural question," which he distinguished from multiculturalism as a governance framework:

> I was never interested in what was called multiculturalism, which is really a government policy towards stimulating people to get on with one another. . . . I was interested in

{ 1 }

Introduction

> what I call the multicultural question. . . . This question is how do people with a different history, a different language, a different culture, different customs, different habits, different ways of holding the body, how do people who are born into a specific culture survive when they are obliged to share space with other cultures? (Hall 2009, 44)

Like Gilroy and Hall and others, we have set out to find evidence of progressive political alternatives to racialized exclusion and inequality emerging within the everyday life of the cities, what we term "everyday equalities." We use the idea of "multicultures" (plural) to signal our view that the "being together of strangers" will take diverse forms across different time-spaces.

Our interest in the fortunes and fate of urban multicultures is inspired by our observations and involvements in the cities where we live and work—a group of settler colonial cities where matters of diversity and difference are an inescapable feature of public life and politics. Established through concerted efforts to dispossess and eliminate indigenous societies, these cities have been destinations for waves of immigrants from different parts of the globe ever since; some recruited to recreate the illusory racial and ethnic homogeneity of imperial societies, others welcomed mainly for their economic contributions, and still others not welcomed at all. As sites of enduring and ever-changing social difference pivoting on relations of race, we contend that settler colonial cities offer not only examples of the challenges posed by and conflict associated with social difference, but also provide new insights into the progressive possibilities of encounters with difference in contemporary multicultures, extending Gilroy's analysis beyond imperial metropoles. To whet the reader's appetite, we offer brief vignettes from the four cities that provide snapshots of mundane, everyday encounters with difference, and of the egalitarian forms of being together in difference that are performed in those encounters.

In Melbourne, university students from different Asian countries and regions, temporary immigrants to Australia, live in large numbers in tiny apartments in the city center, where rents are high. They make their homes here for a few years. Some live in crowded conditions. Some find life in a tiny apartment isolating, for most of the buildings offer no common spaces in which to socialize and make friends. Some of these students express regret at not being able to make friends with young people from Melbourne. Yet many find spaces for socializing in the buildings around them in the central city—most often in the food halls of major downtown shopping malls. There they meet young people from many different countries in Asia, eat together, chat and study. They engage with one another as equals, forming networks together that enable them to escape restrictive private living spaces, the difficulties they may encounter with learning English, and the exclusionary everyday racism they can experience in the university.

In Toronto, the pace of work is intensifying and opportunities for workers in service industries to socialize casually on the job are disappearing. In this neoliberal context, one union tries to combat racialized inequalities in Toronto's large hotels, where minority workers do most of the dirty, demeaning, and dangerous jobs such as housekeeping, dishwashing, and cooking, by organizing and supporting a choir composed of union members (Tufts 2006). Performing at union functions and public events across the urban region, the choir has provided opportunities for encounters among hotel workers that they describe as caring, sympathetic, and uniformly helpful. Since establishing the choir, the union has supplemented its traditional strategies of organizing hotels—most recently the Trump International Hotel and Tower (Fuatai 2016; Kopun 2015)—and of using strikes to secure wage increases and scheduling improvements (Balch 2010) with celebrity endorsements of hotel workers' economic and social contributions (Sidhu 2010) and a successful campaign for a training center that helps new hires qualify for permanent jobs with predictable hours and benefits (Mojtehedzadeh 2015). By breaking down the isolation among hotel workers with little time to socialize on the job, the choir not only gave voice to its participants but helped the union change public discourses about the value of hotel workers, an essential prerequisite for achieving improvements in pay and working conditions.

In Sydney, on the morning of December 15, 2014, a lone gunman took eighteen people hostage at a café in the central business district. The siege lasted sixteen hours, and two of the hostages

4   *Introduction*

and the gunman were killed before it came to an end. During the early hours of the siege, there was widespread speculation about the identity and motives of the gunman, and about whether or not the hostage situation was part of any coordinated attack on Sydney. Early in the siege, the gunman had forced hostages to hold up a black flag with Arabic writing in the window of the café. This was initially reported to be the ISIS flag—incorrectly, it turned out. But given the self-declared religious and political affiliations of the gunman, it was almost inevitable that the siege would be reported on as a realization of the perceived threat of Islamist terror directed against "the West." On the afternoon of the hostage-taking, while the situation remained unresolved and tense, a woman over 900 km away in Brisbane updated her Facebook page with the following two posts:

> . . . and the (presumably) Muslim woman sitting next to me on the train silently removes her hijab.
> . . . I ran after her at the train station. I said "put it back on. I'll walk with u." She started to cry and hugged me for about a minute—then walked off alone.[1]

Her posts were made public by a journalist who was a member of her social network. Inspired by this encounter, a Twitter user in Sydney tweeted the following messages:

> If you reg take the #373 bus b/w Coogee/MartinPl, wear religious attire, & don't feel safe alone: I'll ride with you. @ me for schedule.[2]
> Maybe start a hashtag? What's in #illridewithyou?[3]

Thousands of similar offers by other Twitter users followed, specifying the bus and trains when they would be available to ride with anyone worried about being abused or attacked for wearing clothing that marked them as Muslim (or for any other reason, for that matter). Within forty-eight hours, #illridewithyou had been used in over 450,000 Twitter posts,[4] and had grabbed headlines in local and international mainstream media reporting of the Sydney hostage situation. While we'll never know how many offers to ride together were taken, the Twitter intervention kicked off a debate about whether egalitarian forms of sociality might be able to combat the escalation of racist abuse that frequently accompanies such events.

In Los Angeles (LA), spaces of multiracial activism are central to working beyond its reputation for fraught ethnic, racial, class, and geographic divisions and social inequalities, and its long history of periodically violent conflict between different cultures and races (from the 1965 Watts Riots to those following the 1992 Rodney King beating). Experiences of state violence, discrimination, and deprivation by communities of color have triggered unrest, but also have spawned visionary community organizations, an alternative press, cross-cultural and cross-racial organizing, and new forms of multiracial politics. Female directors of LA worker centers, who coordinated 2015's successful $15 minimum wage and Against Wage Theft campaigns, have been experimenting and enacting inclusive and empowering modes of governance within the city's network of worker centers. They promote and emphasize worker centers as spaces of care, also redesigning the material space of worker centers by bringing domestic elements such as a kitchen into their public space. Through such varied initiatives, worker centers are becoming spaces of learning and negotiating across difference. By addressing prejudice, stereotypes, racism, sexism, and religious intolerance head on and through conversations underwritten by rules of conduct designed to foster coexistence, they become a space of refuge from which public campaigns against inequality in Los Angeles can be launched.

Overarching inequalities are all too visible in the contexts in which each of these encounters takes place. Yet forms of *everyday equality* nonetheless emerge through them, in the togetherness that is performed by participants as they interact across their differences, undertaking certain tasks. On streets and train carriages in suburban Sydney, the geopolitics of military intervention in the Middle East and the micropolitics of embodied copresence are drawn into relation. Yet public transport riders form supportive and hopeful groups through the use of social media, premised on the idea that public transport should be safe for everybody and anybody. The capacity of hotel workers in Toronto to sing together is influenced by the complex politics of their union's struggles with the city and their hotel employers. Yet the singers find great support and companionship in their choir, which becomes a foundation for asserting further political demands. Immigrant students seeking housing in inner Melbourne find themselves living (literally) in the middle of the profitable high-rise districts built recently by developers for investors, and its difficult regulatory aftermath. Yet they congregate in collective spaces of the central city that are available to them, forming empowering networks as they socialize. Protesters against the demonization of the immigrant labor force in Los Angeles sometimes fall foul of police when demonstrating. Yet the efforts of their grassroots organizations have created a supportive community, whose actions are expanding their capacity to organize demonstrations and protests and enhancing their voice in the metropolitan area. In focusing on such instances of being together in difference as equals, then, our aim is not to gloss over the racisms and structural inequalities that stubbornly persist. Rather, our aim is to honor the hard political labor that produces and sustains new forms of being together, on the basis that they have much to teach us about the meaning and practice of equality in our times and places.

This project of seeking and understanding political alternatives to racialized hierarchies and inequality that might emerge from everyday urban encounters with difference has taken on even greater urgency in recent times. Nationalist politicians and social movements attacking immigrants and seeking tighter and more punitive migration and border controls are on the rise across the globe. They are spurred on by media representations that frequently focus on the multicultural city as a site of disorder and violence, and attribute such outcomes to the presence of migrants (and often their descendants), whose racial and cultural differences are said to be incompatible with local norms and laws.

In this book, we argue that forms of "being together" with difference in any given urban context should not be premised on the assimilation, toleration, or even celebration of "difference" or "diversity." Neither the eternal privileging of the norms and values of hosts over those of migrants, nor the celebrations of migrant cultures that embrace their "contributions" to host societies while

Introduction 7

leaving structural inequalities in place, will do. Rather, as scholars concerned with urban social justice, we approach the question of urban life and the "being together" of diverse urban inhabitants from an *egalitarian* standpoint. Taking an egalitarian view does not mean imposing a fixed, timeless, philosophically derived definition of equality on to empirical reality and assessing whether the real world "measures up." Rather, it means embracing the priority of equality while seeking to understand its manifestations across time and space as it is enacted in particular historical and geographic circumstances. So we ask: what does equality look like in circumstances where inequality is fundamentally (if not exclusively) a product of processes of racialization and racism against immigrants and their descendants?

Drawing on both theoretical reflection and urban ethnographic research, we offer the formulation "being together in difference as equals" as a normative frame for reimagining the meaning and pursuit of equality in today's urban multicultures—a frame that highlights those circumstances in which people who are strangers to one another establish forms of being together from a starting point of their equality with one another without erasing their differences. We observe the emergence of forms of being together in difference as equals across the different spheres and spaces of contemporary urban everyday life, and seek to identify and analyze the circumstances in which these forms have emerged.

As we will argue across the chapters that follow, this "being together in difference as equals" is neither a spontaneous occurrence in urban life, nor is it necessarily a peaceful situation that is premised on the avoidance of conflict and contention. Rather, it takes shape through emplaced assertions and enactments of equality that confront the status quo and seek to supplant it with new ways of being together in difference, through the hard work and care of people who draw on a range of organizational resources and structures to sustain their efforts. Of course, such efforts are not guaranteed to succeed, nor are any successes guaranteed to be permanent or to be replicated beyond their particular context. But herein lies precisely the analytical and political intent of our book: to contribute to the durability and extension of egalitarian political formations that are emerging in the urban multicultures that we

8   *Introduction*

study by understanding their emergence and characteristics, and by highlighting their significance and potential resonance in other urban contexts.

Encounter as Ontology, Epistemology, and Methodology

A key claim of the book, developed in different ways across its length, is that answers to the question of how people live together in contemporary cities of diversity can be found through close examination of *encounters with difference* that take place in the course of everyday urban life. We use the concept of encounter as a centerpiece for understanding and studying urban multicultures, but also everyday urbanism more generally. Everyday encounters across difference are central to the formation and perpetuation of urban multicultures. It is through encounters that urban dwellers experience, negotiate, and transform difference. In talking about encounters with *difference* we do not simply mean that everyone is dissimilar in terms of gender, age, class background, sexuality, ethnicity, religion, and other axes of social positionality. Rather, difference refers to social variations that are articulated, politicized, regulated, and judged. Evaluated as much by institutions as by individuals, social difference is the foundation of social hierarchy. Urban life is lived through an influential web of these ways of differentiating us that are termed difference. A focus on encounters with difference in the mundane everyday illuminates both the challenges of living together with difference as equals and the potential of living together with difference and enacting equalities. Even in cities of great inequality, we argue that such everyday encounters can catalyze new ways of living in difference that both redefine and advance the cause of equality.

While we elaborate on our approach to encounters with difference and their political potential in subsequent chapters, some introduction to our active use of the concept is necessary as a prelude to describing the book and its structure. Our use of the concept of encounter goes beyond the self-evident point that, in urban multicultures, people interact with individuals from different cultural backgrounds, sometimes in fleeting ways (such as in shops and on public transport) and sometimes repeatedly (as in sports clubs and

Introduction

community groups, at work, and in residential neighborhoods). Instead we propose encounters with difference as an ontology, epistemology, and methodology in theorizing everyday urbanism.

First, *we consider encounters with difference as a centerpiece of urban ontology.* The mix of city life, with its ceaseless social interactions, is central to contemporary urban studies. By highlighting the "throwntogetherness" of urban places, Doreen Massey (2005, 149–62) captured the sense in which interactions with difference characterize daily life in cities around the world. The concept of encounter with difference makes a statement about the formation of everyday urbanism. In taking this view of the centrality of encounter to the lived world of the urban everyday, we are choosing an ontological view that urban life is material, embodied, and performed; it is activity that occurs in interactions and only because of them. We thus consider everyday urban life as an ongoing process of emergent formation, rather than as predetermined. In doing so, we locate encounters with difference within all the spheres of everyday life in a city, rather than primarily in certain kinds of bounded settings like public spaces. Urban mix and throwntogetherness is not experienced only in squares and streets. Urban inhabitants encounter others as they go about their everyday lives, which involve many and various activities and priorities. Encounters with difference take place in the process of activities like making a home, working in paid employment, riding a train, and participating in urban activism (each of which we discuss in detail in this book). We can expect the kinds of encounters, and their associated politics and possibilities, to vary across different spheres of urban everyday life. As such, each warrants its own investigation.

Second, *we deploy the concept of encounters with difference in this book as an epistemology;* our way of building knowledge about everyday urbanism. We use our expectation of the presence of encounters with difference in urban life as a lever, a hypothesized occurrence, to theorize and document the kinds of social relations that occur in the process of making a home, being at work, participating in publics, and getting around—whether these relations are directly mediated by institutions, are the product of continued habits, or are conscious shifts in direction by those interacting. We look for encounters with difference that make up the urban world in their variety, and look also for their unexpected outcomes and political potential. In this book we take the following questions about encounters with difference as our epistemological entry point to the study of everyday urbanism and its multicultures. The first set of questions relates to urban life and its everyday dimension. How do encounters with difference vary across different spheres of daily activity? A second set of questions concerns the temporality of encounters. What kinds of being together emerge from encounters that are more fleeting, like those on public transport, in contrast with other encounters that are sustained and repeated, like those associated with making a home or earning a living? How do past encounters impinge on the present? A third set of questions asks about the different spatialities that shape encounters with difference: what are the relevant and different spaces within the city, the wider geographical and historical contexts in which encounters are embedded, and the local and extralocal connectivities among individuals and places? This last question is especially important. The encounters that we examine in the cities of our concern are quite particular to their contexts, and yet they have a broader resonance because their particularity articulates with and is mediated by broader political-economic and settler colonial structures and forms of oppression.

It follows that although the time-spaces from which we write in this book have certain specificities, the events and practices we narrate could be told from many more cities. The broader urban geography of our project, the way we approach the spatiality and temporality inherent in different forms of encounter that foster being together as equals across difference, is influenced by ongoing lively debate about the limitations of such research. This debate cautions against universalizing the experiences of a narrow range of cities, in particular cities of the Global North, to constitute "the urban" (Jacobs 2012; Robinson 2006, 2013; Roy 2009; Sheppard et al. 2013). Postcolonial urban scholars in particular have questioned the assumption that urban theories and concepts developed in Europe and North America apply to cities of the postcolony. These debates have important implications for our claims in this book about the geographies and politics of urban multicultures.

Introduction

Among other things, this work encourages us to think carefully about the particular places in and from which we write—a selection of cities in the so-called Global North, as we have noted, located in nations with histories of imperialism and settler colonialism. We thus agree with the argument that knowledge production is necessarily situated, and that all knowledge is initially local, shaped by the context in which it is produced (Leitner and Sheppard 2016). However, certain local knowledges gain hegemony and stake claim to universal status. It is not our intention to make such claims about the knowledge produced here. While we write from and through Northern cities and centers, we do not claim that the knowledges we produce have universal applicability. Rather, our goal is to uncover both the distinct forms that encounters with difference in these cities take and the performativity of everyday equality that they can engender, even in this era of neoliberalism. We see our findings as serving as a provocation for comparison with other sites and eras that triggers the identification of generalizable practices that shape the world we seek to apprehend.

Third, *we approach encounters with difference as methodology.* Informed by the ontology and epistemology outlined above, we deploy a historically grounded, multisited, collaborative global ethnography to juxtapose urban encounters with difference across different contexts. Indeed our collaboration is itself a research practice of encounter. We understand ethnography as "an eclectic methodological choice which privileges an engaged, contextually rich and nuanced type of qualitative social research, in which fine grained daily interactions constitute the lifeblood of the data produced" (Falzon 2016, 1). Traditionally, ethnography has been associated with the lone researcher immersed in a single research site, with the aim of gaining a deep understanding of a particular locality and community. In contrast, the multisited, collaborative global ethnography deployed in this book involves a spatially dispersed field with multiple sites, in which the urban everyday is extended and connected in complex ways to extralocal processes and larger scales (Burawoy et al. 2000; Falzon 2009, 2), and in which the research is being conducted by a team of researchers themselves practicing research as encounter. Indeed collaborative research, including ethnographic research, has been on the rise since the late twentieth century, offering a number of advantages over the single researcher in terms of the knowledge produced, such as the sharing of experiences and interpretations between the researchers that contribute to a more holistic understanding of the research topic, as well as the diverse skills and energies that researchers bring to the topic (Jarzabkowski et al. 2014). Collaborative research and writing, however, also presents its challenges, as we have experienced. It requires often lengthy negotiations across our differences in terms of interpretation and writing (and time zones!) and necessitates trust and flexibility and an openness to learning from each other.

The Structure of the Book

The approach to encounters with difference in urban everyday life as ontology, epistemology, and methodology is reflected in the structure of the chapters that follow. In chapters 1 and 2 we further develop the ontological claim about the centrality of encounters with difference to urban life, and make a case for the study of encounter as a means to produce knowledge about the politics of equality in contemporary urban multicultures. In chapter 1 we situate our work within the broader literature of urban studies that theorizes forms and outcomes of encounter. We then offer a relational understanding of urban encounters which emphasizes that encounters with difference, though of-the-moment, occur within a temporal and spatial context in which their participants are embedded in a range of institutional settings and political rationalities. Conceptualizing how these institutional settings and political rationalities are brought to bear in encounters with difference in the cities of our concern, and the politics associated with this, will be a major concern of our analysis. Also important will be a recognition of the performative and contingent nature of the urban encounters emerging in these settings.

In chapter 2, we take up the question of the political potential of encounters, examining how the study of encounters with difference in the city might be informed by, and informative of, a politics of equality that is fit for our times and spaces. Contending that a normative concern with equality is crucial for the development of

Introduction   13

new and more just ways of living in difference, we offer the concept of *being together in difference as equals* as a frame for reimagining the project of equality in today's urban multicultures. This draws on a concept of equality that is given meaning and political significance only through its enactment in particular historical and geographic circumstances, with equality not so much a "goal" to be attained (as in "we want to be equal") as an assumption to be verified through forms of action by people identifying and acting together as equals in their everyday urban lives. Thus, building on the argument developed in chapter 1, our aim in chapter 2 is to push thinking about urban encounters beyond their appearance as part of some apparently disorderly throwntogetherness. Rather, we envisage urban encounters with difference as instances in which we might identify, examine, and encourage the emergence of relations of everyday equality that address the particular forms of racialized inequality that characterize the urban multicultures we consider. We build on three overarching principles: First, equality is enacted or performed, expressed materially and bodily. It is not manifest simply in changing attitudes toward others. Second, a focus on being together in difference as equals involves considering how people develop and enact communal commitments rather than paying attention to individualized subjects acting in their own self-interest. Third, enactments of equality respond to, and are shaped by, their particular context. Concepts of equality evolve in response to the emplaced social orders in and against which they are enacted. As such, to understand people being together in difference as equals requires attention not only to everyday urbanism, but also a focused appreciation of the broader geographical and historical context and processes.

In chapters 3 through 6 we offer a series of theorized ethnographical accounts of encounters with difference and enactments of equality across four different spheres of everyday urban life— making a home, making a living, getting around, and making publics—in the four settler colonial cities of Melbourne, Toronto, Sydney, and Los Angeles. While each of these chapters considers quite distinct forms of encounter in different urban contexts, each of the chapters operates with a similar structure. First, since urban multicultures vary across time and space, each of the cities in consideration is positioned within their specific historical and geographical contexts. The primary cities in which the empirical studies of urban multicultures in this book are situated occupy particular time-space positions that affect everyday urban life and its political possibilities. Located in countries of settler colonialism, with long histories of colonization, dispossession of indigenous peoples, waves of diverse settlers, and liberal democracy, these cities are known for their ethnic, racialized, and religious diversity, intermittent violence, and their often problematic attempts to manage it. Inhabitants frequently encounter difference in these urban multicultures as a part of their everyday routines and their efforts to remake the urban spaces in which they live (Valentine 2008). But as we will see, they each have their own particularities that shape (if not determine) the politics and possibilities of encounters in their everyday lives.

Each of these chapters then considers the specifics of the encounters involved in its chosen sphere of everyday life in some detail. Making a home in Melbourne is examined in chapter 3 through the encounters across difference of migrants who have arrived in the city in the last five decades, some more recently than others. We look at encounters within the dwelling, and encounters outside the dwelling in the activities and places surrounding the dwelling. Two things are clear. First, encounters with difference in making a home are more often than not long-term, repeated, and with people who become familiar, rather than being fleeting and with people who remain strangers. Second, encounters in making a home are framed influentially by the morphology of the housing available and by institutional priorities favoring home-ownership and investment. We draw on rich case studies from the literature about making a home in Melbourne. These demonstrate the mutual caring of migrant neighbors in the diverse suburb of Dandenong in contrast to the lives of physical and social separation and perceived inequality lived by public and private tenants in a refashioned public housing estate in inner-city Carlton. They show how long-term intergenerational encounters within households respond to difference within families, and how migrant dwellers create in the form of their housing what might be considered "equality" statements, establishing their presence in the city as their dwellings sit in streetscapes alongside the dwellings of others. The enduring encounters involved in making a home insert migrants into the everyday activities of the city, where interactions with difference do not erase that difference but render it familiar and a basis for emergent forms of solidarity and equality.

Chapter 4 investigates the politics and political potential of encounters with difference that take place at work locations. Although workers from diverse backgrounds are compelled to interact at work, in Toronto, Canada, stringent regulations and repeated interactions often fail to promote equitable encounters. Using examples of room attendants in large hotels, grocery store cashiers, and live-in caregivers, our analysis demonstrates how the spatiality and temporality of work compels specific types of interactions among adults from diverse backgrounds. The increasing pace of work and its physical arrangement often discourages the sociable interactions among workers and between workers and their managers that might alter contemporary social hierarchies. We find that nonstate actors concerned with employment issues, especially unions and community associations, have important roles to play in fostering encounters with emancipatory potential. They can provide opportunities for workers to acknowledge and negotiate their cultural differences as equals through a shared commitment to improving working conditions.

In chapter 5 we examine Sydney's public transport system as both a site and an enabling infrastructure of encounters with difference. A focus on public transport gives us another distinct window onto the politics of equality in urban multicultures. Perhaps in contrast with making a home or making a living, the encounters associated with public transportation are frequently fleeting and unfocused. This generates particular challenges for the enactment of equality in difference. The chapter examines three examples of efforts to address the accessibility of public transport in that city, each of which involve different kinds of actors and actions engaging in efforts to influence the nature of "being together" on public transport. First, it considers communications campaigns by transport providers seeking to specify and eliminate various forms of "bad behavior" on public transport, and considers the ways in which these efforts engage (or not) with problems of racist discomfort, abuse, and violence on the network. Second, it examines the emerging trend of passengers themselves using mobile and social media to document and discuss instances of racism on the network. Finally, it looks at a community organizing campaign to make public transport more affordable to people seeking asylum. Across these examples, we see that enacting a form of being together in difference *as equals* on public transport is not simply a matter of passively sharing a train or a bus with strange others. Rather, it involves a kind of political labor that makes public transport a matter of public concern, in order to be able to politicize and contest its entrenched inequalities.

Written from Los Angeles, chapter 6 examines the making of multiracial publics through spaces and sites of activism. It provides insights into challenges and possibilities of encounters and negotiations across social difference, and into enacting equality in both the routine everyday and through organized collective action. We examine two such sites: the Immigrant Workers Freedom Ride of 2003, originally envisioned in Los Angeles before spreading rapidly to other U.S. cities, and Los Angeles worker centers that have emerged during the past twenty-five years and catalyzed multiracial campaigns, such as the recent raise-the-minimum-wage campaign. Both sites exemplify how the construction of egalitarian political spaces requires inclusive modes of governance, spaces of care, spaces of learning to negotiate across difference, and spaces of publicity. We examine the role of worker centers' nonwhite female leadership in constructing and enacting new forms of order that enable being together in difference as equals. We also demonstrate that enacting multiple spatialities is crucial to facilitating and mediating the construction of multiracial publics: including macro- and microgeographic contexts, the construction and configuration of quasi-sovereign material spaces in buses and worker centers, and extralocal connectivities and mobilities.

The final chapter of the book offers a set of concluding reflections that seeks to build upon the different insights about encounters with difference that emerge from the substantive chapters' focus on different spheres of everyday urbanism in four different cities. What have we learned about the prospects and practices of being together in difference as equals through our ethnographic

Introduction

investigations, and what applicability might these lessons have for multicultures in other urban contexts? Reflecting on the findings of our case studies, we offer six propositions for a praxis of everyday equality to realize a being together in difference as equals in urban multicultures. It requires:

Resisting and struggling against dominant modes of conduct through new practices that transgress those normalized ways of doing things;

Hard work, determination, learning, and ethical and political commitment on the part of participants;

New organizational infrastructures to promote and support practices that enact equality from the bottom up;

The creation and observance of codes of conduct, especially prescriptions about respect and openness toward difference;

Political horizons with distinct temporalities, requiring time and endurance;

The making of distinct spatialities and infrastructures.

We offer these as propositions, not as iron-clad laws, to provoke comparisons and responses about what is going on in many other cities—the places in which you may live and from which you may write.

{ 1 }

Encounters with Difference in the Urban Everyday

A Relational Approach

THIS IS THE FIRST OF TWO chapters in which we elaborate in more detail the conceptual and political foundations of our book. Having established in the introduction that we are using the idea of encounter as a pivotal dimension around which to build knowledge about city life and its potential for enactments of equality in difference, or everyday equalities, in this chapter we develop a theorization of urban encounters themselves that informs the empirical studies to follow. Over the course of this chapter, we set out a *relational* theorization of encounters—insisting that while encounters are observable moments of interaction and "being together in difference" that take place across distinct spheres of urban everyday life, such moments are profoundly shaped by their geographical, historical, and political contexts. We develop this relational theorization of encounters in three steps. First, we situate encounters with difference in both the spaces and times of the urban everyday. Second, we emphasize the role of the wider geographical and historical context—the broader societal and cultural structures as well as the nature of their specific contexts in shaping encounters with difference. Here, we focus attention on the governing institutions, especially the state and dominant political rationalities at multiple geographic scales, an aspect that is given little attention in the encounter literature. Finally, we emphasize that encounters nonetheless have a performative and contingent nature. This is vital to the *political potential* of encounters with difference to disrupt existing forms of racialized inequality—a matter that we will address in chapter 2.

{ 19 }

The Space-Time of Encounters with Difference in the Urban Everyday

From early accounts of the city as a "way of life" in urban sociology (Simmel 1903; Wirth 1938) to ethnographic accounts of "everyday life" in urban environments (Goffman 1961) and efforts to grapple with ideals of city life (Jacobs 1961), urban studies has seen a recent revival of interest in conceptualizing urban encounters (Wilson 2017). This revived interest has in large part been driven by researchers who, like us, are concerned with racial and other social hierarchies in cities. Several have turned their attention to encounters with difference, seeking to understand whether or not these might contribute to breaking down racialized oppression and hierarchies (e.g. Amin 2012; Fincher and Iveson 2008; Matjeskova and Leitner 2011; Sandercock 2003; Valentine 2008; Wilson and Darling 2016; Wise 2009; Young 1990). Demonstrating the richness and complexity of these ordinary urban encounters and making them visible allows us to see how they both "make difference" and "make a difference" (Wilson 2017). This work—some of which we have conducted ourselves, some of which we have been inspired by, and some of which we are reacting to—shapes the approach to encounter that we take in this book.

In recent writing, there has been a growing emphasis on the need for a *multisited* approach to encounters with difference in urban everyday life. Much early writing about encounters and everyday urban life focused on the "public spaces" of cities as a key site for the "being together of strangers"—no doubt because being "part of the crowd" was thought to be one of the defining features of modern urban life that distinguished it from other historical and geographical contexts (Simmel 1903; Wirth 1938). Of course, public spaces do remain important for our enquiries into the encounters that make up the political geographies of urban multicultures—they remain sites in which urban inhabitants are confronted with differences of many forms, not least those associated with ethnicity and "race." However, the recent literature on encounter has helpfully drawn our attention to the emplaced materiality of encounter, suggesting that it unfolds differently across different activities. For instance, Amin's work on the multiethnic city emphasized the

Encounters with Difference in the Urban Everyday   21

importance of "micro-publics" that formed around activities and places like childcare and community services (Amin 2002). Influenced by that work, Wise's research on "everyday multiculturalism" has considered encounters in shopping mall food courts and suburban backyards (Wise 2009, 2010). Indeed, our own previous work has emphasized the significance of multiple sites of encounter and interaction—Fincher and Iveson (2008) focused on neighborhood centers and public libraries as spaces of encounter alongside more conventional public spaces associated with festivals; Leitner (2012) has examined the nature of encounter between immigrants of color and white residents at different sites in rural towns as well as the private spaces constructed by diverse grassroots movements for political organizing; and Preston (Romero et al. 2014) has worked on domestic labor and the home as a site of encounter with difference. The activities that generate urban encounters with difference take place in sites that exist on a spectrum from public to private, from the streets, parks, and shopping malls to the bus, neighborhood, office, place of worship, sports field, and the suburban backyard. In some ways, this contemporary emphasis on the diversity of encounters across different sites elaborates on some of Goffman's (1961) early work on encounter, in which he argued that different activity-based interactions generate social groupings that are specific to the activity and its associated encounters. The particular kinds of "being together" of people involved in encounters are not the same as other kinds of social collectives defined by criteria such as shared identity and/or membership.

Time also matters in influencing the dynamics and potential of encounter. Indeed, as Massey (2005) argues, space and time are interconnected dimensions of human experience. As with our discussion of spatiality above, encounters have different temporalities. As Goffman (1961) and many others since have observed, the activities of urban residents have distinct rhythms, which have significance for the dynamics of encounter. Many of our everyday activities involve routines such as trips to and from work, weekly sporting fixtures, fortnightly visits to social security offices, monthly meetings of a reading group at a community center, or annual festivals marking a significant anniversary in the life of a neighborhood or nation. Depending on their rhythm and repetition, these activities bring urban inhabitants into quite different kinds of encounters with others. Some may promote familiarity through repeated and sustained interaction with a fairly stable group of people such as coworkers or fellow church congregants. Others may involve fleeting interactions with people who become familiar to some degree through repetitive, regular encounters (perhaps the librarian, the shopkeeper, or other parents at the school gates). Yet others may involve little more than "unfocused," ephemeral physical copresence with constantly shifting groups of strangers, like those on the crowded metro platform at peak hour.

Another important temporal register that affects the dynamics and outcomes of encounters with difference are past encounters. As Ahmed (2004, 31) contends, encounters with difference are more than immediate face-to-face interactions between different racial groups:

> The "moment of contact" is shaped by past histories of contact, which allows the proximity of a racial other to be perceived as threatening, at the same time as it reshapes the bodies in the contact zone of the encounter. These histories have already impressed upon the surface of the bodies at the same time as they create new impressions.

Here Ahmed shows that as different racial groups come face-to-face with each other in the present, they carry the history of past encounters with them in the moment of "being together." For example, Leitner (2012) describes how white residents' fear of immigrants of color in rural Minnesota is not based on negative personal experience with immigrants of color in the present (until recently, much of rural Minnesota has been primarily a white space), but is shaped by the history of U.S. race relations and racial nationalism, which associates nonwhite bodies with danger and fear. Past associations circulate through stories by gossip and media; they create a "reality" that has profound implications for the dynamics and politics of present and future encounters. As Grosz (2004, 251) puts it:

> Every present is riven by memory . . . equally, the present always spreads itself out to the imminent future, that future

Encounters with Difference in the Urban Everyday 23

a moment ahead for which the present prepares itself by reactivating the past in its most immediate and active forms, as habit, recognition, understanding.

Our discussion of the multisited and multitemporal nature of encounter is reflected in the organization of our book's empirical chapters to focus on encounters with difference in distinct spheres of everyday urban life, each with their own sites and rhythms of "being together": making a home, working, moving around the city on public transport, and making publics (reported in chapters 3, 4, 5, and 6). But this raises still further questions about how such diversity can be best approached through the study of urban encounters.

In his classic studies of encounters between strangers, Goffman (1961) sought to understand their dynamics through close ethnographic observation. From these observations, he derived a number of insights that remain relevant for our consideration of urban encounters with difference. For instance, Goffman drew a useful distinction between *unfocused* and *focused* interactions (Goffman 1961, 7). Walking down a street might involve passive copresence, with a variety of people going about their business without much focused interaction with others on the street, and is an example of unfocused interaction. Working, on the other hand, might involve a group of people sharing a focus of attention on a single task, and is an example of a focused interaction. An analysis of urban encounters needs to pay careful attention to the moves between focused and unfocused interactions in different spheres of urban life. Encounters with difference may oscillate between focused and unfocused interaction—for instance, a street or a train carriage may be occupied in the presence of others in an unfocused manner, but then an event or initiative in that place may trigger more focused interaction. Or conversely, much of the working day for many people only involves unfocused interaction with others, rather than a sustained interaction, for example around a shared task.

Close ethnographic observation of the kind practiced by Goffman continues to be influential in contemporary studies of urban encounters with difference. Much of the recent work on encounter has been interested in documenting the micropractices of everyday encounters in their diversity, and identifying their different features and circumstances (Darling and Wilson 2016; Valentine and Sadgrove 2012; Wilson 2011; Wise and Noble 2016). However, while much can be learned about encounter through close ethnographic observation, we believe it is also necessary to pay attention to the wider geographical and historical contexts that shape the circumstances in which encounters take place. To this end, the next section elaborates on the crucial role played by institutions and ideologies that operate beyond the geographical and temporal scale of everyday urban encounters.

Governing Encounters with Difference

Encounters with difference are not only shaped by the spatiality and temporality of the urban everyday, but also by broader societal and cultural structures. Here we highlight the role of dominant political regimes and their institutions and policies at multiple geographic scales that shape both urban inequalities and either encourage or limit encounters with difference. For instance, national migration regimes are crucial in shaping both the population composition of any given city and inequalities between citizens and migrant populations through the differential allocation of rights to work, welfare, and other urban services. Similarly, national housing policies and the operation of housing markets are crucial in influencing how urban populations are (or are not) spatially sorted and concentrated by class, ethnicity, age, and other factors. We could think of many more examples (and indeed, we will offer many more examples in the chapters to follow). We contend that the latter reach deep into the encounter—not simply as geographical context, but as constitutive of the encounter, shaping the purposes of encounters and the subjectivities of their participants. For example, we shall see in our discussion of getting around how both national migration policies and state transport policies profoundly shape the encounters with difference that take place on public transport in Sydney by determining who has access to ticket concessions and how trains and buses are policed. As such, our approach to urban encounters with difference is not only *multisited*, it is also *multiscaled.*

Discourses, policies, and management techniques deployed by both governmental and nongovernmental institutions have a bearing on encounters with difference and engender both positive and negative effects. One dominant national policy of governing difference since the mid-twentieth century has been *multiculturalism* (we noted the distinction between our use of 'multiculture' and 'multiculturalism' in the introduction). Multiculturalism as a policy comes in different incarnations, ranging from nation-states celebrating diversity while encouraging and even demanding assimilation to the dominant culture, to nation-states promoting awareness and tolerance of diverse cultural heritages and practices (Banting and Kymlicka 2010; Bloemraad 2011). Critics of multiculturalism policies in Australia, Canada, and the United States have highlighted the fact that while enabling ethnic and racialized minorities to retain their cultural heritage and practices, the policies have also contributed to a reification of minority cultures and identities, and have rarely tackled the social inequalities and inequities associated with cultural difference, particularly racialized difference (Banting and Kymlicka 2010; Hage 1998; Koopmans 2013; Vertovec and Wessendorf 2010; Wright and Bloemraad 2012). In settler colonial contexts, where "dispossession and settlement are performed and creatively enacted every day" through property regimes and relations (Blatman-Thomas and Porter 2019, 42), the question of how forms of multiculturalism that seek to govern immigration interact with matters of indigenous recognition and sovereignty is also complicated and fraught (Snelgrove et al. 2014).

Multiculturalism is highly spatialized. Both the substance and implementation of multiculturalism policies often vary between different tiers of the state (Fincher et al. 2014; Leitner and Preston 2012). The multiscalar and diverse forms of multiculturalism that prevail in a single site will affect encounters with difference, although the specific pathways of influence are sometimes difficult to unravel. We also note that tensions among local, regional, and national views of multiculturalism may affect encounters with difference unevenly in the various sites of everyday life, such as homes, workplaces, transportation modes, and nonprofit and public spaces.

Currently, multiculturalist policy frameworks that have been in place for several decades in Europe, North America, and Australia are being contested and are a topic of heated political debate and rhetoric (Vertovec and Wessendorf 2010; Wright and Bloemraad 2012). Indeed political leaders in a number of European countries have called for abandoning multicultural policies, suggesting that they have failed. Claims of "failure" are typically narrated with illustrations from urban neighborhoods where conflict has erupted between inhabitants from different cultural, racial, and religious backgrounds, with blame apportioned to migrants who are said to have failed to "integrate" into their host society and are characterized as leading parallel lives (Fincher et al. 2014).

While obviously significant, multiculturalism and associated policies are only a few of the many state actions and political rationalities that shape encounters involving people from different ethnic, racial, cultural, and class backgrounds in cities (Fincher et al. 2014). Decades of critical writing have demonstrated the ways in which states have been engaged not only in the construction of social differences, but have also reinforced, exacerbated, or mitigated ethno-racial and class hierarchies and inequalities (Pred 2000; Sandercock 1998; Soja 2000; Soss et al. 2011; Wacquant 2008). For example, in terms of the construction of social difference, population censuses have been implicated in the categorization of populations along racial and ethnic lines, forming data that are the basis of much social planning; human resources departments in organizations note the diversity of their workforces by classifying them according to supposed differences, as well (see Ahonen et al. 2014).

In the places and times of concern in this book, the institutional mediation of urban encounters is shaped by the dominance of neoliberal and neoconservative political rationalities that seek to legitimize and delegitimize particular definitions and arrangements of social difference. These rationalities may paint certain encounters with difference as inappropriate, requiring active resistance to stage such encounters (as we will see in the examples in later chapters). Neoliberalism and neoconservatism are two dominant political rationalities that warrant separate examination in our analysis of encounters with difference in urban multicultures (Brown 2008). While neoliberalism's market-led regulatory restructuring imposes market rationality on the state and other social institutions, neoconservativism emphasizes the importance of a strong state that will ensure a return to an imagined past characterized by consensus concerning social norms and standards (Brown 2008; Soss et al. 2011). Each political rationality promotes a distinct stance toward the sociocultural difference that is at the center of our analysis.

Neoliberals view the diversity of cultures as an asset, as a valuable commodity to be deployed, for example to attract visitors and investors to a particular city (Fincher et al. 2014). They applaud the efforts of immigrant businesses to market themselves as exotic attractions for visitors and residents alike. At the same time, neoliberals often disregard how the state's development and promotion of ethnic commercial precincts can threaten the livelihoods of the immigrant businesses themselves. Similar contradictions are apparent in development strategies that posit diversity as a major attraction for financial investment in the built environment. The gentrification literature has demonstrated how investment by wealthier households in working class neighborhoods often contributes to the displacement of working class residents and the dissolution of their local social networks (Bridge et al. 2012). Despite the attraction of diversity for many gentrifiers, there is little social interaction across social classes, particularly when the working class population is also racialized (Davidson 2010; Fraser et al. 2012).

In contrast, neoconservatives see cultural diversity as an interim stage, to be tolerated while newcomers assimilate to the dominant culture. Neoconservatives tolerate diversity but rarely, if ever, view it favorably. The rise of neoconservative politicians is associated with statements that policies of multiculturalism (designed to ensure retention of minority cultures) have failed and should be ended, and racial profiling for Muslims and other nonwhite minorities should be intensified. A strong state is charged with disciplining and punishing those who persist in being different or deviating from dominant social norms (Brown 2008). For example, some European states have censured expressions of religious and cultural difference, such as wearing the hijab in public and maintaining extended family structures (Crosby 2014). French debates in 2016 about the wearing of "burkinis," or the banning of headscarves in the schools

28 *Encounters with Difference in the Urban Everyday*

of some Swiss cantons in 2014, are cases in point. Poor, immigrant, and racialized minorities are offered opportunities to reform, with those who prove unwilling or unable subjected to regulation, coercion, and sanction. Similar instances have emerged in North America and Australia in the treatment of Arab Canadians, Arab Americans, and Australian Muslims, both in the wake of 9/11, and following the election of neoconservative governments (Hage 1998; Nagel and Staeheli 2004, 2008; Poynting et al. 2004). Not only does this neoconservative rationality underpin direct policy changes, it also exerts an indirect influence on the atmosphere that shapes how urban inhabitants perceive one another and appropriate behavior toward the "other." For example, President Trump's verbal denigration of people of color, especially the name-calling and racial slurs directed against Mexican immigrants and Muslim Americans, and more generally people of color in the United States, has triggered an avalanche of racist talk and acts against people of color on the Web and on the streets of U.S. cities.

Neoliberalism emphasizes individual achievement and responsibility. Thus inequalities in wealth and well-being along class and racial lines are attributed to failings of individual effort. Consider, for example, the proclamations of a conservative think tank in the aftermath of Hurricane Katrina, blaming the disproportionate and devastating impacts of Katrina on poor and elderly African Americans on their individual shortcomings rather than on vulnerabilities created by a long history of racism in New Orleans (Peck 2009). Neoliberalism and neoconservatism take no account of the uneven playing field that renders poor, racialized minorities, particularly minority women, vulnerable to disasters (Roberts and Mahtani 2010; Seager 2006). Rather than redress inequalities, state intervention is intended to transform the vulnerable into self-sufficient political subjects who are capable of caring for themselves even in the face of disasters, such as Hurricane Katrina, while complying with middle-class mores (Peck 2009). Others have described the formation of a neoliberal paternalism aiming to produce subjects who are self-regulating and self-reliant market actors and consumers (Soss et al. 2011).

Interestingly, in the governance of Melbourne, Sydney, Los Angeles, and Toronto, major urban centers that hold dominant positions

Encounters with Difference in the Urban Everyday 29

in their respective national economies and politics, we observe not only the impact of neoliberal and neoconservative interventions at the national and subnational scales, we sometimes also see the implementation of local interventions that may diverge from them. Even though local governments in all four cities are the least powerful level of the state, they have demonstrated an unexpected capacity to both resist and reconfigure national immigration and integration policies (Fincher et al. 2014). For example, fifteen of the local governments that constitute the Los Angeles urban region are sanctuary cities in which municipal employees do not enforce federal detention orders (Los Angeles Almanac n.d.). Conversely, in Toronto, where the largest municipal government has approved a sanctuary policy, the police services have resisted implementing it and referred people who do not provide evidence of legal status to federal authorities (Keung 2015). In Sydney and Melbourne, national and state governments charge local governments with responsibility for incorporating cultural diversity into the provision of local services, urban planning, and community celebrations (Thompson 2003). The local mandate to recognize and promote cultural diversity often conflicts with an apparently neoliberal broader discourse calling for a small and efficient state, self-sufficient and economically productive immigrants, and a persistent tendency to promote the assimilation of newcomers (Forrest and Dunn 2010).

The neoliberal, institutional framing of encounters with difference in cities has been accompanied by the unloading of responsibility for social service provision to nongovernmental organizations (NGOs). The initial "roll back" of state services in the 1980s produced its own set of economic and political contradictions which, in turn, demanded the "roll out" of new institutional arrangements to "mask and contain the deleterious social consequences . . . [of the] the deterioration of social protection" (Wacquant cited in Peck and Tickell 2002, 389). In the United States, where the trend is well documented, this era of "roll out" is evident in the surge of registered nonprofit organizations since the early 1980s from several hundred thousand to more than 1. 5 million in 2017, providing services in areas such as education, healthcare, housing, mental health, community development, and immigration, among others

(NCCS 2013). Some time ago, Jennifer Wolch described this institutional arrangement as "the shadow state": "a para-state apparatus comprised of multiple voluntary sector organizations, administered outside of traditional democratic politics and charged with major collective service responsibilities previously shouldered by the public sector, yet remaining within the purview of state control" (Wolch 1990, xvi). While these organizations have taken on responsibility for social service provision, their activities are to varying degrees controlled and regulated through state funding requirements, auditing, and a regime of competition that prioritizes organizational survival and growth over service provision (Salamon 1995). To meet these standards, organizations have increasingly professionalized, implementing corporate "best practices" and management techniques and hiring highly skilled staff. Within this context, scholars have documented how NGOs can serve as sites of state social regulation and control, implementing neoliberal and neoconservative agendas and reinforcing social hierarchies (Ilcan and Basok 2004; Mitchell 2001). Yet NGOs also have the potential to challenge dominant notions of difference and diversity. More recent work on nonprofits has sought to accommodate the multiple relations and possibilities of the state–civil society relationship (Cope 2001; DeVerteuil 2017; Trudeau 2008). Thus, NGOs have the potential for considerable hosting of, and experimentation about, ways of being together with difference as equals, as later chapters show.

In the analyses of encounter in different spheres of everyday life in chapters 3 through 6, we will be using a multiscalar approach that draws attention to the ways in which the actions of people and institutions are influenced by dominant political rationalities. This, we argue, is crucial in order to situate the observations we may make about the different kinds of encounters that take place in distinct spheres of everyday urbanism in our four cities.

To sum up, in this chapter we have we set out an approach to everyday life in urban multicultures that focuses on the ways in which urban activities inevitably draw us into moments and routines of "being together" with different others. While we share many scholars' interest in documenting the everyday complexity and

Encounters with Difference in the Urban Everyday 31

richness of urban encounters with difference, we seek to expand this interest into a more relational approach that has two key elements. First, we situate encounters and their participants in the space and time of the urban everyday, highlighting how encounters shape and are being shaped by distinct spaces and times in which they take place. To participate in urban life is to engage in a diverse range of activities that involve others—like traveling, working, shopping, worshiping, neighboring, community and political organizing, and much more besides. A key dimension of the activity-based interactions with strangers is that they generate a particular kind of "being together" that is specific to the encounter. Second, we turn to the governance of encounters, and argue that interrogating the role of institutions, especially state policies and discourses, is crucial for theorizing encounters with difference in urban multicultures. Here, we focus especially on the significance of multiculturalism, neoliberalism, and neoconservatism as influential rationalities in the actions of state and nonstate actors that shape the context in which encounters unfold.

The relational approach we have outlined draws attention both to the contexts and powers that shape encounters with difference. However, we do not wish to suggest that encounters are predetermined by the everyday activities that generate them, or by their situation within broader historical and geographical processes. While the participants and contexts of encounters are shaped by a range of forces and processes from outside the space-time of the encounter, and while dominant norms may even make encounters in certain contexts quite predictable, the dynamics of any given encounter have the potential to exceed their context. As the body of critical scholarship on everyday life makes clear, everyday life as it is lived also contains the ingredients for its transformation (Amin and Thrift 2002; Fincher and Iveson 2008; Lefebvre 2001). Under conditions of rapid social change and increasing inequalities, encounters with difference may reinforce and entrench stereotypes and prejudice rather than reducing them (Matjeskova and Leitner 2011; Valentine 2008). At the same time, encounters with difference have the potential to destabilize existing hierarchies, stereotypes, and prejudices and generate emancipatory forms of being and struggling together that challenge dominant social divisions and hierarchies. The contingent nature of encounter opens up the possibility of both inscribing and disorienting us from deeply held stereotypes and prejudices (Leitner 2012). Judith Butler (1990, 138–39), for one, captures the subversive possibilities of encounters in her discussion of the performativity of the cultural practices of drag and cross-dressing. She describes the circumstantial contingency of such performance to disrupt the naturalized relation between sex and gender, that is, how the disruptive success of any performance depends on its context (its audience, time, and place, or its encounters, we might say). Encounters with difference share this circumstantial contingency. And it is this contingent dimension of everyday urban encounters with difference, the possibility that they will generate new social formations that disrupt their spatial and temporal context, that lends them their potential political significance. As Rancière (2009, 282) puts it, in any given context of oppression and inequality, "the experience of emancipation consists in locating another time in that time, another space in that space."

In the next chapter, we move on to examine the political potential for encounters to generate new forms of being together that disrupt the social hierarchies and assimilationist policies that help to entrench racialized inequalities in our cities. First, we engage with normative conceptions of the politics of equality and difference, and then we examine the opportunities offered in the urban everyday in experimenting with and enacting an egalitarian politics of difference: "being together in difference as equals."

{ 2 }

The Political Potential of Encounters
Being Together in Difference as Equals

IF THERE IS INDEED POLITICAL POTENTIAL in the encounter, what is the nature of that potential? In our view, this political potential emerges from the capacity of urban inhabitants to enact a particular form of "being together" in their urban encounters—what we call "being together in difference as equals." This normative concept arises from our particular interest in understanding how urban inhabitants work against racialized forms of oppression and inequality in cities. Of course, we realize that ideological constructions of racial and cultural (including religious) superiority and inferiority are by no means the only source of oppression in urban life. They intersect with inequalities premised on other identity attributes as well as class hierarchies. But in our contemporary "age of migration," racialized forms of oppression and inequality (often deriving from differences in religion, ethnicity, and nationality as much as skin color and other phenotypical markers of race) offer an entry point for examining intersectionality while simultaneously recognizing that they are significant enough to warrant our focused attention (see for example Amin 2012; Castles and Miller 1993; Gilroy 2004; Sandercock 2003; Valentine 2008; Wise and Velayutham 2009). While encounters with difference are events and performances (sometimes momentous, sometimes banal) that can reinforce those oppressions and inequalities, they are also crucial time-spaces for enacting everyday equalities in multicultural societies.

In the rest of this chapter, then, we develop this concept of "being together in difference as equals." Being together *in difference* for us means living together with culturally and racially different others in our daily life and in the collectivity of communities

{ 33 }

and neighborhoods without either losing our identities or having some identities privileged over others. A political and practical commitment to *equality* is a prerequisite for realizing this way of being together in difference. To live and work in difference as equals is an alternative to dealing with our differences through either assimilation or status hierarchies. The former (assimilation) makes equality dependent on the eradication of difference, while the latter (status hierarchies) make difference a source of inequality. We argue that this commitment to everyday equality is not only a hope for a future city, but a way of being together in the present, even in broader urban contexts characterized by inequality. As we will see, to be together in difference as equals is not easy, nor is it free of conflict. Rather, enactments of equality in difference emerge when urban inhabitants find ways to negotiate across their differences in building everyday egalitarian relations and identifications with one another, and when they take that equality as the basis for political interventions in the face of racialized inequality and oppression.

In what follows we engage with the scholarship of a number of theorists whose work is relevant and has inspired us to chart a way forward in understanding and imagining the political potential of encounters with difference. We also discuss the forms of learning, work, and care that are required for such an ideal to be realized in urban encounters with difference. Having developed this concept, in later chapters we consider instances in which a being together in difference as equals has emerged through encounters as they are constructed and unfold at different spheres and spaces of everyday urban life in the four cities of our focus.

Encounters with Difference and Equality

The literature on urban encounters with difference is populated with a wide variety of normative and political concepts, which are too often taken for granted and used interchangeably rather than critically interrogated and developed. "Successful" or "meaningful" encounters are frequently equated with outcomes like "tolerance," "respect," "getting along," "social cohesion," "community," "social inclusion," "hospitality," or "cosmopolitanism." Perhaps the lack of clear specification of what makes for a "successful" encounter is a function of the fact that many hopes for the political potential of encounters are more focused on the "bad" things that need to be overcome rather than on the good things that might emerge in their place. That is, the question that seems to drive much of the attention to, and hope for, encounter is the question of whether contact with the Other can reduce prejudice and stereotypes.

Indeed, in discussions about the political potential of urban encounters, it is hard to over-state the influence of the "contact hypothesis" (Neal and Vincent 2013). The hypothesis that racial prejudice and stereotypes can be overcome through contact with the Other has almost assumed the mantle of common sense in popular and scholarly discourse on multiculturalism, not to mention policy frameworks enacted by a variety of state and nonstate institutional actors. The contact hypothesis originated from the writings of Gordon Allport (1954), a psychologist, and posits that interpersonal contact between members of different social or cultural groups can reduce stereotypes and prejudice and improve attitudes toward each other, which in turn may result in improved relations between groups. Interpersonal contact is supposed to facilitate getting to know and gaining knowledge about the Other, which in turn may reduce anxiety about, and fear of, the Other. Contemporary proponents of the contact hypothesis have suggested close and intimate interactions with a previously othered subject will not only lead to positive attitudes toward that individual, but will also scale up to positive attitudes toward the entire minority group (Hewstone 2003; McLaren 2003; Pettigrew and Tropp 2000).

The contact hypothesis is the subject of increasing critical commentary. Recent scholarship has challenged not only the scaling up argument, but more generally has been critical of the unequivocally optimistic conclusions of the dominant strand of contact scholarship about the positive effects of contact (Matjeskova and Leitner 2011; Valentine 2008; Wessel 2009). Valentine finds that proximity and contact do not necessarily lead to respect for different others, and that they can even cement divisions and prejudice. Her research on white majority prejudice finds that everyday civility—the fact that people are usually polite to each other—can sit alongside sustained prejudice, the latter fueled by resentment at the resources expended on supporting culturally different citizens. Valentine's research emphasizes the ambiguity of the encounter— that it may be a source of progressive or regressive outcomes, with a wide set of variables making any outcome contingent and unpredictable. Matjeskova and Leitner (2011), in their study of spaces of encounter between local German residents and ethnic German immigrants from Russia in eastern Berlin, found that sustained and close encounters are enabled in spaces of neighborhood community centers, where immigrants and native residents work side-by-side on common projects, and engender more empathy and positive attitudes toward individual immigrants. But these positive outcomes were not scaled up to the group. Instead of a scaling up, they observed a rather different phenomenon, namely an exemption of individual immigrants from negative group stereotypes, referred to by social psychologists as the re-fencing of evidence. These findings point to a broader limitation of classical contact research—it focuses on experimental research designs, and contact as it is staged in these experiments hardly compares to the "contact as it is practiced, experienced, and regulated in everyday life" (Dixon, Durrheim, and Tredoux cited in Matjeskova and Leitner 2011, 720).

We concur with these critiques. However, we also note that some of the rather naïve political hopes for "contact" were actually not present in Allport's (1954) initial work on the contact hypothesis. In fact, he emphasized that positive effects via the overcoming of prejudice may only be realized under certain conditions including *equal status* of those in contact, shared common goals, and lack of competition. Such conditions can be constructed in quasi-experimental designs, but are not present in contemporary urban multicultures. Indeed everyday contact between members of different social groups is always shot through with deeply entrenched, unequal power relations. And yet, perhaps Allport's focus on equality is helpful in suggesting a revised approach to the political potential of urban encounters with difference. Even in the "real world," there may be scope for urban inhabitants to create the precondition of equal status specified by Allport. In doing so, they may enact a politics of equality, or what we call being together in

The Political Potential of Encounters

difference as equals, and in the course of it facilitate more positive types of encounter and progressive political outcomes.

The Politics of Equality and Difference

In this book, we seek to develop a clear description of the political potential of encounter, beyond vaguely specified hopes for the emergence of "tolerance" or "acceptance" through contact. We argue that a normative concern with *equality* gives us a greater critical purchase on the politics of encounter in urban multicultures. For a book on urban multiculture to have a normative orientation focused on the politics of equality might at first seem unusual. The political project of equality is still often associated with the eradication of unjust differences in wealth. At a time when economic inequalities are widening in many places, and when these economic inequalities clearly intersect with the racialized oppressions that are our focus, the dimension of equality is hugely important. But we join those critical theorists who insist that a concept of equality that is politically fit for our times and places must also take account of those injustices rooted in ideologies of racial, religious, and cultural superiority, as well as those rooted in economic inequality and other forms of oppression. In short, "equality" means more than "economic equality." And equality is not incompatible with difference. As Stuart Hall (2000, 10) has argued:

> The multicultural question has taken us beyond the confines of our traditional political conceptions and vocabularies. [It has] taken us into a new political space in which what classical political theories tells us are incommensurable have never the less to be practically contemplated.

Like Hall we argue that "it's possible to have a politics which reaches for equality between people but which does so by recognizing their differences" (2009, 13).

Our political commitment to the normative ideal of equality, and our understanding of its meaning, is informed especially by our engagement with feminist social theory. In work that spans several decades, feminist thinkers Nancy Fraser and Iris Marion

Young sought to *re-imagine* the meaning and politics of equality in light of the experience of emancipatory social movements, including those against sexism, racism, and homophobia. As Fraser (2008, 59) puts it:

> The dimensions of justice are disclosed historically, through the medium of social struggle. On this view, social movements disclose new dimensions of justice when they succeed in establishing as plausible claims that transgress the established grammar of normal justice, which will appear retrospectively to have obscured the disadvantage their members suffer.

So, the actions and thinking of social movements have drawn attention to forms of oppression that are distinct from (while related to) economic inequality. In so doing, they have challenged the "established grammar of normal justice" that is concerned exclusively with economic equality. Fraser's term "normal justice" stands for those existing ways of thinking about justice and equality that come to be widely accepted dogmas before being challenged as inadequate by those involved in social struggles. The dogmas of "normal justice," she argues, must be open to dispute. The task of the critical theorist of equality is to avoid the kind of dogmatism that sets any conception of justice or equality in stone: "Whoever dogmatically forecloses the prospect [of the emergence of new forms of justice] declares his or her thinking inadequate to the times" (Fraser 2008, 59).

But the denial of such dogmas gives rise to its own conceptual challenge: we still need some kind of criteria for interrogating and articulating *new* justice claims and equality concepts that might emerge from social struggle. Here, Fraser argues that a form of normative "monism" is in fact warranted. For her, the normative principle of *parity of participation*—"social arrangements that permit all to participate as peers in social life" (Fraser 2008, 60)—must be held constant, outside of the justice frameworks and arrangements that might achieve it in any given historical-geographical context. That is, she argues for an approach to justice that "combines a multidimensional social ontology with normative monism"

(Fraser 2008, 61). Effectively, the "normative monism" that Fraser recommends is one that entrenches a normative principle of equality at the heart of emancipatory politics, while recognizing that the meaning and practice of equality will have to change in order to confront different historical-geographical forms of inequality and injustice. For Fraser, this meant adding *recognition* (and more latterly, *representation*) to *redistribution* as strategies for enacting equality and achieving social justice (Fraser 1997a, 2008).

In a similar manner, Iris Marion Young's ground-breaking work in her 1990 book *Justice and the Politics of Difference* provides an instance of holding on to a normative commitment to equality while rethinking its meaning in order to confront emergent political circumstances. Importantly, Young conceived of her work as an attempt to grapple with the challenges of achieving the political goal of equality in socially heterogeneous societies. Her work on the politics of difference remains particularly helpful for thinking about the politics of equality and its relationship to racialized, ethnicized, and nationalist forms of difference.

Justice and the Politics of Difference was conceived as an attempt to answer the question: "How can traditional socialist appeals to equality and democracy be deepened and broadened as a result of these developments in late twentieth-century politics and theory?" (Young 1990, 3). Like Fraser's "normative monism," Young's book has as its founding assumption "that basic equality in life situation for all persons is a moral value" (Young 1990, 14). Her framework has as its ultimate goal a rethinking of equality through group difference. Put most simply, she argues that "equality, defined as the participation and inclusion of all groups in institutions and positions, is sometimes better served by differential treatment" (Young 1990, 195). While this particular formulation of her social justice framework comes from a discussion of affirmative action in employment, her insistence on the importance of the recognition of difference for equality is applied and developed across a range of social domains:

> A culturally pluralist democratic ideal . . . supports group-conscious policies not only as means to the end of equality, but also as intrinsic to the ideal of social equality itself.

Groups cannot be socially equal unless their specific experience, culture, and social contributions are publicly affirmed and recognized. (174)

The "dogma of equality" that Young had squarely in her sights here was the reduction of equality to matters of distributional justice. As she put it:

> A goal of social justice, I will assume, is social equality. Equality refers not primarily to the distribution of social goods, though distributions are certainly entailed by social equality. It refers primarily to the full participation and inclusion of everyone in society's major institutions, and the socially supported substantive opportunity for all to develop and exercise their capacities and realize their choices. (173)

This has strong resonance with Fraser's emphasis on participatory parity. While Fraser and Young had their differences (Fraser 1997b; Young 1997), what is important to us here is their shared and unshaken commitment to theorizing a politics of equality. For them, the challenge of oppressions based on differences such as those associated with ethnicity and nationality does not require us to jettison a concern with equality. Rather, it should force a reconceptualization of equality that is fit for our times and places. Such a reconceptualization must begin with the notion that difference is not necessarily an impediment to equality, but might in fact be a condition for its realization.

The focus on equality in Fraser's and Young's work resonates with more recent writing on politics by the likes of Jacques Rancière—up to a point. Like Fraser and Young, Rancière situates equality at the very heart of the political. He describes his approach to politics as a "method of equality," one which is "specifically aimed at detecting and highlighting the operations of equality that may occur everywhere at every time" (Rancière 2009, 280–81). Equality is seen by Jacques Rancière as the very foundation of democracy, which seeks to establish a particular form of authority or "title to govern." Democracy is based on the notion that no particular groups of people

The Political Potential of Encounters

41

are better equipped, or naturally born, to rule. Democracy is distinct from the rule of the best (meritocracy), the rule of the experts (technocracy), the rule of the wealthiest (plutocracy), and so on. It is an alternative to those "governments of paternity, age, wealth, force and science, which prevail in families, tribes, workshops and schools and put themselves forward as models for the construction of larger and more complex human communities" (Rancière 2006, 45). Democracy is the rule of the people, premised on nothing more than the *equality* of each with all.

In an echo of Fraser and Young above, Rancière insists on the centrality of equality to democracy while simultaneously insisting that equality has no essential, unchanging meaning across time and space. Rather, he argues, the politics of equality is "always emplotted in historical configurations" (Rancière 2009, 287). Importantly, then, the meaning of equality is neither timeless nor placeless. Rather, equality is given meaning and political significance only through its *enactment* in particular historical and geographical circumstances by groups of people who claim that some aspect of an existing sociohistorical and sociospatial order (what Rancière calls the "police order") denies their status as equals. Yet perhaps this is where Rancière departs somewhat from the likes of Fraser and Young. For Rancière, equality is not so much a "goal" to be attained (as in, "we want to be equal") as an *assumption to be verified* through forms of action that contest undemocratic forms of authority founded on inequality (as in, "we are equal, and our equality is not recognized within society as it is presently organized and governed"). This involves a process of political subjectification, in which people refuse the roles and parts that they are meant to play in the existing social order *by identifying and acting together as equals.* Such an approach to the politics of equality, then, focuses our attention on the ways in which people develop new ways of being together as equals. It connects to our discussion of encounters with difference in the previous chapter, where we noted that encounters can enable distinct forms of identification to emerge among participants that might be particular to the encounter, and different from the people's ascribed identities that are often fixed and fairly immutable.

Of course, we must add race, ethnicity, and nationality (not to mention gender, sexuality, and so on) to Rancière's list of undemocratic titles to govern based on "age, wealth, force and science." They are crucial sources of oppressive authority—especially in settler colonial contexts such as those we write from in this book, where "political imaginaries are fundamentally premised on the idea of a severed link with Europe and the idea that a 'new' society is being constructed on settled lands" (Hugill 2017, 5). Indeed, it would be hard to think of a more foundational form of naturalized authority than the entrenched notion that "the people" has an ethnic and/or national qualification that rules some people in, and some people out, of its scope. So, a politics of equality fit for our times needs to confront the naturalization of ethnic, racial, and/or national "titles to govern" that persists across so much of the world. As Ash Amin puts it:

> The grip of the imaginary that each society exists as a homeland with its own people, known and loyal to itself (and distinct from strangers in another land) remains vice-like. But could it be that if cosmopolitan societies hold together, they do so around plural publics and as the result of active work by collective institutions, integrating technologies, and constructed narratives and feelings of togetherness, rather than around givens of historical community? (2012, 1)

The challenge for a politics in the name of equality, then, is precisely to point out the contingency and injustice of forms of authority and norms of togetherness that are premised on these "givens of historical community" associated with colonization, race and culture that Amin seeks to overturn.

While we find the likes of Hall, Fraser, Young, Rancière, and Amin especially helpful in thinking through the politics of equality and difference in contemporary multicultures, their work provokes several questions about *how* political possibilities of equality and difference might be realized across the diverse spheres and spaces of everyday urbanism. What particular forms of "being together in difference as equals" might be emerging through everyday urban encounters in our contemporary age of migration to confront and

The Political Potential of Encounters 43

challenge hierarchies based on race, religion, and ethnicity that are very much entrenched in the existing order? How can our "being together" in cities escape the pull of preexisting forms of racialized inequality, and enact forms of being together as equals and strangers? We now turn to these matters through a discussion of politics and encounter as these are situated in the everyday.

Everyday Equalities: Being Together in Difference as Equals in Everyday Urbanism

In Lefebvre's ([1991] 2001) influential conceptualization, the everyday is crucial to political change. Taking up the idea of the everyday has us focus on the forms of social practice in which we frequently engage, how they are embedded in and affected by the places and times in which we live, and the power relations of the institutions with which we interact and by which we are governed. Political change begins by people's actions revealing and then altering everyday life, creating new social practices and institutions. Accepting this broad premise, it follows that a focus on everyday encounters with difference in cities is essential to understanding how people reveal and begin to alter social practices that entrench inequality. As Merrifield (2013, 33) puts it in his discussion of the politics of encounter:

> The notion of encounter is a tale of how people come together as human beings, or why collectivities are formed and how solidarity takes hold and takes shape, and also how intersectional politics shapes up urbanly. The encounter is like a twinkling, radiant, cosmic constellation, an expression of the plurality of participants who conjoin with an open form (and forum), within a dynastic structured coherence, within a configuration that makes itself rather than simply lies there, preexisting, in a passive state.

Merrifield himself is primarily interested in emerging forms of being together that contest the capitalist logic of exchange and exploitation. But we need also to consider the forms of being together that might address ethnicized and racialized forms of inequality and oppression. If contemporary urban life brings us together in our differences, how might that togetherness in difference also be a togetherness as equals? What role might everyday urban encounters have in fostering forms of "being together" that may act as the building blocks for a politics of equality in contemporary urban multicultures?

Our concept of being together in difference as equals is offered as a frame for reimagining the project of equality in the context of urban multicultures. We propose that everyday—or what some scholars might call ordinary (Staeheli et al. 2012) or quiet (Askins 2015)—urban encounters can play a significant role in being together in difference as equals because of the contingent dimension they necessarily involve. The everyday offers vital opportunities for people to experiment with different ways of being and acting together that are foundational dimensions of the political. These experiences may create new politics, new subjectivities. As Rancière insists, politics (which certainly involves encounters by definition) "stems from a multiplicity of microexperiences of repartitioning the sensible, a multiplicity of operations" that have "reframed" the identities and interests of participants (Rancière 2009, 277). This is simultaneously a process of "displacement" and "dis-identification" with existing roles and authorities and the creation of new "distributions of the sensible" and political subjectivities.

The political significance of everyday urban encounter is also a feature of some of Young's work on the politics of equality and difference. The influential chapter "City Life and Difference" in *Justice and the Politics of Difference* identified the emancipatory potential of city life in the following terms:

> In the city persons and groups interact within spaces and institutions they all experience themselves as belonging to, but without those interactions dissolving into unity or commonness. City life is composed of clusters of people with affinities—families, social group networks, voluntary associations, neighborhood networks, a vast array of small "communities." City dwellers frequently venture beyond such familiar enclaves, however, to the more open public

The Political Potential of Encounters   45

of politics, commerce, and festival, where strangers meet and interact. (1990, 237)

Indeed, Young develops a normative ideal of the city by identifying several positive outcomes associated with everyday urban encounters with difference. "Social differentiation without exclusion" describes a situation in which group differentiation exists, where "groups do not stand in relations of inclusion and exclusion, but overlap and intermingle without becoming homogenous" (239). "Variety" refers to the diverse activities that good neighborhoods support, which "draws people out in public to them" and thereby encourages them to "go out and encounter one another on the street and chat" (239). "Eroticism" speaks to the "pleasure and excitement of being drawn out of one's secure routine to encounter the novel, strange and surprising" (239). Through such encounters, "one could learn or experience something more and different" (240). Finally, "publicity" speaks to an urban public realm in which people must recognize the existence of difference:

> Because by definition a public space is a place accessible to anyone, where anyone can participate and witness, in entering the public one always risks encounter with those who are different, those who identify with different groups and have different opinions or different forms of life. The group diversity of the city is most often apparent in public spaces. . . . In such public spaces people encounter other people, meanings, expressions, issues, which they may not understand or with which they do not identify. (240)

In his book *Life as Politics* (2010), Asef Bayat, writing from the Middle East, goes a step further than Young, in terms of the nature of political agency and the power of public space:

> Solidarities are forged primarily in public spaces—in neighborhoods, or street corners, in mosques, in workplaces, at bus stops, or in rationing lines, or in detention centers, migrant camps, public parks, colleges and athletic stadiums— through what I have called "passive networks." (22)

Passive networks "refer to instantaneous communications between atomized individuals, which are established by that recognition of their commonalities (e.g. common predicaments, shared dress codes, tastes, etc.) directly in public spaces or indirectly through mass media" (22).

Bayat draws our attention to the political potential that can arise from the most banal and everyday interactions, such as the passive networks between individuals that make up what he calls non-movements of the urban dispossessed. It is the latter that he has termed "the quiet encroachment of the ordinary,"

> [which] encapsulates the discreet and prolonged ways in which the poor struggle to survive and to better their lives by quietly impinging on the propertied and powerful, and on society at large. It embodies the protracted mobilization of millions of detached and dispersed individuals and families who strive to enhance their lives in a lifelong collective effort that bears few elements of pivotal leadership, ideology, or structured organization. (15)

The geographies of urban encounter that Bayat includes in his account are more varied and precise in kind than those evoked by Young. Young's focus is on "open and accessible public spaces" (1990, 119). However, urban encounters with difference are by no means exclusively (or even mostly) staged in open and accessible public spaces such as the street, plazas, and public parks. Indeed, as we noted in the previous chapter, some scholars have argued that there is less political potential in the public spaces of the city than there is in the "micro-publics" that form around shared projects that have their home in less grand everyday institutional settings, such as residential neighborhoods and work locations (Amin 2012; Bayat 2010; Wright et al. 2004).

The political potential of the mundane everyday has also been highlighted in recent scholarship on citizenship by feminist political theorists and political geographers. In their analysis of this relationship between citizenship and politics, Staeheli et al. (2012) suggest that they are "simultaneously constituted through encounters with law and daily life." They argue that "small actions, chal-

The Political Potential of Encounters 47

lenges, and the experiments to which they give rise can lead to varied forms of contact and engagement that hold the potential to nudge established patterns of control and authority and to anticipate new political acts" (630). This is not to say that any small action in the mundane everyday is "political," but it is to say that politics can and does indeed have an ordinary, everyday dimension.

Our own emphasis in this book on the many contexts and the varied geographies in which urban inhabitants encounter others only adds to the arguments about city life and the mundane everyday in encounters with difference. It shows that many urban activities and contexts draw urban inhabitants into encounters with difference that hold out the potential for everyday enactments of equality, to the extent that they transcend forms of domination and oppression associated with racialized inequality. However, the political potential of everyday encounters is not so much the "scaling up" of encounters from the "micro" to the "macro," but the construction of new kinds of everyday equality born from the experience of urban encounters through related processes of political subjectification and action. Through repetition and institutionalization, new expressions of political subjectivity may become habitual over time, and a part of an accepted way of doing things and a new form of social order.

The Work of Being Together in Difference as Equals

As we begin to investigate the potential for "being together in difference as equals" in urban life, it is important to recognize that this potential is not guaranteed to be realized in everyday urban encounters. Some recent literature on urban multiculture has focused attention on the qualities of urban encounters characterized by equality across difference. This literature suggests that the making of everyday equalities, and indeed the development of habits about this, is hard work—it involves labor, learning, and care.

Neal and Vincent's (2013) study of friendship development between the parents of school children from different ethnic and religious backgrounds in a British locality demonstrates the ongoing *labor* involved in avoiding withdrawal from difference, and the effort required for cultural translation between group members. They emphasize that maintaining interactions between people of cultural (and indeed class) differences requires competence, dedication, and skill on the part of participants in the interactions. Similarly, Amanda Wise's study of neighboring practices between people who have to "negotiate the 'accident' of propinquity in shared multicultural spaces" (2009, 21) draws attention to the particular labor and skills that enable the emergence of what she calls "transversality." Drawn from feminist theory (Cockburn 1998; Yuval-Davis 1999), this term denotes a politics of encounter in which participants are both "rooted" in their own membership and identity while also "shifting in order to put themselves in a situation of exchange with those who have different membership and identity" (Wise 2009, 23)—not unlike the "being together of strangers" envisaged by Young.

While such "exchanges" in Wise's work do not have an explicit orientation toward equality, her discussion of transversality is informed by a concern with how people *work* to produce alternatives to ethnicized and racialized hierarchies, in order to find another basis for their "being together" in the city. In her research, Wise finds that certain individuals in a neighborhood or community of interest can often play an important role as "transversal enablers"—people who have developed the skills and habits to "assist in creating threads of connection across cultural difference— for themselves, and for their communities" (24). They play this role through activities such as exchanging gifts, creating opportunities for the production of cross-cultural commensality and spaces of intercultural care and trust. Here again, then, the production of encounters that involve being together in difference as equals depends on the development of practical skills that enable transversal political orientations to emerge. Yuval-Davis (1999) emphasizes that transversal enablers are simultaneously *rooted*, aware of their own positioning and identity, and *shifting*, putting themselves in the position of those who are different with whom they are engaging in dialogue. In a transversal politics, shifting and rooting always aim to reduce unequal power relations and promote inclusion.

Some of this labor is *emotional* labor. The literature conceiving encounter as an embodied experience draws our attention to the emotions unleashed in encounters with difference in everyday

The Political Potential of Encounters   49

urban multicultures (Darling and Wilson 2016; Nayak 2010). Embodied practices and encounter are shot through with emotions that play an active role in how the encounter is felt and acted upon, and thus the kind of work it does. As Ahmed (2004) reminds us: "Whether something is thought of as agreeable or hurtful involves thought and evaluation at the same time it is 'felt' by the body. [The] process of attributing an object as being or not being 'agreeable' involves reading the encounter in a certain way" (31). As such, emotions are involved in drawing and potentially reinforcing or transgressing social boundaries, stereotypes, and prejudice. Leitner (2012) for example has shown how encounters between white residents and immigrants in small towns in Minnesota are often marred by racism and elicit strong emotions, primarily fear and anxiety, which have negative effects on subsequent social interactions. Emotions such as fear "mediate, in concrete and particular ways, relationships between the psychic and the social, and the individual and collective" (Ahmed 2004, 31). As such, there is an emotional dimension to the work performed, and the skills required, in building new forms of being together in difference as equals in the urban everyday.

Of course, the kinds of skills discussed by Yuval-Davis, Wise, Neal and Vincent, Ahmed and others must be acquired and learned. This process of *learning* is the focus of McFarlane's (2011) *Learning the City*. He emphasizes that learning about others is not only a process of translating knowledge, but requires coordination, and can also "entail shifts in ways of seeing—where ways of seeing is defined not simply as an optical visuality, but as haptic (meaning touch) immersion" (16). His work is especially useful in drawing attention to the importance of "organizing devices" in these processes of learning (19). McFarlane's focus on the importance of organizing devices in learning draws our attention once more to the significance of institutions (broadly defined). Organizing devices such as written documents are themselves produced and circulated by a range of actors and institutions with different capacities and interests. McFarlane has also demonstrated how nongovernment organizations play a crucial role in facilitating inter- and intra-urban learning and exchange across difference. As such, we note that institutions such as NGOs, and tiers of and individuals within the state may be engaged in contesting Rancière's "police order" through encouraging and facilitating encounters with difference and promoting equality. Thus it is not simply a matter of "the state" versus "civil society." Fincher and Iveson (2008), for instance, argue for the significance of institutions such as public libraries and government-funded neighborhood centers in enabling encounters with difference (see also Matjeskova and Leitner 2011). Amin (2012) has also made a case for the significance of institutions and their role in providing both integrating technologies and infrastructures as well as circulating distinct narratives of togetherness.

A further element for enacting being together in difference as equals, *care and caring*, is emphasized by feminist political theorists and feminist geographers (Lawson 2007; Tronto 1994). Tronto maintains that care needs to be a centerpiece of a democracy that rests on the view that "we are equal as democratic citizens in being care receivers" (Tronto 2013, 29). The development of an ethic of care for others can be seen as fundamental, definitional, to the everyday enactment of equality across difference. At its most basic, the development of resistance to racialized inequality that occurs through habitual practices of recognition and inclusion in encounters with difference in the everyday is an act of collective caring.

This is a matter of our ability to take responsibility for our own societies and their inequalities. Such caring involves recognition of the embeddedness of contemporary injustices in ways of being in the past, and being careful not to erase these pasts from memory as new futures are imagined. Says Tronto (2013, and see 2003) speaking of racism and sexism:

> Those who have benefited from past injustice have a great incentive to forget that fact, whether they perpetrated injustice or were simply bystanders who benefited from the unjust acts of others. And those who have been so harmed cannot grasp how the world can go forward simply by ignoring or burying the past. (127)

And this leads to our final point—that the work of "being together in difference as equals" may also involve *agitation* and its associated conflict. If, as Rancière insists, politics involves confronting

The Political Potential of Encounters

inequality by introducing *dissensus* into naturalized social orders, we should not anticipate that this will be a "happy" process. Unlike normative appeals to "social cohesion" and "tolerance" that are often inscribed in state-led multiculturalisms, our ideal of being together in difference as equals is not about "making the shift from unhappy to happy diversity" through contact and encounter in which differences and disagreements are resolved amicably (Ahmed 2007, 123). To enact equality in a context of inequality is not a process in which people "gently invite their interlocutors to a pleasant, turn-taking conversation; rather, they must coerce and compel their quarreling "partners" to acknowledge them as equals" (Sparks 2016, 425). Or, as Hall (2007, 152) says rather more bluntly about the pursuit of equality in difference:

> Don't think it is going to be what is called, these days, social cohesion—which is a polite form of assimilation of "the other," and represents in effect the abandonment of the multicultural principle. There is going to be nothing cohesive about it at all. It's going to be a bloody great row. Any form of democratic life—and I'm not talking about political democracy only now—is a big, staged, continuous row. Because there are real differences, and people are deeply invested in them and so they have to find ways—difficult ways—of negotiating difference, because it's not going to go away.

Of course, the form that such rows might take is certainly not determined in advance—as we shall see in the chapters to follow, agitations can range from arguments among family at the dinner table to national and international campaigns involving disruptive marches and occupations.

Following the lead of those scholars discussed above, our empirical investigations across our four cities will pay attention to the kinds of labor, learning, care, and agitation that have been practiced in efforts to establish new, egalitarian forms of being together in difference.

In this chapter we have offered the concept of "being together in difference as equals" as an alternative to dealing with and managing our differences through either assimilation or status hierarchies. Building on the insights from the authors discussed in this chapter, we have argued that the political potential of encounter with difference in the urban everyday involves a combination of being together with culturally and racially different others without either losing our identities or having some identities privileged over others, along with a political and practical commitment to equality. These everyday equalities are not only a hope for a future city, but a way of being together in the present, even in broader urban contexts characterized by racialized inequality. Of course, there is no guarantee that the political potential for "being together in difference as equals" will be realized, or that enactments of this form of everyday equality will reverberate across time and space to transform societal inequalities. The matter of whether this will occur, and how it might be done, is an empirical question. We hope that the ways of thinking about encounter that are demonstrated in chapters 3, 4, 5, and 6—where encounters are shown to be variously fleeting or sustained, one-off meetings or repeated, formally organized or unintended, involving many or few participants—may be a useful frame for thinking about ways in which the practice of equality in difference might occur.

This approach directs our discussion about encounters with difference in the chapters to follow, in which we will seek to reveal instances of being together in difference as equals in different spheres of everyday urban multicultures in Melbourne, Toronto, Sydney, and Los Angeles. We do this with a view to identifying the praxis of equality that can be discerned in these encounters. We observe very different kinds of encounters across these four chapters, in the processes of making a home, making a living, getting around, and building publics. And yet, across this diversity, we find what we believe to be shared practices and institutional arrangements for enacting everyday equality. In the final chapter, we will draw these observations together to offer a series of propositions about this praxis of equality in urban life.

{ 3 }

Making a Home in Melbourne

IN THIS CHAPTER, we discuss making a home as an everyday activity in which people are together, often as equals and across difference, in urban multicultures. Encounters at various spatial scales are present in every stage of the task of making a home. For as well as being places of interaction between householders, homes are sites of constant outreach to the neighborhood and beyond. There is a special time dimension to making a home, as well, that distinguishes the interactions involved in making a home from the interactions of other everyday activities in the city, like getting around on public transport. For encounters in home-making occur over extended time periods more often than being fleeting. Within the dwelling, home is made in those encounters that occur repeatedly between family or household members and visitors; beyond the dwelling home is made as encounters occur over long periods with neighbors, shopkeepers, service providers. We note as well that being together in difference as equals, where this occurs in the encounters of making a home, is the product of hard work, learning, and care. Through these encounters and the hard work and care they involve, everyday equalities are enacted.

Our discussion focuses on the encounters with difference of migrants in metropolitan Melbourne as they make their homes there, having brought their families and their cultural distinctiveness to Melbourne's suburbs (by which we mean its local government areas outside the central business district [CBD]) in the decades since the mid-twentieth century. The chapter is organized as follows. We begin by orienting the discussion of home-making in Melbourne by referring generally to the kinds of encounters with difference that take place in the course of making a home in urban multicultures. Then, after providing some contextual background to

{ 53 }

housing patterns and issues in Melbourne's urban multiculture, we offer a series of short case studies to shed light on the interactions, or encounters, that are a major part of these home-making processes and the everyday equalities they involve. We note that four of these five short case studies are drawn from the rich literature about making homes in Melbourne written by our past students and close colleagues, rather than from our own original empirical studies.

The first three of these case studies are about people making home together in Melbourne's *neighborhoods* (the often-distinctive areas of everyday interaction and activity that occur within suburbs), across their differences. In these cases, reaching out to others in the neighborhood is a key part of making home. We recount Michele Lobo's portrayal of newly arrived migrants in the Melbourne suburb of Dandenong. Here, encounters recognizing others have developed over many years as people have actively supported their neighbors, forming a kind of inclusive culture of place that can be seen as being together as equals across difference. We note from the work of Iris Levin and her colleagues the example of the social mix replanning of an existing public housing estate in Carlton, imposed by government in partnership with developers. Insofar as this planning is failing to provide possibilities for encounter across difference for public tenants and private owners, it is actually an example of how not to make home and how to preclude being together. And we observe in a third example, sourced in our own research with colleagues, the manner in which the form of apartments for foreign students in the CBD fringe of Melbourne influences the students' use of nearby facilities and infrastructure. Our attention focuses here on the interplay between the physical settings of dwellings in cities and the possibilities of encounter and being together as equals to which these physical settings may give rise.

Then, in the final two short studies, we take up home-making encounters at a different spatial scale, examining encounters in which home is made in the social relations within dwellings. A first case, drawn from the work of Mariastella Pulvirenti in the 1990s, demonstrates that intergenerational differences within the family households of Italian migrants have occurred over whether homeownership is to be preferred to renting and whether heterosexual relationships are to be preferred to same-sex relationships in the making of a home. The "home rules" (Susan Smith's [2008] term for the micropolitics householders create about how their everyday lives should be lived) of the first generation of migrants are being questioned here by the second generation. Sometimes the generations come together as equals after a time of considering their differences on this question; sometimes the hierarchy of the family precludes this. In the second case, from the research of Iris Levin (2010), a focus on the physical form of migrants' houses in suburban Melbourne demonstrates how migrants have achieved with their houses a tactful fitting-in to the streetscape. Over lengthy periods they have participated in encounters using the building materials and plantings of the local streetscapes of Melbourne's suburbs, accommodating to these in their own dwellings as their houses express their presence as equals in the streetscape.

Making a Home in Urban Multicultures: Encounters in the Neighborhood and the Dwelling

As we will see in the case studies to follow, many different activities are involved in making a home. In this chapter, we are especially interested in the home-making process for migrants. When one is newly arrived in a place and is an outsider, as migrants are, many kinds of encounters with difference are necessary to these activities. In the perspective advanced in this book, interactions or encounters with others within the dwelling and outside it underpin, even constitute, the making of home. Think about the encounters involved in each of the following aspects of making a home: finding a secure place to live that one can afford, and furnishing it; locating resources like local schools, parks, and libraries that are required to live comfortably in the local area; fitting in with how things are done in that new place—shopping, meeting neighbors, perhaps joining local clubs or places of worship. Making a home includes setting up things inside the house, looking in, and also setting things up outside the house, looking out. Each aspect of it can involve negotiations with other people across differences, at the various scales of social engagement that making a home requires: within the home itself, in and around the immediate surrounds of the house, and across the broader neighborhood, suburb, or metropolitan area through which housing is distributed spatially. Certain tasks can also involve interaction with the material world: with unfamiliar products that may be used locally in housing construction, or with equally unfamiliar plants used for fashioning and using household gardens. All this can produce anxiety, as well as joy and satisfaction. It can necessitate engagement with household budgets and financing by banks. Jacobs and Smith (2008, 517) suggest the idea of an "assemblage of dwelling," to which we might refer when talking about making a home in order to capture the many emotional and material elements, actions, and encounters that constitute that process. And making a home is not over once one has completed a set of initial actions after moving to a new place. It goes on as one continues to live there. It is a long-term endeavor. Home is ever made and re-made, as things change and new developments in our lives occur. As Blunt and Dowling (2006, 23) have it:

> Home does not simply exist, but is made. Home is a process of creating and understanding forms of dwelling and belonging. This process has both material and imaginative elements. Thus people create home through social and emotional relationships. Home is also materially created—new structures formed, objects used and placed.

Of course, the creation of home by people is mediated, even shaped, by the many features of their context. In the cities of which we write in this book, complex institutional environments make housing, and thus homes, more readily accessible to some than to others. In Australia, and the city of Melbourne about which this chapter is written, home-ownership and owner-occupation have long been both institutional priorities and the preferred form of housing in the population (Cook et al. 2016). Australian cities evolved with low-density suburbs, constituting what Davison (2016, 105) terms "a large suburban peasantry" as people used their suburban lots to grow food and store garden and house-repair equipment. Even in poorer suburbs, people who could use their backyards to grow food and for recreation had a reasonable quality of life. Since the

1990s, however, housing prices have grown rapidly in the major cities like Melbourne. Access to housing, and especially to home-ownership, is now a major dimension of inequality in these cities. The large suburban housing lot is becoming a thing of the past, rarely present in new housing developments in the suburbs of the metropolitan fringe. National policy has provided opportunities for investor purchase of housing (including high-rise apartments) that owners will rent out (supported by negative gearing, which is the tax deductibility of investment expenses). The real estate markets of Australian cities have drawn homeowners and renters into the globally connected investment platform that housing in many countries has now become (Rogers 2016; Smith 2008). This is widely regarded as having contributed to high housing prices in the private rental and home-purchase markets, and to the exclusion of many from the quality of housing they might have expected some decades ago. Affordable housing is very scarce.

We emphasize that such institutional demands and expectations are actively present, and influential, in the encounters involved in making a home. Finding a dwelling one can afford and access can depend on housing policies, including subsidies to homeowners and investors, provision of public rental housing (or not), implementation of plans for a social mix of housing tenure types. Powerful private sector organizations, particularly banks and real estate agencies, also influence the availability of housing and its financing. Local council and state government allocations and planning priorities make available (to different degrees) in Australian cities facilities like parks, schools, libraries, food markets, and social services. Access to these features can render neighborhoods more homely, and at the same time can help neighborhoods host encounters with difference between newcomers and longer-term residents. Activist and community groups can support their constituents materially and politically.

In our five short case studies about the encounters of home-making, not all of these things are evident in each one. But the presence of institutional priorities about home-ownership and its investment potential sit clearly in encounters reported within the dwelling and within the neighborhood, notably in the example of the social mix policy being applied to a public housing estate in

Carlton and in the example of intergenerational conflict over Italian parents' commitment to home-ownership rather than renting for their sons and daughters. Those priorities are even seen in the slow evolution of migrants' homes in the city's suburban streetscapes, for migrants seek over the long term to belong in Australian society as homeowners. In this, they exhibit the same general preferences as the whole population, even as they bring diverse ways of living to suburbs. The presence of local planning priorities and the resources that public services and public (or collectively available) spaces can provide for those making a home are also evident in our cases here. For foreign students, spaces for encounter across difference are found in food courts and communal kitchens; in Dandenong's public food markets both acknowledgment of difference and being together with that difference occur frequently.

Though we might assume that the making of home is primarily a process of creating a haven of familiarity for those dwelling in the home, a place of comfortable refuge in an unpredictable world, in fact any assumption that home-making solely involves interacting with and reproducing the familiar may be called into question. Considering what home means to migrants, Ahmed (1999, 339–40) criticizes how such a way of viewing home calls for "a definition of home that is itself impossible":

> It stabilizes the home as a place with boundaries that are fixed, such that homes become pure, safe and comfortable. However encounters with otherness which . . . would engender desire, cannot be designated in terms of the space beyond home: it is the very opposition between "home" and "away" that we must call more radically into question. . . . The problem with such a model of home as familiarity is that it projects strangeness beyond the walls of the home. Instead, we can ask: how does being-at-home already encounter strangeness? How does being-at-home already engender desire?

In a discussion of the formation of a community of writers from different parts of Asia who lived in the United Kingdom in the mid-1990s, Ahmed (345) describes how the very lack of a common

Making a Home in Melbourne

59

identity between participants and an acknowledgment of their foreignness or strangeness to each other itself became the basis for the making of a community or homely environment to share together. Perhaps it is this that we see in the long-standing making of home in Dandenong by refugee and migrant groups of great diversity of background and experience, so evocatively presented in Lobo's (2009) writing and used as our first case study. Resisting any denial of the familiar as central to making a home, however, Marotta (2011) points out that migrants deal simultaneously with the strangeness of the host and the sameness (and sometimes also strangeness) of members of their familiar group; encounters with difference can be found in both sets of interactions, as home-making proceeds.

In this chapter we ask, then, how does making a home—that process of seeking secure shelter and situated belonging in a place, in which we are all involved in some way—involve encounters with difference in urban multicultures? How are social relations of equality enacted in the encounters with difference that occur when making a home, even as those making a home must do so within a housing market characterized by inequality? Making a home as a continual process of creating a space that is familiar but in which heterogeneity is encountered may be one of the ways of "gathering diversity into a functioning commons" (Amin 2012, 11), though it will not be without conflicts. In the encounters involved in making a home that we discuss below, those that include difference are clearly negotiated and intended, not merely accidental or fleeting, although not necessarily preplanned. They may have some well-understood rules of participation, and indeed may be subject to "home rules" of the kind Smith (2008) describes, as well as other culturally specific expectations. They may involve learning by participants about the way things are done in a neighborhood or place, even though this learning may take place over a very long time, and even across generations. They are often grounded in relationships of care.

In migrants' everyday lives, we will see that making a home gives rise to encounters and often negotiation with difference at two principal scales: (1) within a neighborhood area that groups diverse residents and neighbors alongside the infrastructure around their housing, and that may also include institutional stakeholders like local governments or housing authorities; and (2) within the individual dwelling and its suburban garden, where encounters occur between householders—often of the same family—over the daily tasks of social reproduction. These are both scales at which making a home can be seen as involving the intersection, or encounter, of the social relationships of being homed with the things (i.e. material technologies and forms of financing) that are "houses" and neighborhoods. In focusing on these scales of activity in the making of home, we follow Jacobs and Smith's (2008, 517) point that "the acts of 'housing' and 'dwelling' [and, we might add, making a home] are a co-production between those who are housed and the technologies, architectural and financial, they use."

A further scale of analysis in the making of home that might be considered is the metropolitan area as a whole, where housing of different kinds (physical form, size, tenure type) is distributed, which is occupied by population groups with varied characteristics (wealth, racial and cultural background, household type) in circumstances of greater or lesser segregation, all of this with the support of housing and other urban policies. And of course, even though the making of home is understood as a grounded process that occurs through residents being materially located in buildings and in parts of the city, their actions and interactions also occur online. The "homes" they make are therefore further embedded in networks quite beyond the physical scales we have named here. In this chapter, however, we choose to examine the encounters of migrants at a more intimate scale that involves them and their homes directly in the activities of everyday life.

Housing in Melbourne's Migrant-Based Multiculture

The major cities of Australia, especially Sydney and Melbourne, whose metropolitan areas each have populations of more than 4 million people, have since the 1950s been the favored destination of Australia's migrants. The composition of the migrant population in these cities differs slightly, with some national groups favoring one or the other. Within each city, particular migrant groups may cluster in certain suburbs, though they are not highly segregated.

Immigrants usually locate together in suburbs that have residents of a variety of cultural, regional, or national backgrounds. Different migrant groups may have a particular relationship to areas of relative affluence or disadvantage within these metropolitan areas. In general, though, in the metropolitan area of Melbourne over the past fifty years, newly arrived migrants have often started their new lives in poorer areas like the inner ring suburbs (which were not affluent until their gentrification from the 1970s onwards), certain pockets in the northern, southern, and western suburbs, and more recently the suburbs of the outer metropolitan fringe. They have moved to more affluent, often middle-ring suburbs over their lifetimes, as their economic circumstances have improved. Recent migrants, even those who are affluent when they arrive in Australia, often find themselves situated in a housing market of marked inequality, with high housing prices. There are inadequate supplies of social housing. Migrants' experiences of being together as equals in the encounters of their daily lives must therefore be understood within the broader inequality of their setting.

Australian census data presents information about grouped individuals in the population; this is not, of course, data about encounters or actual interactions between those individuals. Population data from the census does, however, provide useful background information for a study of encounters, especially by providing information about changes in the demographic context over time in which those encounters might arise in different parts of the urban area.

This data has been used by some scholars to demonstrate that the residential locations of migrants to Australia's major cities, including Melbourne, exhibit the overall pattern described in spatial assimilation models: an initial spatial clustering when a migrant group first arrives, which disperses over time, particularly as subsequent generations spread out to live among other groups in the city (Edgar 2014; Forrest et al. 2006). Edgar uses ancestry rather than birthplace data about migrants in Sydney and Melbourne (from the 2011 census), thus being able to include the locations of people from three generations who identify with a particular migrant origin. The index of dissimilarity values emerging in Edgar's study, she suggests, make it clear that large-scale segregation of the kind evident in research on U.S. cities does not prevail in Australian cities. The very great diversity of immigrant groups in Australia over decades is one reason for this finding, Edgar maintains, with a regular spatial progression of later groups through the areas of cities previously occupied by earlier-arriving immigrant groups, and with some members of all groups remaining in these locations to make up a cultural mix. Forrest et al., using earlier data, also find "no general evidence of any long-term spatial entrapment" (461). There is always the caution, however, that reliance on quantitative data to demonstrate ethnic concentration or dispersal, and the assumption that assimilation (dispersal) is the desired outcome of any migration process, may fail to see that some long-standing spatial co-locations of people of similar cultural backgrounds are a supportive and positive thing for them, and that the visibility this concentration brings to cultural diversity can also be of benefit to residents of the city as a whole (Dunn et al. 2007).

Since the mid-twentieth century, commentators have often seen Melbourne's metropolitan area as made up of "the inner city" and "the suburbs." The inner city comprises municipalities (which are actually suburbs, in fact) circling the CBD—for until the construction of high-rise apartment buildings from the mid-2000s to house the new boom of university students from overseas, few people actually lived in the central business district. These inner-city municipalities have the majority of the oldest housing in Melbourne, which has been generally of higher density than housing in what is thought of as the suburbs, those newer places farther away from the CBD. The suburbs of the city, outside this inner ring, have long been known for their single family housing on sizable lots. (Suburban housing on big lots has long been the norm and the aspiration for many households, even now that higher density housing is growing in suburban settings.) These suburbs are the home-places of the "suburban peasantry" mentioned previously. Such low-density suburbs, varied in age and character as they are, create the sprawling cities for which Australia is known. In Melbourne it is at the suburban fringes of the metropolitan area that much of the city's strong population growth, including migrants, is being accommodated. The newest, outer fringe of suburbs is poorly

Making a Home in Melbourne   63

served by public transport compared to those suburbs nearer the city center, and schools and social services are constantly needing to respond (belatedly it always seems, despite planning efforts) to the high levels of population growth occurring there. Inner-city areas are well served by public transport infrastructure and social services like hospitals and parks.

As in so many cities in countries with major immigration, there has been a profound link between migrants in Melbourne and the city's less affluent urban locations, in Melbourne's case the inner city. Newcomer migrants arriving in Melbourne after World War II could afford to live in inner-city areas because the dilapidated old Victorian villas and terrace houses there were less desirable parts of the housing market. Those existing residents who could were selling up and moving to suburbs farther out, or moving into the public housing being built in high-rise form on land from which old housing had been cleared. The old housing of the inner city was cheap for newcomers to rent and to buy—and home and land purchase was what many migrants wished for (see, for example, Pulvirenti's 1996 study of Italian migrants' focus on home-ownership). Italian and Greek migrants in particular, prominent migrant groups in Melbourne in the 1950s and 1960s, created a special presence in the inner city. (Urban historians document this time as the beginning of the gentrification of inner Melbourne and also of the activism of groups opposed to the urban renewal policies of the state government's housing authority, which was intent on clearing the inner areas' old housing and building high-rise public housing in its stead [see Davison 2009; Howe 2009].)

Because of the spatial concentration and straitened circumstances of these newly arrived migrants, activist and service organizations emerged in Melbourne's inner city in the 1950s and 1960s that supported migrants as they began to establish themselves. Housing was part of the remit of these organizations, though not their only concern. Tenants' organizations and support groups in the inner city worked with and for migrants as they did with other residents. The women's refuge movement began to find safe homes for needy immigrant and refugee women from the mid-1970s (Murdolo 2014). Organizations formed by migrants themselves were active in service provision roles that supplemented what was available from government. Many of these organizations remain active (see Jupp 2002; Hinz 2010).

By the late 1970s, when any remaining manufacturing work was leaving the inner city and when gentrification was beginning to raise house prices, many migrant homeowners sold up and bought homes in the suburbs farther away from the CBD (Howe 2009). Even then, "home" was understood in terms of financial security and financial opportunity in the inner Melbourne context; making a home was forming a financial asset as well as a place to belong, as our case studies in this chapter reflect. If some migrants had managed to find housing in publicly owned rental units when they first arrived in Melbourne, this was temporary and they moved into the private housing market as soon as possible. Such public housing was always a relatively small proportion of the total housing stock in the city. But since the 1970s, with the growing influence of neoliberal ideologies in housing policy and provision, the proportion has been further reduced, with the creation of new publicly owned units not keeping pace at all with population growth and rising demand. Forming a home, for new migrants in Melbourne, has generally been about achieving home-ownership in the private housing market, in the same way that this has long been the aspiration for longer-term residents of Australian cities, and private ownership is the form of housing tenure principally supported by public policy (Troy 2012).

Evidence about the housing tenures in which Melbourne's migrant groups are now living demonstrates the move to home-ownership among migrant residents, where they can make this happen. This is illustrated in Figures 1 and 2, which depict the circumstances recorded in the Australian census in 2016 for selected birthplace groups, some of whom are long-term migrant residents (from the 1950s or 1960s) and others more recently arrived. In Figure 1, the long-term residents from Italy and Greece are shown to have the highest rates of outright home-ownership; higher rates of renting occur among much more recently arrived groups from Somalia, Ethiopia, Afghanistan, Pakistan, Bangladesh, India, and Iraq, many of which include refugees. Migrants who are not long-term residents but whose birthplace groups have a significant middle-class component, such as mainland China, Sri Lanka, and India, tend to be homeowners with mortgages, as do groups present since the 1970s, like those from Lebanon, Turkey, and Vietnam. In Figure 2, renters' circumstances are shown, and it is evident that people from Somalia and Ethiopia, with their major refugee components, are concentrated in the public housing rental sector. Previously disadvantaged migrant groups from Turkey, Lebanon, and Vietnam retain a strong presence in that housing. Most renters are in the private rental sector, renting from real estate agents.

Beyond the inner city, Melbourne's suburbs are diverse. They are old and new, with mainly low-density housing of different

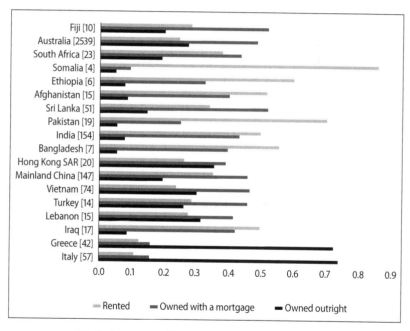

FIGURE 1. *Birthplace groups' housing tenure, metropolitan Melbourne, 2016. The graph shows the percentage of individuals in selected birthplace groups in metropolitan Melbourne in 2016 who are renting their housing, own it outright, or own it with a mortgage. On the y axis, the numbers in brackets to the right of the birthplace names indicate the overall size of each birthplace group in Melbourne, in thousands. (Source: Australian Bureau of Statistics 2016. Table constructed using the ABS Table Builder function, March 2018.)*

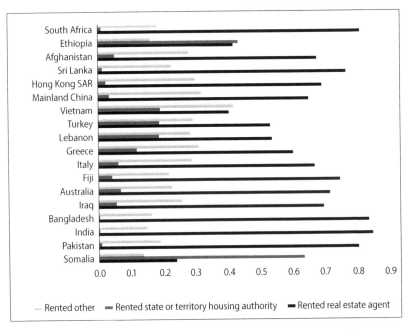

FIGURE 2. *Birthplace groups' forms of renting, metropolitan Melbourne, 2016.* The graph shows the forms of rental housing selected birthplace groups occupied in metropolitan Melbourne in 2016, including renting in the private housing market from a real estate agent; renting a public housing unit from a government housing authority; or other, which includes renting from a nongovernment social housing organization and renting directly from a landlord without going through a real estate agent. (Source: Australian Bureau of Statistics 2016. Table constructed using the ABS Table Builder function, March 2018.)

styles and prices set on blocks of land of varying sizes, and they are experiencing the incursion of high-rise or high-density housing at different rates. The newer suburbs on the metropolitan fringes include some master-planned estates, in which developers promise that "communities" will be built.

From the 1970s, many migrants who were factory workers chose to locate in suburbs that were close to the big (then) manufacturing centers of automobile production in the (then) outer north of the metropolitan area. Now, in the early twenty-first century, migrants (other than students) usually locate first in non-inner suburban locations to establish their homes, often attracted by the presence of those from their own cultural communities. Thus, for example, the central eastern suburbs are now increasingly home to a large middle-class mainland Chinese population. Refugee hubs in Melbourne have long been located in outer southeastern Dandenong and inner western Footscray, places where government-owned housing was initially provided for refugee newcomers, and services supporting them were established. Though inner-city public housing remains important for some refugees from Africa and the Middle East, outer suburban localities now host recent refugees and asylum seekers in growing numbers, though big apartment blocks of public housing are not available there for this purpose.

In Melbourne's outer fringe suburbs, populations of great ethnic diversity are settling. These are both first- and second-generation migrants, seeking out the affordable house and land packages made available by developers in these new suburban locations. One example is in Whittlesea, in the state government designated "growth corridor" of Melbourne's northeast, where migrants of Vietnamese, Indian, Sri Lankan, Chinese, and Filipino ethnicity live together in considerable numbers (Khan 2014). To the west of Melbourne in particular, and to the southeast and north, similar groupings of migrant households are found in the rapidly growing outer suburbs. The birthplaces of the overseas-born groups in each of Melbourne's local government areas shows the persistence of major migrant groups in certain sections of the city: China-born in the central east and southeast, Italy-born in the northern suburbs, India-born in the southwestern suburbs. But in all municipalities there are numerous overseas-born groups of almost equal size and percentage in the local population, providing a varied cultural landscape across the metropolitan area (Australian Bureau of Statistics 2014).

Thus, the making of home in Melbourne has since the 1950s been an increasingly suburban experience, with many newly arriving immigrants now finding themselves in suburbs on the urban fringe. That being said, the inner-city area of Melbourne has had a special relationship with migration as a place where many migrants first stayed when they arrived between the 1950s and 1970s, where they were supported by activist and service organizations,

68   *Making a Home in Melbourne*

and from where many launched their suburban lives with financing from the sale of their homes to gentrifiers. With the exception of particular immigrant groups like students from overseas who live primarily in high-rise housing near their university campuses, homes are now being made by migrants largely in the suburbs, for some in those suburbs that are financially more accessible, but for others also in the suburbs of the middle class. These homes are made within institutional arrangements that give priority to home-ownership. They occur within spatial settings that are not highly segregated ethnically. Despite the tendency to the formation of ethnically specific enclaves that might occur soon after the arrival of big migrant groups from the one place of origin, who seek out their familiars for comfort as they begin to make their way, the evidence for Australian cities (including Melbourne) demonstrates that, over the two generations that follow, these spatial concentrations ease.

The precise encounters with difference that a migrant might experience when making a home, and the ways that everyday equalities might be expressed in those interactions, will vary according to a range of factors, like the time of one's arrival into a particular housing market and economy or one's location in a building, street, and suburb with conationals or with a variety of others. In the following cases, we consider interactions in the making of home in Melbourne at two scales, to examine what the significant encounters with difference, and their associated enactments of being together as equals, might be in this particular urban activity.

Everyday Neighborly Caring in Dandenong

In our first case, we consider a place to which migrants from all over the world come as their first location in Melbourne (and many stay on), and the emergence of a bottom-up neighborhood culture of recognizing others that has developed in which people routinely support and include others. Within the local streets of Dandenong, a super-diverse, migrant-receiving suburb in southeastern Melbourne, making a home together is the task and activity of families from more than 150 nations of origin who work at being neighbors. Their home certainly includes their individual houses, but is

Making a Home in Melbourne   69

not defined utterly by them. We draw here on the work of Michele Lobo (2009), who recounts the stories of residents of Dandenong from a variety of cultural backgrounds and lengths of residence in that suburb, and their interactions as they make a home there. She interprets their actions as "shifting the boundaries of whiteness" in that location, something that could be seen as the enactment of social relations of equality. Certainly there is active encountering across difference. Mutual caring is a manifestation of equality here—it is equality being practiced.

It is clear that Lobo is seeing inclusion and hope for a better future in the way that her interviewees talk about their home-making; she converses with people who appreciate the different lives that have been lived by the people around them, and value their spatial proximity in local streets and apartment buildings. Being a good and caring neighbor, and recalling how neighbors helped in one's own first days in Dandenong, appears to motivate migrant residents to engage in convivial encounters with difference. Lobo quotes China-born Lisa, who lived in Dandenong for eighteen years after coming to Australia:

> I mix up, you know. It's like you know, when I live in Dandenong South, it's my right hand side the neighbour is from Yugoslav[ia]—very good people. And my left hand side, one old lady from India—yeah, very good lady. You know, since I moved from there, you know, during the holiday time, Easter and Christmas time, I still go there and visit them. (182)

Others, more recent arrivals to Australia and the area, note that sometimes different languages, dress, and customs can be a barrier to communication between people living in neighboring apartments, but that simple daily greetings can readily be made. Longer-term residents often showed care for those newly arrived in Dandenong. Lobo recounts her experience of neighborly care and assistance at a time of a fire emergency in her own flat in Dandenong:

> When I was a resident of Dandenong, a fire broke out in our flat and our neighbors who had recently migrated

70   *Making a Home in Melbourne*

> from Serbia and Bosnia, who spoke little English, thought nothing of risking their lives to help me. They did their best to put out the fire and protect me from harm. Reflecting on this moment now, I see the neighborly care that they extended towards me as something difficult to understand and explain because we had not developed a deep friendship. This is the care that people show towards one another that creates a strong emotional attachment to Dandenong. These practices of care contribute to a feeling of belonging that was apparent when residents made comments like "For me [Dandenong] is good," . . . "it's a home type of feeling." (184–85)

Humor, as well as care, is a way of getting along in public encounters with those of different cultures, Lobo found. It defuses possible misunderstandings. She recounts a frequent scene at the huge local food market, where one vendor and his customers "often engaged in banter that depended on cultural and ethnic identifiers but which was playful and irreverent" (187). In his long conversations with his customers, the vendor often tried to guess the country his customers came from, even introducing different customers to each other using this information, all this in a joking manner.

Encounters with difference, as noted by Lobo, very often involved daily exchanges as neighbors and consumers around the local area's streets and public spaces. Friendly, reasonably caring styles of communication were vital to the inclusion experienced. There is surely a form of intimacy in this kind of belonging, in knowing how the local place works, and feeling comfortable and comforted by that knowledge, in trusting one's neighbors to respect one's civility as well as acknowledging one's difference. Lobo found the communication reported by her interviewees recognized and valued the fact that Dandenong has a history of receiving new migrants from all over the world, and retains many of those people within its boundaries.

Just as Ahmed (1999, 345) remarked, acknowledgment of everyone's strangeness is a way for people to bond, to form home together, and to belong. This is readily possible in a migrant-receiving suburb of great cultural diversity, as Lobo reports for Dandenong, though conflicts occur as well. Not only is home being made here, but an everyday equality is being enacted in the banal interactions of neighborliness and use of public spaces and shops. Although an acute everyday focus on the countries from which people come and the varied cultural backgrounds they have can label people as different and as other, nevertheless this is also something they have in common; they are equal in their variation. The "imagined community" of Dandenong is not founded on nationality, but on a distinct form of equality in difference—it is imagined by its inhabitants as a place where *anyone* can make a home, no matter where they are from, without a requirement for people to erase or assimilate their differences.

Around a neighborhood, then, especially one in which cultural differences are so visible and long-standing, making a home can occur at a scale beyond the home unit itself. The positive ways home and belonging can be made in such a place are based on repeated, everyday encounters. Local practices of caring for newcomers, and being civil to them, can create the warmth and comfort that are central to a feeling of being at home. The politics and social relations of equality being practiced and developed in Dandenong, in Lobo's account, derive from the way that new arrivals are enveloped in an ongoing culture of learning that names and draws upon difference (and sometimes stereotypes it too) and presents an "all in this together" kind of feel. Of course, tensions are always there aplenty, as well as hope and care.

Limiting Encounters with Difference in Carlton

Our second case stands in stark contrast to our first. Here, we have an example of the "social mix" replanning of an existing public housing estate, imposed by government in partnership with developers, that is limiting possibilities for encounter with difference and is reinforcing status hierarchies and inequality between public tenants and private owners (we draw for this case upon the 2015 analysis by Arthurson, Levin, and Ziersch). In inner-city Carlton, a place that was central to the urban activist movements of the 1970s and to which post–World War II migrants from Italy and Greece came in large numbers, social mix is currently being applied to a large high-rise public housing estate—one of those very estates against which activist movements in the 1970s protested.

This large redevelopment project places privately owned rental housing units alongside publicly owned rental units. This is a social mix project, transforming an existing estate of high-rise and medium-density public housing units into a mixed-tenure housing estate of high-rise apartment buildings. The Carlton estate was home at the time of the 2011 census to about 1,700 public housing residents. The social mix project included construction of both public and private housing units to replace eight public housing apartment blocks, construction of a retirement village and aged-care center, development of new public parks, gardens, and landscaping, and gradual renovation of the remaining high-rise public units (Arthurson et al., 494–95).

Social mix (or housing mix) policies are a reaction by urban policy-makers to the spatially concentrated presence of low-income people in certain housing and certain areas. Higher-income residents, and often homeowners, are encouraged to locate in rebuilt housing spatially proximate to long-standing low-income residents, often renters in public housing. This is justified as a means to reduce concentrations of poverty. The number of low-income residents in the location may decline as a result of this process. Debate exists about whether governments intend primarily to create the conditions for gentrification in urban settings by combining households of different income (and sometimes ethnic and racially identified) characteristics so that gradually wealthier households will overtake the area, or whether governments really are committed to improving the lives of lower-income households by helping them to make homes in a broader community of people across their differences even though the research evidence demonstrates plainly that such interaction does not occur. The edited collection by Bridge et al. (2012) lays out this policy territory clearly, and provides an evidence-based academic critique of it.

As the first construction phase in Carlton progressed, the original intent of government to provide a "salt and pepper" social mix of public and private tenants through all the buildings was abandoned. This occurred under pressure from the private sector developers who were partners in the project and wanted to hide the public housing component of it (the public housing tenants are more likely to be of racialized minorities, many having come fairly recently from certain African countries as refugees to Australia). Accordingly, the new apartment buildings (not including an aged-care facility) each accommodate occupants of a particular housing tenure—either public tenants or private tenants (who may be owner-occupiers). Arthurson et al. (2015, 498) quote a local service provider who was dismayed at the sales pitch being presented to potential private investors by the marketing staff of the real estate developers on site:

> They weren't selling it as one of the most amazing opportunities for social inclusion, one of the most amazing opportunities to experience, on a deep level, being in a multicultural community, getting to know people who are black and getting to know people from another country and know people on a different social level. No, it's not about that, it's about getting an inner-city unit.

One of the manifestations of the shift toward the interests of developers in the design and construction of this site is the fate of a small garden area on the estate. Where the original intention was to create shared public space around the buildings, now this small garden is visible to all public and private tenants from their windows, but accessible only to private renters/owners. Arthurson et al. (499) describe how an extra retaining wall has been built to prevent public tenants from having access to the garden:

> The garden, then, is a small public space that bears the imprint of the development industry's interest in having these inner city apartment buildings available to investors in the private market, untrammelled by the possibility of interacting with lower-income people of different ethnicities. This interest has swamped any concern that government may have expressed in the past about mixing tenants of different housing tenures in the interests of social inclusion.

74 *Making a Home in Melbourne*

Interestingly, private sector residents interviewed by Arthurson et al. comment that while they might have made an effort to meet residents who were public tenants if they had shared the same building, they would not make the effort if public tenants lived in other buildings. They also stated that social inclusion had been less of an interest for them in locating in these buildings than obtaining an inner-city apartment and making a good real estate investment. For their part, public housing tenants on the estate said that they did not expect to mix socially with residents in the privately owned apartments, even expressing some sympathy for these private tenants who had paid so much money for a small apartment. They imagined the residents of the private housing as being busy, and as having good jobs and friends of similar incomes.

Even though emotions of dismay are expressed by community workers who had high hopes for this program, the residents themselves, when interviewed, seem resigned to the inscription and normalization of status hierarchies and inequality that is going on here, and the limitations on encounters that will ensue in the making of home in this place. They seem to have accepted that tenants of the publicly owned buildings will have less beneficial conditions in their housing environment than will tenants or owners in the privately owned units; they have accepted not being together as equals, but being separate and unequal.

These public and private housing tenants express the same divergent feelings about their housing and the role of housing in their lives as August (2014) found in her study in Don Mount, Toronto. There, market (private) housing residents in this gentrifying locale of social mix had different expectations of the activities around and purposes of housing than did some returning residents of subsidized housing. Almost paralleling the case of Melbourne's Carlton estate, in which the garden is off-limits to residents of public housing and available only to private market residents, in the case of the Don Mount housing estate the expectations of private housing residents that public housing tenants (usually of different ethnicities and cultures than their own) would not hang out in public spaces were actively stated and patrolled. Indeed, the exclusion of renters, newcomers, and those of fewer resources does not have

Making a Home in Melbourne 75

to be part of a government-organized social mix in housing. As Gow demonstrates (2005) in his close study of the residents of a strata-titled apartment block in western Sydney, owners living in their apartments themselves used their membership in the owners' association to attempt to regulate the use of public spaces around the building by tenants, many of whom were recently arrived refugees. The owners issued threatening directives about parking and areas where children could not play to tenants of the building, their strategy being, says Gow (397), "to direct the block into privatized and closed spaces." On this occasion, the directives seem to have backfired, causing tenants to gather together to express their solidarity in opposition to limitations on their use of public spaces around the building—this solidarity being formed across their differences and language barriers.

Redeveloping housing contexts like that in Carlton make particularly clear the role of institutions in establishing how one conducts a life and makes a home in and around housing. The messages implicitly delivered to residents through the way this social mix program is evolving form a grammar of living, to use Smith's (2008) term, indeed. Not only is making a home a process internal to a household. It also involves, very centrally, encounters with neighbors, and processes sometimes of differentiating oneself and one's familiars from them. Policies of social mix might have been expected to demonstrate positive encounters. Certainly the rhetoric of social mix in policy suggests that social inclusion is its aim, and its expectation is that higher-income residents will actively seek to support and engage with lower-income residents. The evidence of what actually happens in situations of social mix shows, however, a different reality, that is commonly more akin to what Arthurson et al. found in Melbourne. As Shaw (2012) demonstrates in an excoriating review of the redevelopment of inner Melbourne's public housing estates (including the Carlton one), the efforts of government to avoid financial risk through public-private partnerships have meant that developers have had a strong say in the layout and marketing of the redeveloped estates. Diversity in tenants of the resulting housing has reduced. The kinds of units available to public tenants have changed so that large families are less able to be

76 Making a Home in Melbourne

accommodated. And there is no question that state-led gentrification is an inexorable product of the market-oriented redevelopments in these now-coveted inner-city locations.

Private Apartments and Public Venues of Central Melbourne

As a third example, we consider student migrants living in high-rise apartment buildings on the fringe of Melbourne's central business district, and focus our attention on the interplay between the physical settings of cities and the possibilities of encounter and being together as equals. Here, we examine how students' socializing and encounters with one another and with others in the city are influenced by the physical form of the new apartment housing that has been built with university students in mind. For student migrants living in these apartments, making a home involves socializing in the big private shopping malls of the downtown area nearby, because there are rarely communal spaces for socializing in the student housing they are occupying. We note that young people, here students, are in a life course stage in which making a home is about forming friendships and conquering loneliness; it also involves developing a workable identity (Fincher 2011).

Australian universities, including those in Melbourne, are increasingly dependent on revenue from international student fees to supplement shortfalls in state funding for their core operations (Fincher and Shaw 2009). But as universities target the international student market, what is life like for the students who become temporary migrants in cities like Melbourne? Documentation of the morphology of a large sample of apartment buildings intended for the student market in the first decade of the 2000s demonstrates that the stand-out features of the buildings, located on the fringe of central Melbourne, are the small size of the apartments (which are usually studios with a bed or two, a desk, a tiny kitchenette and bathroom, and minimal storage space) and the lack of communal space, with none of the spaces common to student housing elsewhere in the world and indeed in student housing elsewhere in Australia, such as communal kitchens, lounges, and study areas (Fincher et al. 2009). This situation came about because of the way the construction of the apartment buildings was financed. The buildings (some of them pictured in Figure 3) were developed in the commercial market, and individual apartments in them were pitched at investors seeking relatively low-cost entry to the housing market within the prevailing institutional climate that allowed negative gearing (tax deductibility for housing investment costs) for investors. Cheap, no-frills apartments were what investors sought: large numbers of the apartments in these buildings were purchased with loans of almost 100 percent of the value of the properties.

One may readily conclude that the construction of these apartment buildings was primarily about the generation of assets for investors in real estate, rather than the production of housing for student migrants. Students' homes were never the major aim here, as the flexibility of the housing was important so that it could be sold as single apartments in the case of a future decline in demand from students. In such a circumstance, communal facilities would serve no purpose. So, "the temporary nature of this accommodation is not due solely to the temporary status of their student residents, but to the typologies of the buildings themselves which make them perform as temporary dwellings while masquerading as permanent" (Fincher et al. 2009, 55). International students, particularly from different countries in Asia, tend to be funneled into these apartments by the agents of universities, who play a major role in the housing choices provided to students. International students are also limited in their capacity to choose housing farther away from campus by their ineligibility for concession fares on public transport (an issue related to those discussed in chapter 5— see Fincher and Shaw 2009).

The morphological features of this housing (tiny apartments, no communal spaces) propelled student residents to study and socialize in communal spaces elsewhere—especially in the food courts of the nearby enclosed private shopping malls. These spaces became students' lounge rooms. One student from China, who had been living in Melbourne for three years, reported that she enjoyed these accessible parts of two big shopping malls:

FIGURE 3. *Investor financed and student-occupied apartment buildings, Swanston Street, central Melbourne. (Source: Fincher et al. 2009; photograph by Kate Shaw, used with permission.)*

> Because I can do many activities. Like meeting people and doing some shopping . . . even do homework there [in the QV food court]. And . . . we always meet in Melbourne Central. It's easy to recognise. (Fincher and Shaw 2011, 544)

Students emphasized the proximity of the shopping malls to their apartment buildings, and also that they found these places comfortable social spaces in which to be with friends. Accordingly, the food courts and scattered seating in these large shopping malls are associated with students from different parts of Asia who live in the area, who meet, study, and socialize there. Mappings of the preferred places of recently arrived student migrants in Melbourne show the attachment they have to these frequently visited places and how warmly they feel about them (Fincher et al. 2009; Fincher and Shaw 2011). Students from the apartment buildings also like

Making a Home in Melbourne 79

the fact that the spaces are secure and well cared-for; being inside and in a secure environment makes their socializing in a new place more comfortable. Accordingly, home and belonging are made via frequent encounters in the accessible and large communal spaces of shopping malls. These are encounters with difference in the sense that the students engaged in them are from a diversity of countries in the Asian region; though they are encounters with the familiar in that all participants are students and have study and forming friendships in an unfamiliar city as the life task they need to deal with. Being together in difference as equals occurs in the socializing of students in these accessible spaces, despite the inhospitable nature of the apartment buildings in which the young people actually reside, and perhaps also despite the formal purposes of those public spaces in which they gather (shopping mall food courts were unlikely to have been designed with homework and study in mind!).

A small number of student apartment buildings near Melbourne's major universities have communal kitchens. Usually these are older, smaller buildings, and less well-advertised to incoming student migrants than the larger buildings whose morphological features we have mentioned. Students from buildings without communal facilities flock to join residents of the buildings with kitchens in cooking together, making a home through the establishment of friendships in this simple activity. Hear a student living in one of the buildings with a communal kitchen:

> C [a small, older, cheaper student apartment block] is a place where we have share kitchen and share common room. So basically I meet my friends while we're cooking. So we start the cooking and made friends and our group got bigger and bigger. Friends just came from being friends of my friends . . . some of them are from [building] U which is just a stone-throw away from C. (Fincher et al. 2009, 31)

In this example, young people from a number of countries in Asia (primarily China, Singapore, and Malaysia) who are establishing social lives in Melbourne as new migrants set about making home by making friendships with other young people. In this task they find themselves taking advantage of the facilities in the broader neighborhood, principally because the apartment buildings in which they live do not have communal spaces where their socializing can occur. In accessing and appropriating these spaces, they are collectively making a home in the city in a manner that escapes the restrictive housing and educational markets that tend to interpolate them as having no life beyond individualized dormitory study. They are finding ways to be together as equals across their different national and ethnic backgrounds and forming networks of friends; the networks are formed through the doing of daily tasks of study and eating together. Some students join student societies to press for improvements in the facilities offered to international students, and make alliances and friendships in this way. Many join churches with an active mission to international students (Fincher 2011). Most students find friends more simply, through the daily social and educational tasks that they are required to perform.

It is not evident yet that these ways of being together in difference as equals have translated into an effective political movement of international students who are concerned about housing and who are making organized claims on the relevant city institutions in support of their attempts to make a home in these tiny, privately rented apartments. But there are signs that institutions are increasingly aware of certain problems that can befall student migrants in the private rental sector in Melbourne. (It is, of course, in the interests of such institutions to protect the lucrative flow of these young migrants to the city and its universities and businesses.) Universities, local governments, and state government consumer affairs agencies now warn international students very visibly about their rights as tenants, particularly the issue of how to have a "bond" returned at the end of one's rental lease (for landlords may refuse to refund this amount to unsuspecting tenants). The local government of Melbourne's CBD has, in the wake of researchers' assessments of the apartment buildings it allowed to be erected for students (such as those shown in Figure 3), recently established design rules for the building of student housing where previously it had none. This awareness on the part of city institutions has come about because of students speaking up together, to their university teachers and to the members of church communities they have

Making a Home in Melbourne

joined, as well as because these institutions seek to protect their own benefits from the flow of students to the city. Local governments, particularly in central Melbourne, now consult with international students to develop strategies to support the students in the city. Organizations formed by and for international students are growing in confidence and in presence on university campuses, with interests in a range of issues, one of which is housing. These students' being together in difference as equals through their own housing experiences, their own attempts to make a home, has contributed to the formation of a growing student voice in the city, even though this could not be termed a fully-fledged, housing-oriented, visible activist movement. A concerted effort by students from overseas may create a group that long-standing advocacy organizations like Tenants Victoria particularly support and deem vulnerable in the private rental market.

Being Together in Making a Home, Intergenerationally

Our next two cases consider the kinds of encounters with difference that take place within, and with the physical objects of, the dwelling. Encounters with difference can occur within a dwelling that has already been made a home over an extended period by other family members or housemates. As we shall see, there is nothing uncontested or homogeneous about home-life within dwellings, and difference can occur within its walls and gardens and with reference to the clashing expectations of diverse household members. Of course encounters within dwellings are the product of outside influences and past histories brought into the home from outside it as much as they are interactions produced entirely in the moment and within the confines of the dwelling itself.

In the first of these cases, we consider intergenerational differences within family households of Italian migrants over whether home-ownership is to be preferred to renting and whether heterosexual relationships are to be preferred to same-sex relationships in the making of a home. The "home rules," to use Smith's (2008) term, of the first generation of migrants are being queried here by the second generation, with being together as equals a possible casualty. We draw on Mariastella Pulvirenti's (1996) account of the importance of home-ownership to first- and second-generation Italian Australians making a home in Melbourne. An acceptable and "proper" home cannot be rented, in this first-generation "home rule," but must be owned. Further, an acceptable family life must be lived in such a home, and needs to be grounded in a heterosexual relationship, preferably in which the couple are parents to children. Pulvirenti showcases negotiated encounters between the generations about these aspects of making a home, especially the negotiations involved in establishing the role of home-ownership in defining an acceptable family life. Some young people, children of first-generation Italian immigrants, followed their parents' views on the importance of owning housing and not renting it; others did not. First-generation Italian immigrants to Australia from the 1950s, who were often from rural areas in Italy and arrived as migrants with few financial resources, placed great stress on becoming established as new residents via home-ownership and employment. They also emphasized the heterosexual, family-prioritizing social relationships that earning and buying housing were intended to support. Second-generation Italian Australians, however, were sometimes not so dedicated to this mix of housing tenure and closely prescribed family mores. (Heterosexuality, as diaspora studies have pointed out, is often given a central place in making a home, especially where that process is aided by religious affiliations, e.g. Fortier 2000).

In Pulvirenti's (1996) study of first- and second-generation Italian migrants in Melbourne in the 1990s, many younger family members lived with their parents while they saved. Said Vicky, one of the interviewees:

> We put off marriage until we could afford to buy land or buy a home. . . . We lived with my parents for three years while we built. They didn't ask for rent or anything like that. My father did all the tiling, the bathroom, the floor tiling. . . . Save, save, save, everything went into the house. (166–67)

Yet other second-generation Italian Australians were less keen on the linked ideas of home-ownership and heterosexual marriage.

Making a Home in Melbourne 83

Thus their encounters over and within their parents' homes were more fraught and had to be actively negotiated. Nadia, who moved out to rent, said:

> My parents think it's stupid to be paying rent . . . my dad wasn't very supportive. . . . He didn't agree with me moving out of home and he took the attitude that the door was one-way and I could never go back once I left. (174–76)

Some gay or lesbian second-generation interviewees resisted the "heterosexual home-ownership matrix," as Pulvirenti terms it. Said Anna:

> Mum kept saying . . . "When you have your own house, your own husband, blah, blah, blah, then it'll be your own house and I'll come and visit." Then it became over the years, when it became sort of quite clear to her that I wasn't actually looking for a husband . . . it became "Well I don't care if you don't have a husband as long as you're living in your own house and you haven't got all those strange people in there, then I'll come and visit." (187–89)

On the other hand, for Claudio, buying a house was the way out of his family home and its expectations of a life of heterosexuality:

> It dawned on me one day, that I wasn't going to grow up, stay at home and be gay. . . . So I figured this was going to be my ticket out. Just a little bit before I actually bought the house I'd met my partner and I knew that I wanted to live with him. . . . So ultimately that's what made me buy the house. . . . It wasn't because I really wanted to buy a house. (201)

Rejecting the "heterosexual home-ownership matrix" within these migrant families occurs through encounters between parents and their children that are in fact encounters across generational difference. In the quotes it is possible to see some young people (for example, Anna) having conversations with their parents over quite long periods that actually shifted the parents' thinking somewhat. Learning was occurring. Others (for example, Claudio) worked out a way forward (again over a lengthy time) that did not confront his parents as directly as did other interviewees (for example, Nadia) who had to move out of her parents' dwelling in order to be housed as she wished. Respecting and caring for one's parents, as well as living the life one wanted, was the task of the second-generation interviewees involved in making a home for themselves that involved encounters with difference.

Becoming equals across their generational differences and sometimes across their different sexualities by disrupting the places that had been assigned to them in both family and social orders took time for these young people. It is possible that in some dwellings, parents and adult children were together as equals as they resolved their different views about housing and making a home; more likely, it was not until the adult children moved out of the parental home that this equality within the family was achieved. Evidently, while it has been important for first-generation migrants to maintain their cultural priorities and resources in the face of broader racialized inequality beyond the home and the family, this very cultural maintenance has also been experienced as oppressive by some of their children who have sought to diverge from their parents' priorities.

The Physical Form of the Dwelling in the Making of Migrant Homes

As a second example we turn to the question of the material form of a dwelling unit, which is important in the making of home, along with other elements such as interior furnishings and the layout of gardens. A literature has emerged (e.g. Levin 2016; with reference to kitchens, see Supski 2006) that documents the manner in which migrants may establish homes whose physical characteristics reference "home" in their country of origin, or the important memories they have of their original country or home culture. We draw here on Iris Levin's (2010; 2016) documentation of this process in Melbourne, with reference to migrants from Italy and

China, where one of the important encounters with difference is the manner in which these migrants integrated the form of their housing with local expectations, at the same time referencing elements of their place of origin and the ways houses and home there looked and were used. The encounters emphasized here are not merely with other people in the new location, which in fact would be encounter at the scale of the neighborhood. Rather, the encounters emphasized are those that migrant dwellers have with the materials, plants, and forms (as well as the social relations) of making a home that they draw into the physical form of their individual dwellings in Melbourne.

Regarding the forms and locations of immigrants' houses, Levin found that long-standing Italian immigrants in the mid-twentieth century worked side-by-side with friends and family members in Melbourne to build their houses in certain suburbs, using those materials available in Australia that suited the forms of building construction with which they and their Italian friends were more familiar and that they could afford. In contrast, recently arrived professional middle-class Chinese immigrants in Melbourne chose to buy homes through real estate agents specializing in Chinese clientele, locating in suburbs of Melbourne in which their conationals live in numbers alongside middle-class non-Chinese. These locational and building decisions involve encounters with the familiar and the comfortable in dealing with conationals, and are brought to bear in the form of the dwelling produced. Encounters with difference with the building forms and materials used in the Australian context are also reflected in the physical form of the dwellings and gardens.

In Levin's work it is clear that the immigrants she interviews are not asserting in the physical form of their dwelling a visible statement of ethnic identity, pushing it into the streetscapes of their new country to change things there. Rather, theirs is a much more nuanced and long-term encounter between the physical forms of old and the physical forms of new. As Levin is able to show, the settlement of these immigrants is not only inward-looking and a search for links to the past; it is also from the start a hybrid experience of engagement with their new country, and deliberately so. This settlement, as expressed through the physical form of the

FIGURE 4. *A Victorian-era house in inner Melbourne. On this house, traditional veranda posts have been removed by migrant occupants and replaced with posts evoking the trunks of locally native eucalyptus trees. It has "modernized" window and door treatments, concrete-rendered brickwork, and a Victorian-style wrought-iron fence. Compare to the gentrified and renovated Victoria villa next door. (Photograph by Ruth Fincher.)*

house, is a mixture of origin and destination in the lives and hope of the immigrants, an active and lifelong encounter of pasts and presents. Figure 4.4 shows one example.

Lorenzo, one of Levin's interviewees, identifies an "Italian spirit" in his dwelling because its large spaces remind him of Italian houses he lived in during his childhood, and because of the furniture made in Italy with which he has furnished it (Levin 2010, 113–14). Others placed eagles and lions in front of their houses when they moved from the inner to the outer suburbs of Melbourne to denote their European origins and their success. Some of the interviewees, however, see their housing in Australia as Australian in character. As Levin (116) notes: "Loretta's front façade corresponds perfectly with the Australian setting in which it is located, whereas her backyard consists of an Italian vegetable garden." Clearly the manner in which the "suburban peasantry" of the Australian city used the land around their houses was something with which Loretta had plenty of sympathy. Another interviewee of Italian background, Otto, included in his 1960s suburban house some Mediterranean features (a white balustrade and concreted-over front garden space), but it is nevertheless quite at one with the varied suburban streetscape surrounding it.

Italian migrant interviewees living in the Victorian terrace houses of inner Melbourne modified the front façades of their houses with potted plants and terracotta, but the overall Victorian house remained the same. Many created outside veranda spaces for socializing in their Melbourne houses, and modified kitchen spaces to allow socializing as well, as they had in Italy years before. Thus the immigrants interviewed had created social outcomes in the houses in Melbourne that were familiar to them from their childhoods in Italy, but not by rigidly replicating housing trends from the past (Levin 2010, 2016).

There is a mixture here, and Levin concludes from her research that in most houses she saw, when her interviewees showed her around,

> there were not any significant modifications of the visual appearance of the house. Most of the houses are part of a continuous development of streetscapes in Melbourne, thus they do not stand out and wave an Italian flag, in contrast to the common literature which presents Italian migrants' houses as representations of Italian culture. . . . Nevertheless, houses in Melbourne do represent their residents' ethnic identity through a combination of both Italian and Australian characteristics, which makes them familiar and recognisable for their dwellers. (2010, 121)

With her Chinese respondents, Levin was told that none had enhanced the exteriors of their suburban houses to make references to Chinese features, but some had created patio spaces outside reminding them of famous Chinese gardens. All had lived in apartment buildings in China before migration, and none of the features of those dwellings were referenced in the suburban housing they had chosen in Melbourne. Some fêng shui principles had been followed in the interiors of some houses. Chinese immigrants' backyards were not used as household vegetable gardens in the ways of the Italian immigrants preceding them; no suburban peasantry here. Levin (2010, 171) notes that the large Chinese-built suburban "monster houses" disrupting more modest streetscapes elsewhere in the world (especially North America) do not seem to find parallels in suburban Melbourne, at least in the middle-class suburban streets of her report.

In both groups Levin studied, immigrant house-builders and house-dwellers hastened slowly in any physical transformation of their properties. Assertion of an obvious and proud ethnic identity in the publicly visible physical form of their housing seems to have been far from their minds. In the Italian case this may have been because their initial poverty precluded it, and in the more recent Chinese case because locating in suburbs with excellent educational features was a greater priority. Inside their dwellings, memorabilia and decoration sometimes referenced their pasts and their ethnic identities, but little of this was expressed outwardly.

Here we see a gradual absorption of certain Melbourne-situated local histories and habits into the material ways of living of these migrants; they have made their homes through a process of encounter between the building materials and ways of making home that prevailed in their places of origin and those of their current locale. Through migrants' gradual and tactful insertion of their dwellings into different pockets of the built neighborhoods of the city, alongside neighbors who accept their presence, everyday equality and togetherness across difference are being enacted. Perhaps these migrants felt constrained to "fit in" to the streetscapes of their suburbs, from the time of their arrival in Melbourne, and considered they were not the equals of their neighbors in being able to assert an individual presence. Migrants' reluctance to change the exterior of their house profoundly might reflect pressure they felt to assimilate rather than express difference. They did not assert this in interviews, however. Rather, what it appears we are seeing, from Levin's report of her interviews, is a meeting of Italian-ness with

Making a Home in Melbourne 89

Australian-ness in built form choices, and a meeting of Chinese-ness with Australian-ness too. This is one kind of being together in difference as equals, based on encounter and expressed through shaping the physical features of home over a sustained period.

The kinds of encounter reported in this chapter, of making a home at the scale of the neighborhood and at the scale of the dwelling itself, have some distinctive features. They lack the occasional, fleeting, random body-brushing or acknowledging glance that might occur in a trip on public transport or a visit to a one-off music festival in a major public space. Perhaps that is not surprising, since the making of home is a long process of micro-crafting belonging and identity. Being together in difference as equals occurs through repeated encounters with the familiar and the unfamiliar. Many of the encounters reported in this chapter also have an emotional content that demonstrates the importance of care in developing homely situations, and how a lack of care can deny those willing to encounter others and new situations the inclusion they seek. The emotional aspect of encounter is most visible to us when we are capturing comments from relatively newly arrived migrants describing their recent experiences, rather than comments of people talking of the distant past whose hurts may have receded in their memories.

Accordingly, we have observed in the long-standing, migrant-accepting suburb of Dandenong the presence of care and humor as the lubricant that allows many new arrivals from all over the world to make a home with those who have lived there longer. Acts of kindness by neighbors that form relationships, after a fashion, are accompanied by acts of publicly expressed humor by a shopkeeper: even if this is done by calling out the places from which individual customers have come, everyone is greeted and treated in the same way. These are daily exchanges, often repeated; they are intentional rather than fleeting and incidental. They are more the focused interactions of which Goffman (1961) spoke than unfocused interactions. They enact being together in difference as equals in the making of a suburb in which anyone can belong, and in which that anyone is expected to be from anywhere.

In the example of the social mix program in the Carlton public housing estate, we observe the decision by institutional shapers of the program to separate public and private tenants, the former more likely to be recent refugees and migrants, not only separating them into apartment buildings of specific tenures, but preventing access by public tenants to a small park within the development. Now, it is possible that encounters will occur among the privately tenanted or owning residents of certain buildings and the publicly tenanted residents of other buildings. But the social mix promised across the tenure types, in which residents are together as equals, seems unlikely to occur, because the inegalitarian hierarchy between public and private housing tenures is normalized and cemented by these institutionally set arrangements.

Even as we note the significance of the figure of the housing investor who is championed by private sector developers in the social mixing of the Carlton estate, we see this again in the case of student immigrants whose rental housing in new apartment buildings is also guided by that same imperative of the property industry to advantage housing investors. The preferred methods of financing housing, as Smith (2008) has emphasized, are a significant contributor to the fate of those who live in the housing and make their homes there, being one major aspect of the "grammars of living" she conceptualizes. Student migrants seeking friendships but lacking communal spaces in their own buildings have made use of nearby shopping malls as their "living rooms," places in which to hang out and study and make encounters with young people from other places and cultures. The difficulties of being together as equals because of the living arrangements of the individual apartment buildings in both these cases are alleviated for the students by the facilities nearby in the central city's shopping malls. In contrast, these difficulties are exacerbated in the case of the Carlton estate's public tenants by the inaccessibility of the nearby garden. In both cases, encounters and being together as equals are influenced by the actions of property developers.

Within dwellings encounters are similarly across difference, and similarly sustained over time rather than being fleeting. In the intergenerational encounters within Italian Australian households about the value of home-ownership and heterosexual marriage as one makes a proper home, differences are aired over time. They also occur largely in a manner that respects the ongoing social relations of families, even when adult children leave the family dwelling in order to make their own home in a way that may not fit with their parents' "home rules." The heated nature of some of these oppositional exchanges is hinted at, in interviewees' comments reported in the literature. But overall, family relations hold together over time. In the case of migrants building their homes and gardens to reflect some features of their original cultures and places of origin, they also, right from the start of their migrant lives, develop awareness of the different building materials, garden plants, and styles of putting these things together in the streetscapes of suburban Melbourne. The encounter of migrants with the technologies and materials of the suburban house in Melbourne is quite rapid and then long-lasting. A tactful migrant presence in those streetscapes is negotiated, over a long time, in addition to migrants' retaining an emotionally meaningful set of memories from an ever more distant past. Holding these matters in tension, accommodating some matching of the Melbourne streetscape while retaining some features from the past, is the enactment of an everyday politics of equality, of sameness and difference together.

Encounters with difference abound in the making of home in Melbourne. We have concentrated here on encounters engaged in by migrants from many cultures and origins who have come to this city, and have shaped it. Often these encounters are also with whiteness, as Lobo (2009) has emphasized. They are sustained encounters for the most part, repeated, often intentional, not due to chance alone. They are encounters that take place in the context of persistent institutional priorities. The struggles we observe here to enact equality in difference respond to distinct forms of inequality—from White Australian suburban and home-owning norms to hierarchies between public and private tenants, between local and international students, and between straight and queer family members. As a result, these encounters are characterized by particular spatialities and temporalities, the enactment and performance of which can exhibit a variety of forms of being together as equals.

{ 4 }

Working for a Living in Toronto

MOVING FROM HOME TO THE WORKPLACE, we examine the potential of encounters to encourage being together in difference as equals at sites where people from different ethnic and racialized backgrounds earn a living. A politics of equality at work means that the views and interests of workers with the least power and status, workers who are often racialized minorities, are heard and acted upon. It is a particularly challenging goal in workplaces where employers have the authority to decide who works and largely control working conditions and wages. The power differentials are so well known that many state institutions seek to regulate their impacts on workers and their working conditions. We contend that the charged combination of difference, hierarchy, and regulation that characterizes many workplaces in settler colonial cities shapes interactions among workers and with employers, customers, and the general public. In the process of earning a living, encounters may build awareness and respect for cultural difference and ultimately, contribute to a politics of equality. However, encounters may also have little impact on people's views of each other or they may confirm suspicion and reinforce stereotypes. Our goal is to characterize the encounters that occur while people are earning a living, tease out the circumstances that promote equality in difference among workers, and address inequality in the workplace more broadly. We ask how such encounters among workers are constrained and enabled by the institutional and social structures in each workplace and draw attention to the hard work, learning, and care required for being together in difference as equals at the workplace.

We investigate encounters with difference in workplaces in Toronto, Canada, where immigrants from Asia, Africa, the Caribbean, and Central and South America struggle to earn a living alongside their predecessors from every corner of Europe. We start by offering a general overview of the kinds of encounters associated with work in racialized urban labor markets and processes. We then outline current patterns of exclusion in Toronto's workplaces, evident in rising inequality in earnings and incomes and growing reports of unfair treatment on the basis of race, skin color, ethnicity, accent, and religion. Short case studies illuminate the encounters that occur in workplaces that are often more heterogeneous than the places where we live, the public spaces where we gather, and even the recreational facilities where we relax (Ellis et al. 2004; Estlund 2003). In each case, we identify the circumstances under which workplace encounters encourage living in difference as equals and the circumstances in which encounters in the workplace reinforce inequalities rooted in difference. Our analysis acknowledges the varied encounters that occur in workplaces. While many are purposeful, even planned and scripted, others are fleeting and occur by happenstance. The temporality of encounters at work also ranges from encounters like those involved in home-making that are repeated daily over months and years by long-time employees to unexpected interactions precipitated by newcomers in the workplace, technological changes, new regulations, and altered labor processes.

The argument unfolds through three case studies of various workers and workplaces in Toronto: room attendants in large hotels, cashiers in grocery stores, and domestic workers in private residences. The case studies consider workplaces that range in size from private residences where there is only one employee to large downtown hotels that hire hundreds of employees for many different occupations. The labor processes in the three workplaces under study also vary. Domestic workers are charged with numerous different tasks, unlike cashiers who repeat prescribed activities at individual checkout stands and hotel room attendants whose scheduled tasks are coordinated with the tasks of other workers. In all three cases, workers are subject to strict supervision.[1] The case studies comprise a secondary analysis of a growing labor geography literature about Toronto workplaces written by our students as well as our own analyses with colleagues of exclusionary experiences in Toronto workplaces.

The first case study investigates the circumstances that enabled emancipatory encounters among room attendants in large Toronto hotels as revealed in Steve Tufts's analysis of one union's efforts to organize disparate workers drawn from all corners of the globe and possessing diverse skills. Here, the union's support for activities that enabled diverse workers to collaborate in a shared project was crucial for promoting encounters that encouraged living together in difference as equals at the workplace. Despite the overall success of the union's initiative, the case study also illustrates the challenges of achieving a politics of equality in hierarchical workplaces. These challenges are starkly evident in Ekaterina Morihovitis's study of part-time cashiers in Toronto grocery stores that is the basis for our second case study. Many aspects of the labor process foster isolation among the cashiers in a workplace where they have little recourse to other institutional support. Isolation also characterizes the working lives of the caregivers who participated in Silvia D'Addario's investigation of their home and work lives in suburban Toronto. Our attention here focuses on interactions with employers and with other caregivers who come together to deal with the challenges of their temporary immigration status and exploitative working conditions. The case studies acknowledge the significance of workplace encounters for earning a living and in people's everyday lives.

Working for a Living in Urban Multicultures

Encounters in the workplace influence success at work with immediate and long-term consequences for each person's income, livelihood, identity, and sense of belonging. In the settler colonial cities under study, the rise of neoliberalism encourages the view that successful adults are those who are economically self-sufficient. Success in the workplace is shaped intimately by encounters with many different people: workers doing the same job, workers involved in other tasks, employers, customers, and the public. The interactions occur in work locations where ethnic and racial diversity is often increasing as the demands for specific skills intersect with processes of ethnic segmentation that channel workers from specific ethno-racial backgrounds into specific occupations and industries (Parks and Warren 2012). In these contexts, encounters that promote working in difference as equals also facilitate individual economic success, life satisfaction, and well-being.

We pay attention to the various temporalities and spatialities of encounters in each of the workplaces considered in the case studies. Focused interactions, some planned months in advance and others organized more spontaneously, define the texture of many people's work days through meetings large and small, conversations in person, on the phone, and through electronic means, and shared tasks. As Wise (2016) emphasized in her detailed study of a Sydney bus depot, brief chance encounters also occur as people move within and between workplaces, exchanging greetings during breaks and en route to their work locations at the beginning and end of the day. The built form of the workplace shapes the frequency and nature of encounters, as we see in extreme form on production lines. In abattoirs and car assembly plants, where workers are literally emplaced (Broadway 2007; Leitner 2012; Leslie and Butz 1998), interactions occur mainly at breaks. The labor process also shapes encounters in each workplace. Some jobs isolate workers from each other and from supervisors and subordinates, customers and the public, while other jobs require regular social interaction. Shift work and work on a production line with its unforgiving and demanding tempo isolates workers from each other (Leitner 2012; Leslie and Butz 1998). Many service jobs, such as surgical nurses assisting in operating rooms and waiters and waitresses serving banquets in large hotels, compel interaction (Batnitzky and McDowell 2013).

We emphasize how regulation influences encounters in workplaces. In the urban multiculture considered here, the state and other institutions affect major workplace decisions, from hiring and remuneration to working conditions and terminations. The state tries to exert control over encounters in work locations by allowing workers the opportunity to file complaints if fellow workers or bosses discriminate against, physically harass, or verbally abuse them. States insist that ethnic and racial diversity is an important consideration in all workplace decisions, from hiring and setting wages and salaries to decisions to sever employment (Ahmed 2012). With formal regulations, states aim to ensure equal treatment in all workplace decisions regardless of ethnic and racialized differences. Regulations concerning the presence and activities of trade unions also stipulate the nature and format of many interactions and specify roles for workers, employers, and their representatives in encounters. In this regulated context, trade unions increasingly set their own goals and ground rules to deal with cultural difference among members and for members to deal with difference among themselves (Briskin 2003).[2]

Informal regulation also affects encounters at work locations in subtle and overt ways. Employers require "soft skills" (Moss and Tilly 1996, 253), "abilities and traits that pertain to personality, attitude and behavior rather than to formal or technical knowledge," as well as knowledge of taken-for-granted norms concerning how to interact with other workers, employers, customers, and the public, among many others. A steady stream of research has shown that soft skills not only predict, but even cause labor market outcomes (Heckman and Kautz 2012). Since the evaluation of soft skills is largely subjective, employers' stereotypes and the cultural differences between many employers and minority workers often put minority workers at a disadvantage in hiring, earnings, and promotions (Moss and Tilly 1996). In highly diverse workplaces, workers also regulate their behaviors informally. Wise (2016) and Leitner (2012) underscore the ongoing effort involved in reaching a social consensus that ensures workers will get along in the face of their cultural differences. In one telling example, Wise notes that casual bus drivers did not participate in the jokes shared by permanent drivers who regularly spent lengthy breaks together. Informal regulation is an ongoing project among workers who must develop practices that will enable them to work together regardless of their cultural differences.

The influence of formal and informal regulation varies across workplaces. The state has more influence in recognized sites of paid work, such as factories, offices, and retail and commercial facilities. Once paid work is unmoored from these sites, formal regulation often has less influence. Formal workplaces are recognized legally as places of work, subject to the regulations discussed earlier, whereas informal workplaces are usually residential locations that are also places of paid work. The mixed status of these locations confounds regulators. For example, some workplaces, such as farms where the owner resides, are excluded from many state regulations, leaving agricultural workers with few protections from exploitative working conditions (Reid-Musson 2017). Even where homework and homeworkers are covered by state and other institutional rules, the challenges of monitoring many small work sites combined with the discomfort associated with regulating activities in private residential locations add to enforcement difficulties. As a result, homeworkers, especially domestic workers, are vulnerable to unreasonable demands for long hours of work, unsafe working conditions, reduced and delayed wages, and unwelcome interactions with employers.

The complex machinery of regulation is implemented and enforced in workplaces characterized by inequalities in power and status. Some hierarchies are based on the differential valuation of skill and experience that often puts migrants and ethnic and racial minorities at a disadvantage. For example, to obtain recognition as a professional engineer, foreign-trained engineers must obtain four years of acceptable engineering work experience in Canada regardless of the amount or nature of their prior experience gained abroad (Ontario 2016). Others reflect seniority, particularly years of service, and still others reflect power differentials between owners and their employees, managers and their subordinates, and trades and production workers. Coworkers may meet sometimes as equals, one of the prerequisites for Allport's assertion that repeated encounter will promote intercultural awareness and understanding (Allport 1954), but it is a rare workplace in which some encounters are not imbued with status differences. These hierarchies are often racialized and gendered, so that minorities and women face inordinate challenges to advancement. Regulation is also confounded by rapidly changing working conditions that place workers outside the regulatory framework, often by defining them as self-employed subcontractors. In the contemporary multicultures that we consider, subcontracting is rapidly reducing the state's power to regulate encounters at work locations (Vosko et al. 2016). For example, information technology (IT) workers in Toronto who often work on short-term contracts are excluded from the state's employment regulations regarding hours of work and overtime.

Our analysis acknowledges the diverse ways that encounters in workplaces produce cultural difference. The case studies of three very different workplaces demonstrate the progressive possibilities and limits of encounter to achieve working together in difference as equals. We begin the case studies by situating the three workplaces in Toronto, outlining the contours of ethnic and racialized difference in the urban region and the current knowledge of inequality and exclusion in Toronto's workplaces.

Working in Toronto: Difference and Discrimination

Canada's largest urban region[3] with approximately 6 million residents (Statistics Canada 2017b), the Toronto census metropolitan area is also home to one of Canada's most diverse populations. Approximately half of the population identifies as a racialized minority,[4] with Chinese, South Asians, and Blacks among the largest individual ethno-racial groups.[5] Smaller minority groups, especially Filipinos, Latin Americans, and Arabs, are growing rapidly, adding to cultural difference in this urban multiculture. The metropolitan area's large minority population is due to its enduring attraction for newcomers to Canada. In 2016, it was home to 3,157,300 foreign-born individuals who made up almost half the metropolitan population, 48.8 percent (Statistics Canada 2017). Consistent with Canada's history as a settler colonial society, the vast majority, approximately 95 percent, are permanent residents. Since 1967, when "white Canada" immigration policies ended, the largest source countries for immigrants have been in Asia, Africa, and Central and South America. Recent immigrants settled in an urban multiculture that already included residents from every country in Europe, along with smaller numbers of people who identified as Jewish, Black, Chinese, and Vietnamese (Kobayashi and Preston 2015; Murdie 2008). European immigrants settled in waves during the eighteenth, nineteenth, and early twentieth centuries, when minorities were alternately discouraged or forbidden from staying in Canada. While European immigrants and their descendants are still among the largest ethno-racial groups, their dominance is diminishing steadily. In 2016, people claiming European heritage and ancestry accounted for only 48.6 percent of the metropolitan population.

The workforce is even more diverse than the residential population, largely as a result of immigration policies that favor working-age adults. The foreign-born who are legal permanent residents of Canada accounted for approximately half of the metropolitan labor force, 48.1 percent, in 2015. With the addition of temporary residents and those who are working without legal status, the share of foreign-born workers likely exceeds 50 percent. Their high percentage in the Toronto labor force reflects deliberate immigration policies. Since the 1990s, the federal government has increased the flows of highly skilled migrants as permanent residents. In 2014, 165,089 economic immigrants accounted for 63.4 percent of all permanent residents settling in Canada. At the same time, the numbers of temporary foreign workers also increased. More than 94,000 received visas in 2014 alone. Like permanent residents, temporary workers are disproportionately from Asia and Central and South America, with the Philippines, India, and Mexico among the top five source countries (Citizenship and Immigration Canada 2015).

As the number of minorities increased, they spread across the metropolitan area, well beyond traditional immigrant reception areas adjacent to the central business district, such as the Ward (Murdie 2008; Ray and Preston 2015), where there is a well-established history of minority succession. In the Ward, poor Irish immigrants were followed initially by Eastern and Central European newcomers who included the founders of the city's vibrant Jewish population. They were replaced by later waves of Southern European, Chinese, and South Asian immigrants. Since the 1980s, minorities have bypassed traditional reception areas such as the Ward, where gentrification and redevelopment have reduced the supply of low-cost housing and attracted affluent and white Canadian-born professionals. Many minorities now settle directly in the suburbs, attracted by the emergence of institutionally complete communities (Toronto Foundation 2016), others end up in suburban high-rise apartments (among Toronto's least expensive rentals), and still others seek the suburban dream as soon as their finances permit.

Racialized minorities now account for a higher percentage of the population in several suburbs (local government areas also known as municipalities in the Toronto metropolitan area), than in the City of Toronto, where traditional immigrant reception areas are located. In five suburbs—Markham, Brampton, Richmond Hill, Mississauga, and Ajax—minorities make up the majority of the population (Table 1). There is no single immigrant corridor to the suburbs. The five suburbs where minorities dominate extend in all directions from the city proper. Ajax is located in the far east of the metropolitan area, Markham, Richmond Hill, and Brampton stretch to the north, and Mississauga is adjacent to the city's western boundary. While many minority residents are foreign-born, growing numbers are the children and grandchildren of immigrants. In this respect, Ajax, where more than half the population identifies as minority and less than 40 percent are foreign-born, may well represent the future in many of Toronto's suburbs.

Table 1. Diverse Toronto Suburbs

	Total Population	Minority (%)	Foreign-Born (%)	Low-Income, 2015 (%)	Median Household Income, 2015
Markham	327,400	77.9	60.7	15.1	$89,028
Brampton	593,640	73.3	53.7	11.3	$87,290
Mississauga	721,600	57.2	54.7	14.7	$83,018
Richmond Hill	193,800	60.0	59.0	15.9	$88,353
Ajax	119,180	56.7	39.3	9.4	$96,949
City of Toronto	2,691,665	51.5	50.5	20.2	$65,829
Toronto CMA	5,583,064	48.8	56.6	15.6	$78,373
Pickering	90,995	42.9	34.7	8.4	$99,701
Oshawa	157,630	16.0	17.7	14.5	$70,211
Keswick-Elmhurst Beach	26,430	9.2	14.0	10.6	$96,648

Source: Statistics Canada 2017c. Calculations by V. Preston.

Despite the growing minority population, however, some suburbs, such as Oshawa and Keswick-Elmhurst Beach, are still dominated by a white Canadian-born population.

Income inequality and income polarization add another layer to the complex ethnic and racialized geographies of Toronto's residential areas and workplaces. Since the 1990s, income inequality has increased (Walks et al. 2016), due in no small part to persistent and growing racialized and gendered income inequalities. Despite high rates of postsecondary education, in 2010, minorities earned less than Toronto residents from European backgrounds and less than expected on the basis of their educational attainments (Pendakur and Pendakur 2015). Minority men earned less than men from European backgrounds regardless of their birthplaces. Gender cut across the effects of ethno-racial background. On average, women earned less than men in the Toronto economy in 2010. These income trends persist in 2015 (Figure 5). Despite the size of the minority population, the median personal incomes of all racialized minority men and women fall below the metropolitan medians for each gender and are substantially lower than the median incomes of white, non-Aboriginal men and women. Comparing the median incomes among racialized minorities suggests there is a double jeopardy associated with period of arrival and minority status. The lowest personal incomes are reported by some of the most recently arrived minorities, specifically Arabs and West Asians. Many minority women also suffer a wage penalty, earning less than their male counterparts.

Gendered and racialized income inequalities in Toronto are exacerbated by neoliberal discourses favoring private market solutions to social issues and business models of public policy and management. Despite the rapid deindustrialization that occurred after 1990, politicians at all levels are committed to promoting a welcoming business climate, often by reducing the costs of public services and cutting taxes. Both actions contributed to rising inequality in the metropolitan area, where the incomes of middle-income and low-income households declined even as the incomes of the affluent stagnated between 1980 and 2012 (Walks et al. 2016). Increasingly neighborhoods are segregated by income, so that households live near others with similar incomes and at a distance

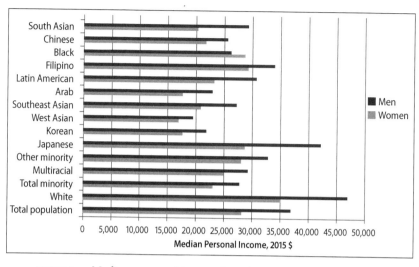

FIGURE 5. *Median personal income for minority groups, Toronto census metropolitan area. (Source: Statistics Canada, 2017b.)*

from those who are richer and poorer. Income polarization is rising more rapidly within the gentrifying City of Toronto than in adjacent suburbs (Walks et al. 2016) even though the proportion of households living in poverty is still higher in the city than in the metropolitan area as a whole (Table 1). In the suburbs, high median household incomes do not always preclude pockets of poverty. In Pickering and Ajax, for example, high median incomes are associated with some of the lowest percentages of low-income populations in the metropolitan area. This is not the case in Markham and Mississauga, where minorities and the foreign-born predominate and the percentage of the population that has a low income is almost as high as in the entire metropolitan area.

The growing income inequality in the metropolitan area underlines the importance of understanding the encounters in Toronto's workplaces that contribute to unequal earnings for minority workers. The urgency of the task is accentuated by evidence that workplaces in the Toronto metropolitan area are more ethnically and racially diverse than residential areas (Ray and Preston 2015). The spatial patterns of ethno-racial diversity also differ between residential and work locations. The neighborhoods surrounding the central business district that are disproportionately home to Canadian-born residents of European background have a diverse workforce. As the city's largest employment node, the central business district attracts workers from every ethnic and racial group in the metropolitan area to fill a vast variety of occupations. In the postwar suburbs such as Scarborough, Etobicoke, and North York, the pronounced ethno-racial diversity of residential locations is matched by an equally diverse workforce (Ray and Preston 2015). In more distant suburbs that mainly developed after 1970, the workforce is more homogeneous than in either the central business district or the postwar suburbs, with the Canadian-born from European backgrounds predominating.

In Toronto workplaces, ethno-racial diversity is highly regulated. About 10 percent of the labor force works in industries that fall under the purview of federal legislation, while the vast majority of workers in the province are governed by provincial policies. Both levels of government have a protective stance, aiming to ensure the fair treatment of all workers. Employment equity policies are designed to redress systemic oppressions related to gender, race, disability, and other markers of difference by ensuring fair access to employment and to advancement in the workplace (Bakan and Kobayashi 2007), while employment standards and health and safety legislation govern minimum compensation, the health and safety of working conditions, and worker's compensation in the event of injury and dismissal (Vosko 2010). With a complaint-driven system, enforcement has been criticized on the grounds that the most vulnerable workers in need of the most protection will be reticent to complain about employers who control their livelihoods.

Ontario provincial legislation specifies the minimum wage, benefit entitlements (including vacation pay), working hours, health and safety obligations of employers and worker's compensation in the event of an injury, and antidiscrimination measures. Although the province's employment equity legislation was repealed in 1995, most employers and workplaces are still subject to the Ontario Human Rights Code that requires equal treatment in employment, unions and vocational associations, and contracts on the basis of race and ethnicity. In addition, the Human Rights Code prohibits discrimination on the grounds of fourteen other personal attributes, ranging from citizenship and place of origin to gender identity, receipt of public assistance, and record of offenses. For workers, rights to organize and the rights of trade unions to bargain on behalf of workers are crucial aspects of the Human Rights Code. Trade unions provide a crucial counterweight to the power of employers in workplaces (Vosko 2010). Bargaining and acting on behalf of employees, unions influence the formal and informal regulation of workplaces, setting the context for working together as equals. The procedures for the certification and decertification of trade unions, the collective bargaining process, and other aspects of labor relations are specified in legislation, principally the Labour Relations Act.

The state also regulates workplaces at the local government level, although the municipal influence is often less overt than provincial and federal regulation. For example, local governments influence the relative locations of residential and work-related land uses through zoning requirements and they affect access to employment through their decisions regarding public transportation and other public services. In the Toronto metropolitan area, local governments often claim to celebrate the ethnic and racial diversity of their populations by encouraging minorities to hold public festivals and develop attractive restaurants and other businesses that will also attract tourists and signal urban sophistication. Many also highlight their commitment to diversity with mottos such as "Diversity our strength." Despite these claims, critics have accused the state of tolerating if not promoting democratic racism, an ideology that allows people to hold simultaneously egalitarian values that society is not racist and nonegalitarian values that favor whites and other dominant groups (Henry et al. 2010). They note the contradictions between the discourse of diversity as strength and the inequalities and inequities that mark the everyday lives and life chances of Toronto's minority residents (Fleras 2014). Persistent and growing racialized inequalities in income, unemployment, and wealth, transit investments that favor predominantly white residential areas, racialized disparities in high school graduation, along with continuing threats to minorities from the police are cited as evidence of the racism experienced daily by minorities despite state rhetoric.

Contrary to official commitments to cultural pluralism and the accompanying regulation of workplaces, they remain sites of discrimination and discomfort for many workers (Banerjee 2008). According to the Ethnic Diversity Survey, the workplace is the most common site of discrimination in Canada, mentioned by 56 percent of those who reported experiencing unfair treatment on the basis of ethnicity, culture, skin color, race, religion, accent, or language in the past five years (Statistics Canada 2003). Although less than one in ten Canadians reports discrimination, more than one-third of racialized minority residents in metropolitan Toronto (37 percent) had experienced discrimination in the five years preceding the survey (Derouin 2004). When asked specifically about discrimination in the workplace, 26.6 percent of Toronto's minority population reported experiencing discrimination (Ray and Preston 2014), a higher percentage than the 15 percent reporting discrimination in other locales, such as streets and shops. The percentage of minority workers reporting discrimination, approximately one in four, was higher than the 6.5 percent reported by workers from European backgrounds.

In addition to unfair treatment, the Ethnic Diversity Survey also asked about discomfort, the feeling of being out of place due to ethnicity, culture, skin color, race, religion, accent, or language in the past five years. Where minority status is the main influence on the likelihood of experiencing workplace discrimination, discomfort in the workplace is affected more by the conditions of employment. Specifically, the probability of being out of place varies across industries and occupations. Unlike reports of discrimination that are made almost exclusively by minority workers, white workers as well as minorities report feelings of discomfort (Ray and Preston 2015). Among white workers, ethnicity has a bearing on their discomfort in the workplace. Eastern, Southern, and Central Europeans who comprise the majority of postwar European immigrants are more likely to report discomfort in the workplace than workers from Northern and Western Europe who are the dominant ethno-racial group in Toronto. There is suggestive but preliminary evidence that place also affects workplace discrimination and discomfort. In the Toronto metropolitan area, workers' experiences in their residential locations also affect workplace experiences. Workers who trust the neighbors are less likely to report workplace discrimination or discomfort, regardless of their individual attributes such as ethno-racial identity and the strength of attachment to their ethno-racial group than workers who have little or no trust in the neighbors (Ray and Preston 2015). These preliminary findings suggest that encounters with difference in multicultures are linked across the sites of everyday life. The findings raise the possibility that achievement of a politics of equality may well require attention to the interrelations among the sites of the everyday.

Census information revealed the broad contours of diversity in the Toronto metropolitan area where cultural difference characterizes workplaces even more than residential areas. Minorities live and work across the metropolitan area, even forming the majority of residents in some suburbs. It also provides insight into the income inequality that places minority workers and residents at a persistent disadvantage in Toronto. The census and survey information describe where people live and work, what they earn, and perceived exclusion in Toronto's workplaces. It says little about how interactions in Toronto workplaces reinforce and challenge inequality. We take up this task in the case studies of three workplaces that follow.

Diverse Workplaces: Hotel Room Attendants

Case studies of the London hotel industry by Linda McDowell (McDowell et al. 2007), Jane Wills (Datta et al. 2012; Wills et al. 2010), and their colleagues reveal common factors that underscore the relational nature of ethno-racial identities. In the hotel industry, South Asian men undertake tasks commonly considered to be women's responsibility in their places of origin. The glamour of the hotel sector combined with the opportunity to work abroad renders these tasks acceptable to ambitious South Asian hotel management trainees. In contrast, Polish women are viewed as ideal room attendants: physically strong, compliant, and uncomplaining. Hotel management acknowledges and even manipulates ethno-racial differences (McDowell et al. 2007). Workers from different backgrounds are considered "suitable" for different occupations and channeled into them. Such occupational segregation also restricts encounters among workers from different national, cultural, and ethno-racial backgrounds. Room attendants interact with other room attendants and their supervisors. Demanding work schedules mean room attendants have few opportunities to encounter workers doing other jobs at reception and in banquet halls and restaurants in London hotels (McDowell et al. 2007).

Resistance to employers' authority has the potential to disrupt stereotypes, by "placing in common a wrong" (Rancière, cited in Davidson and Iveson 2015, 14). Thirty years apart, the experience of going on strike for better pay and to rescind layoffs transformed Asian immigrant women's understandings of themselves and their capacities for action. By striking, the women saw themselves as workers capable of making change despite persistent stereotypes and public representations of them as subordinate and compliant "Asian" women who were secondary wage earners in their households (Sundari et al. 2012). The workers' reevaluation of themselves and their political agency was rooted in support from each other, and in the case of the catering workers, from family and community. Jane Wills et al. (2010) also illustrate how encounters of equals can be promoted by resistance to employers' demands that exploit racialized representations of difference among workers. In London, increasing numbers of low-wage workers are migrants, whom employers and supervisors stereotype and exploit. In a recent campaign for a living wage, workers from many ethnic and racialized groups participated through a coalition of faith organizations united around commitments to social justice. In the United States, the Justice for Janitors campaign also responded effectively to the growing insecurity of custodial work by demanding better working conditions on the grounds that exploitation was racialized and rooted in difference (Savage 2006). These examples suggest that encounters rooted in the shared purpose of resistance can alter naturalized hierarchies in the workplace. Such encounters enable the subordinate to speak and be heard, the key for successful politics according to Rancière (2009).

The efforts of one union, Unite-HERE, to organize diverse hotel workers provides insight into encounters that have the potential to upend the racialized and classed hierarchies that place minority workers at a disadvantage in many Canadian workplaces. Workers in Toronto's hotel industry, like those in London, have varied ethno-racial backgrounds that employers use to reinforce hierarchies of difference (Tufts 2003). In May 2016, jobs for room attendants advertised pay rates of C$13.15 per hour,[6] still among the lowest compensation for any workers in large Toronto hotels. Room attendants are mainly racialized immigrant women recruited for housekeeping tasks that are back of the house and rarely acknowledged publicly by hotel guests or management. One human resources manager emphasizes that her hotel hires recent immigrants as room attendants, regardless of their ethno-racial backgrounds:

> I would say that housekeeping is primarily Filipino. I would say [it is] the biggest group. We have a large Filipino population in the hotel. The next could be Chinese and Middle Eastern. . . . It just depends [on] who comes in off the street. Right now the trend is a lot of Middle Eastern. My understanding is that the gates are open and we're bringing up a lot of people to Canada from there. I interview at least three or four people from the Middle East and India a week. People coming from India are coming through the Middle East on their way to the US. . . . I find that Filipinos tend to be lower skilled [than the] Middle Eastern. (Tufts 2003, 185)

Other social characteristics are also invoked to account for segmentation. English fluency is often emphasized as an essential requirement for front of house jobs. Listen to Michael, director of human resources at one of Toronto's large hotels, who says:

> We participate with the women's immigration placement centres. So when they have people from a certain country with the same experience and background that we're looking for we have no problem hiring them. The only

requirement is English. You have to have it. And I'm talking about you have to be able to converse fluently . . . it's mandatory, you have to have English.

He continues:

> The suite attendants have very minimum contact with our guests. And we drill into their heads that if a guest has any questions they should refer them to the front desk. So English is not a priority for us . . . in that department. (Tufts 2003, 188)

As studies of English-speaking African professionals in Vancouver demonstrate (Creese and Kambere 2003), evaluations of English fluency are socially constructed. Judgments of language fluency reflect racialized stereotypes as much as, and sometimes more than, knowledge of English and ability to communicate in the language.

Managers and executives also attribute the concentration of racialized minority women in housekeeping to workers' social networks. Current employees tell friends and family members from the same ethno-racial group about available jobs and they also vouch for them to the prospective employer. The reliance on referrals for hiring likely contributes to the large proportion of room attendants who are minority immigrant women (Tufts 2003). The hotel industry in Toronto is typical of employers seeking to fill jobs that they consider entry-level and unskilled (Thomas and Ong 2006). Such recruiting often places racialized minorities at a disadvantage because they do not challenge employers' racial stereotypes. Thomas and Ong found that employers who relied on referrals often held negative views about African Americans and favored immigrant workers who they viewed as more reliable and hardworking.

The regular contacts between supervisors and racialized minority women required for both parties to do their jobs did little to dislodge or change gendered and racialized stereotypes in the Toronto hotels that were studied. Tufts (2003) reported several instances in which supervisors discouraged room attendants from applying for better paid and more responsible positions as executive housekeepers and front of the house positions. In Toronto hotels, just as in London hotels (McDowell et al. 2007, 21), frequent and regular contacts up and down the hierarchy of authority reinforced inequality rather than promoting equality. Although frequent, the encounters did not challenge power relations within the workplace, perhaps because managers and supervisors presume they are better qualified than other workers to exert power in the workplace. Routine, regular social interactions are rarely an opportunity for subordinate workers to speak and be heard in the workplace. The power hierarchies of the workplace prescribe when workers may speak and the terms on which they may speak and be heard. They thereby put workers "in their place."

Although repeated interactions among coworkers can encourage equitable working with difference (Harris and Valentine 2016; Kokkonen et al. 2015), this outcome is not guaranteed. Examples from Toronto hotels illustrate the complex nature of the encounters between coworkers and their contradictory and unexpected outcomes. One trade union in Toronto, Unite-HERE, sought to underscore the valuable contributions of hotel workers to the city's economy and its appeal to tourists by recognizing and celebrating their cultural diversity (Tufts 2006). To this end, a choir of union members was recruited to perform at union functions and public events. The choir grew out of an initial performance by an ad hoc group of union members at the International Hotel Workers Day celebration in Toronto where Unite-HERE Local 75 wanted to signal its presence as a progressive union for hotel workers (Tufts 2003).

Dominated by room attendants who had emigrated from the Caribbean, the choir illustrated how hotel workers, even those doing the least desirable and worst-paid jobs, could contribute to the hotel industry's efforts to market Toronto as a diverse tourist destination. To some extent, the union's strategy succeeded. In the subsequent rounds of collective bargaining, employers agreed to contribute one cent for each hour worked by a Unite-HERE Local 75 member to a World Cultural Fund that would underwrite the costs of union members' cultural activities. The agreement fits within the general principles of community unionism since some funds will find their way to community groups and activities in which hotel workers participate. (Unlike many activities that fall under the umbrella of community unionism, the World Cultural Fund is not tied to specific ethno-racial or geographical communities.) The choir was integral to the union's cultural strategy. The union used the World Cultural Fund to hire a choir director and sponsor the choir's performances. Choir practices took place in union facilities and churches, outside participants' workplaces. With strict work schedules that required room attendants to clean a specified number of rooms each shift, there were no opportunities for choir members to meet in their workplaces.

In a pattern that we will see repeated in subsequent chapters, encounters that took place during choir activities strengthened choir members' ties to each other and became the basis for political action. For choir members who were mainly immigrant women from the Caribbean, singing was familiar and appropriate, as Tufts (2003, 344) reports:

> For West Indian people there is struggle all over the world. In any West Indian country it's a struggle. And the only means sometimes to release the tension from our struggle is to sing. So it becomes part of our culture that we sing a lot. In everything that we are doing we sing, because it makes us happy inside and cheers us up. If we are sad it makes us happy.

Choir members participated in a shared project that required regular meetings where they could learn about each other's home and work lives and help each other on the job and outside work. Facilitated by the union that was acting to shore up the bargaining power of its members by emphasizing the value of the diverse hotel workforce it represented, the choir allowed the minority women who participated in it to express their frustration with their jobs and difficult lives in Toronto and share strategies to resist the ongoing demands of employers to increase the speed and volume of work.

The choir's public performances also succeeded in making room attendants, the most hidden and least valued segment of the hotel workforce, visible. In the process, it began the difficult process of changing employers' and public views of them and their work:

No one knows about the union that represents hotel workers. But I think people are listening now. Because if you
notice in our last round of bargaining we're on the news
all over, so people are listening to us. So people are seeing
that we are not just good for cleaning rooms, we are capable
of doing other things. We went to LA to sing and we sang
there and all the people were impressed with our singing.
They commented that our union has so much talent in it
and that's true we have a lot of talents. (345)

Despite its overall success, the choir was viewed with skepticism
by some union officials and even union members who had a somewhat narrower vision of the union's role in workers' lives. Skeptics
worried that the union's efforts to negotiate the World Cultural
Fund and promote the cultural contributions of members would
distract from its principal goal of improving the job security and
earnings of union members. They were also disturbed by the cooperation between employers and the union that they worried might
undermine the union's determination to speak for workers and
their concerns. Some union members also questioned who benefited from the cultural funds. They were not convinced that the
efforts to redefine hotel workers as cultural workers contributing
to Toronto tourism would succeed. They also expressed concern
that only a small number of union members, drawn from only one
of the membership's many occupational groups, room attendants,
benefited from the funds.

Although never discussed overtly, the ethno-racial backgrounds
of choir members also set them apart. The majority were immigrant women from the Caribbean who had been involved with
gospel singing before migrating. For these women, singing was a
familiar activity to combat everyday trials. As Jackie, one of the
choir members, explains:

If you read our history, you would see that music is what we
use to entertain ourselves and get over rough times. We sing
and that's how we do it. . . . You know in this hotel industry
sometimes you have to work 24 hours. You don't know when
you are going to be called in. You don't get to go to church

on Sundays, you don't get to go out much. So after work we get together and we express ourselves and we sing. (Tufts 2003, 344)

Responding to concerns that the choir was exclusionary, choir members tried to recruit participants from other ethno-racial backgrounds. They also encouraged men to join the choir. Choir members went so far as to change the wording of songs to appeal to union members who did not share their background in gospel singing. Despite these efforts, the choir continued to be dominated by female room attendants who were Caribbean immigrants. Although choir participation facilitated encounters among women who shared many aspects of their work lives and personal histories, it offered few opportunities for encounters with difference among choir members. Rather, encounters with difference were more likely at performances where choir members interacted with other performers, members of other unions, and the public.

The experiences of encounter in the hotel industry in Toronto illustrate several important aspects of working toward a kind of being together in difference as equals in the workplace. While the encounters of choir members were facilitated by their shared experiences with gospel singing in the Caribbean, choir members also benefited from interacting with each other on a shared project. Choir members created a micro-public (Amin 2002, 969) in which they shared the common project of participating in a successful choir. Choir activities took place outside the workplace where hierarchies and power differentials were inscribed rigidly. The choir was also supported and nurtured by the union local. As an act of resistance, participation in the choir was imbued with purpose by the union. Choir participants were engaged in encounters that went beyond sharing their individual experiences; they were resisting the authority of their employers and helping to remake the popular image of room attendants and other hotel workers. Within the workplace, state regulation did not always protect the room attendants from racialization. With its support for the choir, the union helped room attendants resist racism by creating opportunities for them to be together in difference as equals, and to assert that equality as the basis for both their own relationships with one another and for challenges to ongoing inequality in their workplaces.

Part-Time Workplaces: Grocery Store Cashiers

A case study of grocery store cashiers illustrates how the labor process, especially the social and spatial organization of tasks and the terms and conditions of employment, limits encounters among co-workers and the progressive potential of these interactions. In the retail grocery sector in Canada, employment is increasingly part time, particularly for women (Kainer 2002). Managers aim to recruit a flexible labor force of grocery store cashiers by hiring only as the workload demands. Work schedules are often announced only a week or two in advance as managers and supervisors respond to changing consumer demand. With the introduction of computer scanning, the workload is also closely monitored and physically demanding. Standing for long hours without a break, repetitive strain injuries associated with repeated movements, and lifting heavy items with insufficient training are common complaints.

A Toronto case study of four grocery stores (Morihovitis 1998) confirmed the precarious nature of work for grocery store cashiers. Hired part time, with 90 percent or more working approximately twenty hours per week, cashiers in Toronto grocery stores are mainly young women between the ages of sixteen and twenty-five. Many work part time while attending high school, college, and university. Given their youthfulness, it is not surprising that the majority of cashiers are single, although the percentage of cashiers who had children ranged from 12.5 percent at one store to 40 percent at another. Managers hire young women specifically to obtain flexible labor that can tolerate the physically demanding job. According to one manager quoted by Morihovitis (136):

> I inherited my staff. I am pleased with 90% and I am not happy with 10%. This is not related with health and safety, but they are not motivated. The majority of the cashiers are female very young . . . 16 to 18 years old. This is usually their first job. . . . No experience is necessary, we can train. If I

could choose my staff, I would hire girls between 16–22. For the simple reason, they are a lot more flexible as far as the work that they can do. You will have less injuries that way. Your older staff will be off longer, I want my staff here working and not at home sick. A younger staff is ideal. A younger staff do [sic] not bring baggage to the store—bad working habits. An older staff brings baggage to the store—bad habits they pick up at other jobs. From a business stand point I would rather have younger cashiers working for me.

Since management pays little attention to health and safety training even though working conditions are grueling and may cause physical injuries, it is crucial that workers be healthy when they start working as cashiers. Although the vast majority of cashiers work part time, they spend about 80 percent of their shifts standing. Since the average work shift is six hours in length, the majority of cashiers are standing longer than current guidelines recommend. Hiring young workers also promotes turnover. Cashiers are likely to quit before repetitive strain and other injuries develop. In the four Toronto grocery stores studied, less than 30 percent of the cashiers had worked more than three years at any of the stores.

Cashiers also have few opportunities for encounters with other store employees. The technology isolates cashiers from each other. With the introduction of scanning, cashiers can be monitored closely, so there are few opportunities to pause during work shifts. The pace of work has also accelerated with the conversion of cashier positions from full time to part time. Managers schedule shifts for cashiers only during periods when they are expected to be fully occupied. Short shifts also mean that workers have fewer breaks where they might socialize with coworkers. Working in isolation, on a part-time basis, with an irregular and unpredictable schedule, cashiers have few opportunities to encounter each other. They may also have an instrumental view of their jobs that discourages social encounters at work. Most cashiers in the case study are young women who are full-time students. Working part time as a cashier is a means to an end, income, rather than a career in which the young women might invest scarce social capital.

Working for a Living in Toronto

Even though prevailing working conditions provide few opportunities for informal socializing on the job, managers count on the social relations among cashiers for recruiting and training. They prefer to recruit through friends and families so that new cashiers have social ties to experienced cashiers. According to one manager that Morihovitis interviewed (1998, 138):

> The working relationship between cashiers who know each other is generally better than with others. They tend to help each other out more . . . a personable environment is created.

Adopting an instrumental view of social interactions, this manager relies on cashiers who know each other prior to working in the store to train each other. Encounters among coworkers are utilized by management to ensure worker productivity that will reduce labor costs.

Recruiting through word of mouth affects the ethnic and racial backgrounds of grocery store cashiers. Although managers say they prefer to hire cashiers who live near their stores, arguing that they are more likely to be punctual and available on short notice, most relied on informal recruiting by current employees and preferred to hire applicants recommended by current cashiers, who are often co-ethnics. Not surprisingly, informal recruiting methods led to clusters of cashiers from individual ethno-racial groups. More than 80 percent of the cashiers from one store identified as Italian Canadian (Morihovitis 1998). In this store, there were few opportunities for encounters with cultural difference among the cashiers themselves. In the other stores, cashiers were from diverse ethno-racial backgrounds. In one, approximately a quarter of cashiers, 26.1 percent, identified as Italian, another 17.4 percent identified as Portuguese, and another 13 percent were South Asian. The ethno-racial diversity in the cashier workforce garnered few comments. Either it was viewed as the norm in Toronto or it was simply not relevant to young women who were coming to work to do a job and leave as quickly as possible.

Cashiers are not always local. At two of the grocery stores, one-third or fewer of the cashiers lived nearby. Indeed, at one store, cashiers commuted an average of twenty-seven minutes to their part-time jobs. Living outside the local market area, cashiers often have different ethno-racial backgrounds than local customers. At one grocery store, 35 percent of nearby residents are Portuguese compared to only 13 percent of the cashiers. At another, even though only 8 percent of local residents are Italian, more than a quarter, 26.1 percent, of the cashiers identify as Italian. Familiarity based on prior social ties enables cashiers to help each other, primarily when they are first hired, but it does not provide a basis for shared solidarity to negotiate improved working conditions. The isolation of cashiers at the workplace combines with their own views that the job is short-term and temporary employment while they complete their education. Cashiers have little interest in learning about their coworkers. In some stores, cashiers are already acquainted but their social relationships are based on shared ethnicity rather than common workplace experiences. Moreover, almost all of the cashiers downplay the significance of jobs that they view as temporary, with a minor role in their current and future lives.

The cashiers' encounters with coworkers and even supervisors do not have the same emotional weight as those mentioned by Das Gupta (2009) and Creese (2011) in their analyses of Black men and women in Toronto and Vancouver, respectively. For Black immigrants, many workplace encounters are marked by competition between people in the same employment position and only occasional cooperation. Cashiers rarely compete since their jobs are convenient, their hours are part time, and working as a cashier is an expedient way to earn extra money for education and entertainment. Most of the young women in Morihovitis's study are full-time students aspiring to other careers. In contrast, the nurses that Das Gupta (2009) and Creese and Kambere (2003) describe are anxious to find a professional niche and achieve career advancement, goals that they struggle to achieve in contexts where finding any job is hard and finding a well-paid job commensurate with one's qualifications and experience is exceptionally challenging. For these internationally trained professionals, employers, supervisors, and even coworkers are perceived as using racist stereotypes to reinforce hierarchies, and their narratives focus on encounters with unfair treatment. They are less likely to mention the banal encounters of the cashiers, who neither compete nor cooperate much.

The union representing cashiers and other workers in the grocery stores, United Food and Commercial Workers, did not facilitate encounters among cashiers as Unite-HERE had done for room attendants in Toronto. Cashiers had limited interactions with each other and even less contact with union representatives, even though several wanted the union to address concerns about the physical demands of their jobs. Eighty percent of the cashiers who had worked more than one year in the four Toronto grocery stores reported musculoskeletal problems associated with excessive standing and repetitive movements (Morihovitis 1998, 96). The high rates of musculoskeletal problems are surprising in light of the youthfulness of the cashiers. Several cashiers felt the union devoted its efforts to improving the working conditions and earnings of full-time, usually male employees while their health concerns, as part-time workers and predominantly young women, were ignored. Interviews with store managers confirmed the cashiers' suspicions that the union had not raised their health concerns during negotiations. One manager commented that health and safety issues had never been raised. Another was aware of the significance of health and safety issues but discounted their prevalence and emphasized the safety measures that had been implemented (quoted in Morihovitis, 128):

> I want to maintain the level that we are at. We have very little injuries on cash. To improve on this would be zero injuries and I do not know if this is possible in a store of 150 employees. This is one of the safest stores [the chain] has. It is the most up to date, it has the latest as far as equipment that is available to us through [the chain].

Encounters with difference by cashiers are very different from those reported by room attendants in Toronto hotels. The cashiers work in isolation, except when they are learning their jobs (Figure 6). Cashiers are seen as disposable workers by employers who rely on

FIGURE 6. *The isolation of cashiers in contemporary grocery stores. (Source: http://www.loblaw-grocery-store-cashier-465765178-steve-russell-toronto-star-getty-compressor.jpg.)*

a youthful and transitory cashier workforce to avoid workplace injuries. The ethnic and racial diversity of cashiers goes largely unremarked by their employers except insofar as it facilitates informal recruiting and training.

The experiences of these grocery store cashiers underscore the impacts of institutional actors on encounters in the workplace. Employers control the labor process in grocery stores and, as part-time workers, the cashiers are isolated at individual cash registers with few opportunities for social interaction. Their isolation is compounded by the perceived failure of their union to address their health and safety concerns. Without institutional support from the union, cashiers do not cooperate to address their working conditions and work schedules. Their frustration reinforces cashiers' insistence that the jobs are temporary and short-term. The cashiers' attitudes to their jobs promotes their isolation from each other, discourages much social interaction at the workplace,

Working for a Living in Toronto

and limits opportunities for encounters with difference that might also generate equality claims.

Informal Workplaces: Caregivers in Private Homes

Around the world, much paid work takes place outside formal workplaces (International Labour Organization 2015; Romero et al. 2014). In Canada, it is estimated that the informal economy accounts for about 2.3 percent of the gross domestic product (GDP) with a total value of approximately $42.4 billion in 2012 (Statistics Canada 2015). Domestic work in private households is often informal (Bernhardt et al. 2013; Fish 2014). Working in residential locations where regulations are enforced rarely, many domestic workers suffer all of the disadvantages of informal work identified by Vosko (2010): limited certainty of employment, limited control over the labor process, inadequate income, and little power to enforce employment standards legislation. A case study in Toronto, Canada, illustrates how the characteristics of domestic work and its residential location affect encounters and opportunities for being together in difference as equals.

In Canada, as in much of the world, the vast majority of domestics work alone, with few opportunities for social interaction other than with the employer and his or her family members and friends (Romero 2011). Encounters with employers take on tremendous significance. The main form of daily social interaction outside their families for many domestic workers, these frequent but informal and unplanned encounters that occur in nominally residential spaces largely determine how much domestic workers are paid, their hours of work and duties, and even their chances to continue working.

The caregiving that is a component of much domestic work also involves tremendous emotional labor as workers tend to the needs of children, seniors, and people with disabilities. The intimate nature of the work and its location in employers' homes, rather than in a formal workplace, complicates the relations between domestic workers and their employers. Employers sometimes make unreasonable and even illegal demands. On the one hand, they treat domestic workers as employees for whom they specify working hours, tasks, and remuneration and at other times, as family members who will provide labor on an uncompensated basis at times that suit the needs of the family (Cranford 2014; Romero 2011; Rosenbaum 2014). Isolation makes domestic workers vulnerable to abuse of all types, including sexual assault (Jureidini 2014). Alone at work and engaged frequently in intimate interactions with their clients, caregiving can become a vocation rather than a job, reducing caregivers' willingness to fight for working conditions and wages (Meintel et al. 2014).

In Canada, the majority of domestics are racialized migrant women, with many originating in the Philippines. Even with legal status, the conditional nature of their visas and being foreign-born compounds the challenges associated with domestic work. Until recently, most domestic workers in Canada entered initially as live-in caregivers who were required to work for two years providing care to children, seniors, and people with disabilities in the homes of their employers before they were permitted to apply for permanent residence.[7] With their paths to permanent residence dependent on satisfying employers who also put a roof over their heads, live-in caregivers are rendered extremely vulnerable to the demands and whims of their employers. According to Anna, a personal care worker in Toronto, quoted by D'Addario (2012, 153):

> They treat you like slaves. As a caregiver they are asking you to do the laundry, asking you to do the washing and you're only paid $9 per hour, that's [pay for] light duty.

Aware that they are being exploited, live-in caregivers often accede to employers' demands in order to obtain permanent residence. Here are several comments from different caregivers:

> They ask for [babysitting] and so I do it for free. She's in the office Sunday and Monday and so every Saturday night she asked me to babysit and go without pay. Because they say every once in a while they need to go out sometimes.
> That is the problem with these employers is they're abusive because they know that the people are under contracts.

And we need the papers and so we have to do whatever. Like 24 months or 36 months because if you change employer then it takes time. It takes time to process the papers or you're losing the time. (158)

As these quotes indicate, insecure immigration status frames many of the encounters between employers and domestic workers. Until they are permanent residents, domestic workers feel obliged to meet employers' demands for additional work and hours, even those that they view as excessive and exploitative. Due to the workers' precarious residency status, employers wield tremendous power over the employee. The power differential does not encourage being together with difference as equals, even when the employer and employee come from the same minority group. Val, who immigrated to Canada as a caregiver to obtain permanent residence, describes her experiences hiring live-in caregivers from the Philippines:

I decided to get a nanny from our country so I sponsored my niece who has been wanting to come over to earn a living and after two years she became a landed immigrant and I can't have any control of keeping her in the house. . . . I hired a [Filipina] caregiver from Spain and she stayed with us for a long time even when she got her landed status. And I enjoyed that because I could work more hours and I can do extra work because there is somebody to rely on in the house. (151)

Despite their shared ethno-racial background and immigration history, Val expresses the same desires for continuity and control as other employers of live-in caregivers. Her interests as an employer override any commitment to ethnic and racial solidarity that might encourage equitable interactions between her and a caregiver.

Domestic workers' knowledge of Canadian society is also shaped by daily interactions with their employers. Many domestic workers learn about ethno-racial difference through everyday interactions with employers and other family members. Here, one woman notes that her employer keeps kosher, so she eats kosher

124   *Working for a Living in Toronto*

food during the week and only eats Filipino food on the weekend during her free time:

> My employer is Jewish so I eat kosher, always kosher. We love to eat rice but in our employer's house we always eat bread and macaroni, pasta. (186)

The domestic workers acknowledge the power of employers to dictate intimate aspects of their lives, including their daily diets. Living with their employers, domestic workers forced to comply with the employer's lifestyle, no matter how different from their own preferences, learn the intimate details of cultural difference. Their knowledge comes from changes in their everyday lives that are dictated by the employer. Awareness of difference does not arise from negotiations where employer and employee act as equals. To preserve their own cultural practices and exercise some autonomy, domestic workers actually leave their places of residence and take on the additional costs of accommodation and food on their days off.

When difference is acknowledged, the acknowledgment tends to reinforce the unequal power relations between employers and domestic workers. The encounter between one domestic worker and her employer, a single parent who asks the worker to work seven days straight with four days off to accommodate the custody schedule for his daughter, illustrates how stereotypes are deployed to reinforce perceived differences between employers and employees. The domestic worker here recognizes the challenges of understanding Canadian accents, describing the difficulties they pose for her and other caregivers:

> Yeah it's difficult because we can speak English but we have different dialects. It's very different like the accents so sometimes when somebody talks to you and maybe you're not familiar with the accents and for you it's like, come again? It's different it's very tough too. (190)

Her employer agrees that there are language barriers, but he essentializes them, attributing the communication difficulties he expe-

Working for a Living in Toronto 125

riences with the caregiver to personality traits that are inherently Filipina:

> We have a lot of trouble communicating. *They* are a little more free spirited whereas *We* are a little more reserved. But she has pretty good English, it's just once in a while. (190)

The employer's comments that emphasize differences between the foreign-born and racialized workers and their employers underline how repeated and prolonged encounters sometimes reinforce rather than challenge inequality in workplaces.

Caregivers' residential locations often compound the unequal power relations between caregivers and their employers. In low-density suburban neighborhoods, caregivers may only know their employers and their families. D'Addario describes the experiences of Mary, who comments on the challenges of suburban isolation where distances are large and difficult to cover. She only knows her elderly employers in the suburb where she lives. Mary compares the limited access to transit of her work location in an outer suburb with the public transportation available in another suburb where she meets caregivers on her days off:

> It's too far here, you need a car or the bus . . . in Scarborough where I travel it only takes two buses, but from here it takes too far. It's very easy in Scarborough but here it's so big. (149)

Despite the exploitation of domestic workers that D'Addario and many others (Hsiung and Nichol 2010; Stasiulis and Bakan 2005) have documented, some encounters between employers and domestic workers are more equitable. These encounters are usually also beneficial to the employer. The employer facilitates the continued employment of the domestic worker by assisting with issues such as visa status, support for families at home, and the worker's health. Employers who assist domestic workers enable workers' voices and concerns to be heard, but their prime motivation is often their own desire to maintain the employment relationship.

To escape the demands of their employers and to combat their loneliness, domestic workers meet outside their workplaces. In Toronto, groups of live-in caregivers rent apartments together to spend the weekends with each other. The accommodations are often spartan, as one caregiver in Toronto explains:

> During the first year when I came over here, I rent one of the apartments along Eglinton. And we are living there exactly 8 live-in caregivers. We live there every weekend so we're paying separately [from] the employer right. If you can see that place it's a basement. No emergency exit . . . we provide our own mattresses because the landlord just leaves us with old mattresses. That's why when the first time we came into that apartment we just used the boxes, just to sleep on that night. (D'Addario, 2012, 187)

Despite the additional financial burden and poor quality of the weekend accommodation, it offers welcome respite, as these four women in conversation explain:

> It's a place to stay.

> Where you can release all your stress.
> Enjoy and dance.
> And eat Filipino food and cook Filipino food. (186)

By distancing themselves from their workplaces and employers, domestic workers exert some control over their hours and conditions of work. In weekend accommodation, women from the same countries of origin cook familiar food and enjoy activities such as dancing that are not possible in the residential spaces where they work and live. Activities at church also provide much needed moral support. Weekend accommodations and church activities enable caregivers to meet as equals with shared experiences of domestic work and immigration despite their class and regional differences (Pratt 2004). Such equality is not achieved very easily between caregiver and employer. As such, these spaces make another place in the city where these workers can escape their identities as domestic care workers and their emplacement in racialized hierarchies, through the production of an alternative domesticity in which they are equals in their differences.

Workplace hierarchies are also challenged by nongovernmental organizations that bring together domestic workers around workplace issues rather than shared ethno-racial identity. At one meeting of live-in caregivers organized by a Filipino organization, two representatives from the immigration department made presentations emphasizing the employment rights of live-in caregivers:

> The written contract is very important, you have to keep it with you and as was mentioned before that is a legal binding document and on that contract it is going to say: what are my duties, what are the hours I work, how much am I getting paid, overtime—when is that put in. That contract will explain to you exactly what you and the employer have agreed upon. So it's very important that when you start working if that employer says that we're going to change around the contract—well you can't just change around the contract. I've heard of cases where the nanny started working and she has to take care of the dog and mow the lawn and clean the windows . . . oh yeah and childcare may be in the afternoon for a couple of hours. That was not what was in the contract. . . . Your primary duty has to be care for a child, or care of a senior, or care of someone disabled. If you're taking care of a senior or a disabled, well you'll be helping them around the house and with daily chores—they may be unable to do so, but the primary reason why you were hired and working and what was approved by Service Canada was primarily to care for an individual. You are not hired as housekeepers you are hired as live-in caregivers to care for in the home. (D'Addario 2012, 154)

The government employee emphasizes caregivers' shared identities as workers in a specific occupation and in particular types of workplaces. The women's rights as workers are highlighted with no mention of their ethno-racial backgrounds. Information meetings such as the one described above underscore the shared interests of

FIGURE 7. *Caregivers protest. (Reprinted with permission of Philip Kelly.)*

caregivers as workers struggling with similar issues. In addition to providing caregivers with crucial information about their rights as workers, the emphasis on their identities as workers offers an alternative platform for organizing and resisting exploitation that is reinforced by statements emphasizing the cultural differences between caregivers and their employers (Figure 7). The meeting described here took place in a church, away from the women's dispersed workplaces. The church is also a location familiar to caregivers and one that employers cannot easily prohibit caregivers from visiting.

Working for a Living in Toronto 129

The mobilization of day laborers, another important and growing segment of the informal economy, provides another example of how nongovernmental organizations can work productively with difference (Visser et al. 2016). The shared objective, to promote change in working conditions, is a microproject similar to those of the worker centers discussed in chapter 6 that animate dialogue among workers who are otherwise culturally and nationally different. Their common struggles to secure immigration status motivate workers to find solutions to misunderstandings and miscommunication that arise through cultural and national differences. Working with live-in caregivers in Vancouver, Pratt (2004) found that the Philippine Women Centre, a nongovernmental organization working to organize domestic workers, emphasized their members' common struggles with working conditions. In Toronto, Intercede: Toronto Organization for Domestic Workers' Rights has a similar approach. Even though Filipinas comprise the single largest group of caregivers in the metropolitan area and they have at times dominated the executive of the organization, its mandate and activities focus on domestic workers and caregivers, rather than a single nationality (Arat-Koc 1999). The organization's activities ask caregivers to meet around the common causes of exploitation and isolation in the workplace and their shared struggles with immigration regulations and family separation, regardless of their ethno-racial backgrounds. Unite-HERE used the same strategy to help hotel workers deal with cultural differences that might have reduced cooperation among workers (Tufts 2003, 2006). The three case studies in Toronto remind us that workplace encounters are highly differentiated, and stratified by social characteristics such as age, gender, and occupation as well as ethno-racial background. Employers identified room attendants by their occupation and class as well as their ethno-racial backgrounds. Age and gender were salient dimensions of identity for cashiers whose ethno-racial background was only important to employers as a means of facilitating the recruitment, training, and punctuality of coworkers. Otherwise, the ethno-racial backgrounds of cashiers are rarely mentioned. Caregivers meet around their shared positionality as isolated and vulnerable domestic workers.

The frequency and nature of encounters depend tremendously on the labor process and the terms and conditions of employment. As Amanda Wise (2016) found in Sydney, encounters among full-time workers are qualitatively different than those among part-time workers such as the grocery store cashiers. As part-time employees, the cashiers had unpredictable shifts and were anxious to minimize their time at work. Brief and instrumental encounters such as occur occasionally among cashiers don't promote being together in difference as equals. Among the choir members, there was time, space, and motivation to consider how to include people who were different from the majority of choir members. In the other cases, one or more of these essential preconditions was lacking. Cashiers had little incentive to socialize and their work offered few opportunities for social interaction. Domestic workers are spatially isolated from other workers with whom they might share common interests.

Power differentials and status hierarchies persist in the workplaces that we studied. Encounters between managers and workers and between employers and workers rarely dislodge stereotypes held by those with power even if encounters are frequent and focused on the shared project of getting the job done. Frequent interaction may promote familiarity but it does not alter prejudices very much or change the stereotypes held by employers and managers (Harris and Valentine 2016).

The case studies highlight the emancipatory potential of nonstate institutions. Despite state efforts to ensure equitable treatment of workers, routine encounters among workers and between workers, managers, and employers rarely enhanced equality in difference in the Toronto workplaces under study. In the case studies, encounters shaped by nonstate institutions concerned with employment issues provided opportunities for enacting everyday equalities when workers acknowledged and negotiated their cultural differences through a shared commitment to improving working conditions. With its financial and organizational support of the choir, Unite-HERE created opportunities for room attendants to meet as equals who shared common interests in choral music and the union, and to take their solidarity back into workplace struggles. The community association serving Filipino immigrants was equally effective in allowing caregivers to identify their commonalities arising from Canadian immigration policies and their working conditions. In both cases, workers also had shared origins in the Caribbean and Philippines respectively that facilitated cooperation and successful being together with difference.

The case studies also illustrate how the temporality and spatiality of work limit the emancipatory potential of workplace encounters. At the workplaces studied in Toronto, the pace of work has accelerated (Theodore 2016), leaving few opportunities for workers to interact informally. When employers encourage workers to socialize, the encounters are strictly limited and purposeful. For example, experienced cashiers are expected to train new hires, a task that invariably involves some social interaction, however, the encounters are limited to those the employer considers useful for training, not the everyday socializing during breaks that Leitner (2012) and Wise (2016) describe in a Minnesota meat-packing plant and Sydney bus depot. Compounding the impacts of work's accelerating tempo, the layouts of many workplaces also restrict encounters among many workers in our case studies. Domestic workers are usually the sole employees in suburban houses, isolated from other workers. Even in large hotels, room attendants have few opportunities to socialize on the job as each is held individually responsible for cleaning a specified number of rooms on each shift. Cashiers work in view of each other, but each must stay at his or her own register and work schedules are designed to ensure employees are busy from the beginning to the end of each shift.

The experiences of choir members and Filipina caregivers underscore the importance of considering the nature, timing, and location of encounters. For the choir members, socializing at choir activities that took place outside the regular work schedule enabled the women to learn about the shared challenges of their everyday lives. Awareness of their commonalities strengthened their commitment to each other and their involvement in union activities. Spaces of refuge were also important for caregivers, who devoted their limited free time to public meetings at churches where they could speak openly about their working conditions. They also spent precious financial resources on weekend accommodation where they could socialize with other caregivers. For both groups of women, informal socializing in spaces of refuge created the solidarity that is often a prerequisite for emancipatory social change.

Any concluding thoughts must acknowledge the limitations of the cases that focus on one labor market segment: low skill and feminized occupations. Recognizing the ways that context shapes opportunities for encounter and the nature of encounters, we have concentrated on cases in a single multiculture so that we might investigate in some detail how institutions shape encounters with difference.[8] The findings underscore the gaps between formal regulation and workplace encounter for some of the most vulnerable workers in the local urban economy.

{ 5 }

Moving around the City in Sydney

IN THIS CHAPTER, we consider moving around the city as another everyday practice of being together in difference that contributes to the experience and politics of urban multiculture. We focus in particular on public transportation, which has a dual significance for us. It is an infrastructure that facilitates access to a variety of activities and services in cities, thereby enabling participation in the kinds of activities that will involve encounters with others. It is also a network of stationary and mobile sites of copresence with others, so that platforms and bus stops and train carriages and buses are themselves sites of encounter with their own distinctive forms and norms. As such, the provision and the experience of public transport matters greatly for our central questions of how ethnic, racial, and cultural inequalities are produced, and how new forms of being together in difference as equals and "everyday equality" can emerge.

As we examine these issues, our geographical focus shifts to Sydney. After consideration of the conceptual significance of public transport for the politics of difference and equality, we provide some contextual background to Sydney's distinct urban multiculture and public transport infrastructure. From here, we present three case studies of attempts to reshape the nature of "being together in difference" on Sydney's public transport. First, we will examine communications campaigns by transport providers seeking to specify and eliminate various forms of "bad behavior" on public transport, and consider the ways in which these efforts engage (or not) with problems of racist discomfort, abuse, and violence on the network. Second, we examine the emerging trend of passengers themselves using mobile and social media to document and discuss instances of racism on the network. Finally, we will examine

{ 133 }

a community organizing campaign to make public transport more affordable to people seeking asylum.

A focus on public transport gives us another distinct window onto the politics of equality in urban multicultures. Perhaps more than making a living or making a home, the encounters associated with public transportation are frequently fleeting and unfocused. While everyday lives for many urban inhabitants may involve regular rhythms of movement, the experience of using public transport rarely involves the kinds of encounters that lead to the formation of lasting attachments and relationships. Indeed, it may not even involve shared attention or focus with fellow passengers. The banality of this regular but fleeting togetherness in difference, and the remarkable extent to which it seems to take place without incident in many cities, could perhaps be indicative of the existence of an everyday form of being together in difference as equals—where public transport emerges as a kind of public space in which anyone can be present.

And yet, we must not romanticize such instances of "rubbing along" without incident. The normalization of certain ways of sharing a train or bus may not necessarily emerge from, or contribute to, a democratic politics of equality in difference. Trains and buses can also be sites where status hierarchies are reinforced through everything from aversive behavior to racist abuse and violence. And we must not lose track of the broader institutional context of these encounters. The geography of public transport infrastructures frequently reinforces patterns of spatial inequality that can correlate with ethnic and cultural difference, and the accessibility of those infrastructures is also shaped by their materiality and cost.

So, as we shall see in this chapter, enacting a form of being together in difference *as equals* on public transport is not simply a matter of passively sharing a train or a bus with strange others. Sometimes, as we noted in chapter 2, "being together in difference as equals" requires care, hard work, and agitation. Our three case studies in this chapter consider the different kinds of actors and actions involved in efforts to make the nature of "being together" on public transport a matter of public concern and political contestation. Through some of these efforts, public transport is made "public" not only with respect to its users or its ownership, but also

Moving around the City in Sydney   135

by making it an object of public discussion, debate, and action. In concluding the chapter, we will offer some reflections on the different kinds of agents, infrastructures, and actions that are engaged in these efforts.

Public Transport and Encounter in Urban Multicultures: Atmospheres and Access

In the contemporary metropolis, people's ability to move between places is a basic condition of everyday life. But this capacity to move is unevenly realized. There is a politics of mobility, and this politics has multiple dimensions.

Unevenness and inequality in our capacity to move is of course profoundly shaped by the provision of mobility infrastructures in any given urban context. Connections are established between places through the provision of footpaths, bicycle paths, roads, canals, tramlines, railway lines, and other mobility infrastructures. Immediately, there are basic geographical questions to ask of these infrastructures: where are such infrastructures located, and which places do they connect? While these are crucial questions, the geography of such infrastructures is only a part of the equation here. There are also questions of accessibility—even where such infrastructures are provided, who gets to use them, and are they equally accessible to all?

The intersection of this politics of mobility with the politics of equality in urban multicultures should be immediately apparent. In interrogating this relationship, we could focus our attention on different kinds of mobility infrastructures. Car driving, for instance, has frequently become enmeshed with the politics of difference and equality in multicultural contexts. Licensing schemes that regulate who can legally drive a private vehicle on the road network can impact unevenly across urban populations. In Sydney, changes that require people to complete one hundred hours of supervised driving in order to qualify for a driver's license have had especially harsh consequences for recently arrived migrants, who may not have access to either a car or a friend/family member with a license who can supervise their learning (Naylor 2010). In California, before a 2015 reform, undocumented migrants were unable to acquire driver's licenses, meaning that many whose livelihoods depended on driving did so without a license. As well as being uninsured, they were also exposed to heavy fines if caught doing so.[1]

However, in this chapter we focus our attention on *public transportation* infrastructure. We do so because of its particular relationship to the politics of equality in the city. In theory, the provision of public transport in the form of buses, trams, ferries, and/or trains ought to contribute to the equalization of access to a basic standard of mobility and connectivity in the city. In practice, however, there are considerable variations between cities in the extent to which equity concerns are prioritized and achieved in transport planning. For example, in their review of public transport plans across North America, Manaugh, Badami and El-Geneidy (2015) note that in many cities, environmental/sustainability outcomes are privileged over social equity concerns in the way that public transportation services are planned and evaluated. Given this, it is important to ask about the extent to which public transportation systems either reduce or exacerbate racialized forms of inequality in the cities where they are provided.

This question has at least two key dimensions. First, the "mobilities turn" across the social sciences has focused attention on the *experience* of different forms of mobility, including public transport. Contemporary scholars working on mobilities insist that human movements through the city should not be treated as "dead time," but rather as experiences of urban copresence with their attendant norms and politics (Bissell 2010; Cresswell 2010; Lobo 2014; Ocejo and Tonnelat 2014; Urry 2007). John Urry, an influential figure in this recent scholarship on mobilities, points out that a concern with the experience of mass public transportation as a site of copresence and encounter is by no means new for those grappling with the nature of urban life. Georg Simmel, for example, noted the distinct features of the experience of urban public transportation:

> Before the development of buses, trains and streetcars in the nineteenth century, people were quite unable to look at each other for minutes or hours at a time . . . without talking to each other. Modern traffic increasingly reduces the majority

Moving around the City in Sydney　137

of sensory relations between human beings to mere sight (cited in Urry 2007, 106).

Likewise, the train carriage and platform were key sites in which Goffman (1961) observed practices of what he called "civil inattention," meaning that people share space with others while developing strategies to avoid focused interaction or attention. So, copresence in trains or buses does not necessarily produce the kinds of encounters that might contribute to the emergence of a "public" in which riders come to imagine themselves sharing collective experiences, interests, and identities with one another. Public transport passengers may share a small space, but they may do so without ever explicitly acknowledging one another's presence, let alone engaging in any kind of interaction or dialogue (Ocejo and Tonnelat 2014).

Importantly, however, this practiced inattention still matters a great deal for the politics of urban multiculture with which we are concerned in this book. What are the norms of encounter in this context, how are they developed and enforced, how are they challenged and contested, and what are the prospects for the enactment of everyday equalities? As Ocejo and Tonnelat (2014, 497) put it in their study of interaction on the New York subway:

> With people from diverse backgrounds constantly entering and exiting, sitting and standing, facing one another, and shifting and bracing their bodies as the train moves, they are bound to come into visual or physical contact with others, or encroach upon their personal space. The subway, then, presents people with a unique space for practicing being a stranger in the city.

Even when it is characterized by inattention and a lack of shared focus, the "being together of strangers" on public transport has an emotional dimension, an *atmosphere*. These atmospheres are complex, multidimensional cocreations that put different kinds of bodies and behaviors "in" or "out" of place on the network infrastructures. For Bissell (2010, 272):

Affect decenters the individual passenger from analysis, and instead prompts us to think about how different configurations of objects, technologies, and bodies come together to form different experiences of "being with" while on the move.

As Bissell and others note, these atmospheres of travel are cocreated by *bodies* in all their diversity—with differences of identity, reasons for travel, and familiarity with the system being among the many significant differences that might coexist within a space of public transportation. Bodily gestures and comportment, ways of inhabiting infrastructure, are just as important as "verbal" interaction with others here: indeed, as we will see, transgressing the rules of good ridership often involves disruption through talking, from verbal abuse to other forms of public address that disrupt the inattention.

The "being together" on public transport is also of course influenced by the configuration of the system and its material infrastructures. Molotch (2012) talks about public transport infrastructures like the New York subway system as a "forest of artifacts"—the design of platforms, carriages, points of entry and exit, the provision of written and verbal instructions and announcements, the staffing and security arrangements—all contribute to the formation of distinct atmospheres on public transport infrastructures. Further, the atmosphere of public transportation infrastructure is also influenced by mediated *representations* of travel that are circulated by various sources, such as the transport authorities themselves, mass and social media, fictional and cinematic narratives, and so on.

Questions of multiculture are rarely far from these considerations of public transport atmospheres in diverse cities like Sydney. Passengers share a carriage with diverse others, and this might come to matter (or not) to the experience of being on transport in a range of ways. As Wilson (2011, 635) suggests:

> In a space of such extraordinary intimacy with others and intense materiality, where bodies are pressed up against each other, seats are shared, and personal boundaries are constantly negotiated, we find an important and often overlooked site of ordinary multiculture, where differences are negotiated on the smallest of scales.

Moving around the City in Sydney   139

For instance, breaches of etiquette and norms of travel in given circumstance might be racialized. Ocejo and Tonnelat (2014) note the ways in which subway riders in New York City sometimes racialize smells, looks, and gestures that they consider "out of place." This can spill over into racialized interactions between passengers. Everything from low-level nonverbal aversive behaviors like people not sitting next to one another or staring to verbal and high-level racist abuse and violence can be part of the experience of public transport for some people, especially those from visible minorities (Anderson 2011; Lobo 2014). Such episodes can reinforce the separateness of, and even the hierarchical relations among, those strangers who find themselves together in their differences on the bus or train. But these episodes—or indeed any events that disrupt the regular rhythms of travel—can also generate temporary socialities and solidarities, when unfocused copresence gives way to people caring for one another across their differences or coming to each other's aid and even defense (Amin 2015). As Bissell (2010) emphasizes, the affective dimensions of our being together as passengers are a collective responsibility.

Of course, the experience of racism on public transport is not only the product of passenger interactions. Racialized profiling by authorities is also part of the public transport experience for some. Fraught encounters between ethnic minority young people and transit police in Sydney trains have been an issue for many years (Youth Justice Coalition et al. 1994). Groups of ethnic minority young people are frequently labeled as "antisocial" in advance of their use of public transport.

While these matters of copresence and atmospheres are vital to our consideration of public transport encounters, it is important that we do not lose sight of more "traditional" issues considered by transport geographers. The fascinating literature on public transport atmospheres has not paid enough attention to the institutional configurations of transport systems, and how they might influence those atmospheres. The other "public" dimension of transport— not as site but as infrastructure notionally provided by and for "the public"—is crucial in determining which urban inhabitants are able to become passengers on the network in the first place.

So, as well as focusing on the atmosphere and experience of

public transport, we need to pay attention to issues of *accessibility*, such as where buses and trains go (and where they don't go), how they are paid for, who is responsible for regulating their operation, and so on. The configuration of the public transport network will shape different people's access to different parts of the city, with their associated activities, services, and infrastructures. As Urry (2007, 98) points out, the route and timetable of public transportation networks act as a "powerful system of governmentality that normatively locates trains, people, and activities at specific places and moments." In other words, they help to order the city and different people's place within it.

And of course, the configuration of the public transport network can interact with racialized housing and labor markets to produce uneven geographies of connectivity and mobility. This was the issue at the heart of the successful Bus Riders Union (BRU) lawsuit against the Los Angeles County Metropolitan Transportation Authority (LACMTA). In a city where bus services are overwhelmingly used by poor people of color, the LACMTA sought to impose a large fare increase on buses to help address the cost-overruns associated with the construction of new rail lines. This worsened an already inequitable situation in which the subsidies for bus riders were significantly lower than subsidies for train riders. A grassroots coalition took action in the courts to stop the fare increases and to increase investment in the bus network (García and Rubin 2004). Increases to bus fares in Rio de Janeiro in 2013 were also widely perceived to exacerbate structural inequalities, and drew tens of thousands of people into the streets.[2]

These two related issues, then, of the *atmosphere* and *accessibility* of public transport will be the focus of our considerations in Sydney. But before we move on to those issues, we will set the scene with some background on the nature of public transport in Sydney and its relationship to the particular urban multiculture that has emerged there.

Sydney's Multiculture and Public Transport

Sydney, which in 1788 became the first Australian location of colonial dispossession and settlement by the British, is currently

Australia's most populated city, and is also home to the highest proportion of migrants of any Australian city, 43 percent as of the 2016 census (Australian Bureau of Statistics 2016).

In chapter 3, we discussed the broader context of migration to Australian cities over the twentieth century, noting in particular that Australia's major cities have been the favored destinations of migrants. Patterns of urban development in Sydney are broadly similar to Melbourne's—especially in the composition of the city as a distinct "inner city" of relatively high-density suburbs around the central business district flanked by suburbs of lower-density housing. But Sydney does have some geographical particularities that are important for the analysis of public transport as a site and enabler of being together in difference as equals.

The locality that is still frequently referred to as the "city center"—the main central business district, or CBD—is not the geographical center of the greater metropolitan area. Rather, the CBD is located around the site of initial colonial settlement on the harbor foreshore very close to the city's eastern coastal edge. The expansion of the metropolitan area over the past two centuries has been shaped by this geography. With very little room to expand to the east, the city has developed along the coast to the north and south, but most expansively to the west. Affluence tends to be concentrated in the areas to the east and north of the CBD, while the region known as Greater Western Sydney now houses around half of the city's population of 4.8 million, and is home to its most ethnically diverse suburbs.[3]

What kind of urban multiculture has taken shape in this context of increasing ethnic and cultural diversity? Certainly, in distinction to the situation some fifty years ago when the White Australia policy was officially overturned at the commonwealth level, state and local governments now regularly celebrate the diversity of metropolitan Sydney and its suburbs. Ethnic, cultural, and linguistic diversity are core elements of place-marketing at local and metropolitan scales, and are frequently celebrated with festivals and addressed in diversity strategies (Dunn et al. 2001).

Academic observers have pointed toward the tentative but substantive emergence of everyday multicultures characterized by mutual learning and transversality in the localities and spaces of diversity in the city (Gow 2005; Wise 2009). However, while political leaders from Sydney have sometimes represented Western Sydney as a model of "successful" multiculture that stands in stark contrast to retreats from state-sponsored multicultures in Europe and North America (Bowen 2011), others are less sanguine about the way the politics of difference plays out in the city. Longitudinal studies find the persistence of racism for many communities in the city (Dunn and Forrest 2007), and critical scholars like Ghassan Hage (see especially 1998) have argued that the city's official and mainstream multiculture tends to be dominated by a white cosmopolitanism that selectively embraces elements of "cultural diversity" while striving to maintain a privileged position for white Australians to "welcome" or "tolerate" the ethnic Other.

Ongoing tensions in the city's politics of difference were laid bare in the notorious Cronulla riots in 2005. These riots, which gained global attention, involved a gathering of over five thousand people in the beachside suburb of Cronulla in response to a call to "take back our beach" from the "Lebs" and "wogs" who were perceived to have intruded into this iconically "Australian" space. The gathering turned violent, as groups of people (some draped in Australian flags, others with nationalist messages written on their bodies) attacked people of color on the beach and in nearby streets and public spaces (Noble, ed. 2009). Any claim that Sydney had fully transformed into an easygoing, nonracist multiculture became hard to sustain in the wake of these events.

This story of migrant settlement and urban multiculture in Sydney intersects with the history of *public transport infrastructure* in interesting ways. Sydney's public transport network presently accounts for a relatively modest 11.7 percent of all trips in the metropolitan area. But importantly, and in distinction to other cities where public transport is a relatively small share of urban transport, there are no simple correlations between income, ethnicity, and the use of public transportation services in Sydney. Public transport is not a form of public infrastructure that is used only or predominantly by the poor. The percentage of trips taken by people across the income range holds remarkably constant: while 13.5 percent of trips taken by people from very poor households with incomes less than $25,000 are taken by public transport, 11.3

percent of trips taken by people from wealthy households with incomes over $125,000 are also on public transport.[4] Nor can it be said that the wealthy tend to be served by trains, while the poor are dependent on buses; again, variations here are minor.

This is not to say that public transport is equally available to all, however. Public transport infrastructure is distributed unevenly across the metropolitan area. A network of suburban train lines planned and developed in the late nineteenth and early twentieth centuries radiates outwards from the CBD into the suburbs in all directions, with the gaps in this network serviced by buses and ferries to the harborside suburbs (Spearritt 1999). More recent suburban expansion to the southwest and northwest of the city has tended to occur without the development of train lines. As a consequence, while the network of public transport services has relatively even coverage across the metropolitan area, the geographical location of *frequent* services is much more uneven, and tends to be concentrated along the rail lines and the inner-urban areas covered by state-owned buses (Troy and Iveson 2014).

The geography of public transport provision and use interacts with the patterns of settlement and diversity in interesting ways. As pointed out above, much of Sydney's ethnic and cultural diversity is concentrated in Greater Western Sydney, where public transport tends to be less frequent. However, because migrant communities have tended to settle in areas with older and cheaper housing stock, first in the inner-urban suburbs after World War II, and then in the "middle-ring" suburbs in the latter decades of the twentieth century and the early decades of the twenty-first (Randolph and Freestone 2012), they often live in areas with access to frequent train services. As a consequence, older suburban rail lines like the Bankstown, Western, Main, and North Shore provide fascinating transects through Sydney's ethnic and class diversity.

For example, consider the data in Table 2 from the 2016 census of the suburban stops along the Bankstown line, which travels from the CBD into the southwest part of the metropolitan area. The place of birth and ancestries of populations along different stops on this line are extraordinarily diverse (both internally and in comparison to one another), as are the incomes and employment profiles. While occupants of trains on this line may never have visited many of the suburbs in which it stops, they may nonetheless share their carriage with a very diverse group of people from localities all along the line. Here, we see the interaction between the two issues of the *accessibility* of public transport and the *experience* of public transport. This suburban railway line enables a relatively accessible form of mobility for inhabitants of ethnically diverse suburbs, and thereby becomes a site of mobile encounters across difference as the train carriages assemble people from different parts of Sydney's distinct urban multiculture.

So, Sydney's suburban railway lines both enable mobility and concentrate diversity within their infrastructures. Not surprisingly, they have therefore also become enmeshed in the contested politics of Sydney's urban multiculture. This is perhaps best illustrated with reference to the aforementioned Cronulla riot. Cronulla is the only major beach in Sydney that is directly accessible by train—other beaches to the east and north of the city are only served by much slower bus services. This has made Cronulla more easily accessible to the ethnically and religiously diverse inhabitants of Sydney's southwestern suburbs. During the 2005 riot, the train line became the site of conflict, with rioters spilling onto the trains at the station and attacking people perceived to be arriving from elsewhere. If "we grew here, you flew here" was one of the racist mottos of the rioters, the train connection to Cronulla was perceived in similar white nationalist terms—with one participant in the riots describing young men of Arab descent as "the filth that crawls off the trains and pollutes our beaches" (quoted in Noble and Poynting 2010, 499). In other beachside suburbs in the east and north of the city in particular, elected mayors and residents have expressed concerns about the potential for a rise in people accessing "their beaches" from other parts of the city. Such concerns about the overcrowding of beaches sometimes have implicit or explicit racist undertones, where the "others" perceived to be threatening the "locals" are migrant communities from the western suburbs. As one reader commented in relation to a recent story about extending the rail network to the northern beaches:

> I'm sure Cronulla was once an idyllic, quiet paradise too.
> Manly, as we know it, will be ruined if trains go anywhere

Table 2. Socio-Demographics of Selected Suburbs on the Bankstown Railway Line, Sydney

Station Suburb	Erskineville	Marrickville	Campsie	Lakemba	Bankstown	Cabramatta
Ancestry, top 5 responses	English 24.6%	English 18.1%	Chinese 31.0%	Bangladeshi 12.9%	Vietnamese 16.3%	Vietnamese 33.0%
	Australian 17%	Australian 15.3%	Nepalese 6.9	Lebanese 7.7%	Lebanese 12.7%	Chinese 24.5%
	Irish 10.9%	Irish 8.8%	Lebanese 5.8%	Australian 6.7%	Chinese 9.5%	Khmer 8.2%
	Scottish 7.9%	Greek 6.6%	English 5.5%	Indian 6.6%	Australian 6.8%	English 4.7%
	Chinese 5.0%	Scottish 5.6%	Australian 5.2%	Pakistani 6.0%	English 5.6%	Australian 3.9%
Median weekly income	$1381	$793	$486	$427	$453	$397
Professionals as % of employment	44.3%	34.2%	16.2%	14.7%	17.2%	10.6%
Percentage using train for journey to work*	37.9%	28.4%	27.0%	23.2%	17.2%	16.3%

(Source: Australian Bureau of Statistics 2016.)

*Note that this calculation does not include people living in other suburbs who use the train station at the named suburb. It nonetheless provides some indication of usage of the train line by residents of the suburbs directly along its route.

146   *Moving around the City in Sydney*

nearby. Never mind how trains help residents, they just bring in the trouble.[5]

Beyond these tensions around the location of public transport infrastructure in the city, there continue to be more general concerns about the experience of public transport and mobility for passengers from visible ethnic and religious minorities. While the copresence of ethnic and cultural difference on the public transport network may often pass without incident, some passengers frequently encounter different forms of racism on Sydney's public transport network. Such experiences may take a range of forms, and have been widely documented. For example, a report on the experience of racism in Australia produced by the Australian Human Rights Commission to mark the fortieth anniversary of the Racial Discrimination Act in Australia found that public transport in Sydney and other Australian cities was a common site in which racism is experienced (Australian Human Rights Commission 2015). That report highlighted in particular the ongoing persistence of racist talk and aggression on public transport, and the thorny question of bystander complicity and intervention in such situations. This racism frequently intersects with gender inequality and stereotypes, with Muslim women being particular targets if they wear clothing that visibly marks their faith (a finding which speaks directly to the story about public transport we told in the introduction). This research pointed out that instances of racism on public transport are not only distressing at the time, but can reduce people's use of public transport and thereby reduce their access to work, services, and social and community events. This report, along with other research (Dunn and Forrest 2007; Noble and Poynting 2010), draws attention to the significance of public transport as a site of "everyday racism" in Sydney. As Noble and Poynting (2010, 490) put it:

> Movement is experienced differentially, and the pleasures and powers it confers are not distributed evenly but linked to relations of inequality and practices of social exclusion.

These authors go on to point out the connection between the intimate encounters involved in sharing a bus or train and larger-scale geographies of inclusion and exclusion—public spaces like the sites of public transportation "function as diverse sites for the regulation of national belonging" (Noble and Poynting 2010, 495) through the aggressive imposition of ethno-nationalist norms of bodily presence and comportment.

The three case studies to follow are all examples of such intersections. Each is an example of the different kinds of work that go into reshaping the experience and/or accessibility of public transport, and each is critically examined in relation to the ideal of everyday equality through "being together in difference as equals" that animates our book.

Policing "Beastly Behavior" on the Network

In the above discussion of the experience of public transport and its significance for urban multicultures, we noted that atmospheres on buses and trains emerge from the interaction of bodies, infrastructures, and institutional interventions by a range of actors. In this first case, we critically examine efforts by transport authorities to police the atmospheres of public transport encounters in Sydney through media interventions on the network. Media—in the form of stickers, posters, and speakers installed on transport infrastructure by operators, billboards paid for by advertisers, and mobile media carried by passengers—are an important element in the "forest of artifacts" that constitutes the public transport network and its atmosphere in Sydney. In recent years there have been several distinct efforts by transport authorities to establish and enforce conceptions of the "good rider" of public transport through media interventions. How do such efforts relate to the politics of difference and equality with which we are concerned? To what extent do they challenge or transform the forms of racist aversion, abuse, and violence that many commuters in Sydney continue to experience on a regular basis when they use public transport, thereby combating the persistence of racialized hierarchies of who is and is not "out of place" on the platform, train carriage, or bus? In the initiatives we will examine here, we will see distinct interventions that relate quite differently to the politics of equality in the time-space of public transportation in Sydney.

148   *Moving around the City in Sydney*

In recent years, informed in part by the creeping marketization of public transportation in Sydney, the New South Wales state government authority responsible for providing and/or contracting public transport services in Sydney has taken a much more proactive interest in what they refer to as the "customer experience" of public transportation. Indeed, in a major reorganization of transport portfolios conducted by the conservative O'Farrell government shortly after its election in 2011, a Customer Experience Division was established within Transport for NSW, with a purpose of "engaging with customers to understand what they value about transport, understanding what they want to see improve and how we can better meet their needs and expectations across all aspects of the transport system" (Transport for New South Wales 2011, 23).

At one level, the formation of this Division within Transport for NSW brought with it a welcome focus on the *experience* of the public transport journey itself, beyond its functionality. As the 2011 Transport for NSW *Corporate Plan* (2011, 25) put it, the "customer experience" was broken into two related elements:

> Firstly, there is a functional benefit we deliver in helping move people and goods between origin and destination. Secondly, there is the experience of the journey itself, which stimulates an emotional response. Overall this produces a level of satisfaction that we aim to improve over time.

This orientation does have the potential to address some of the issues of accessibility and atmosphere identified earlier in this chapter, where we noted that access to public transport is not only shaped by its location, but also by the experience of using it. "Interaction with other users" appeared as one of the core elements of the "customer experience framework." Given the documented persistence of interpersonal racism on the transport network, this explicit focus on the experience of using public transport might have engaged with the experience of encounter and being together on trains, buses, and ferries.

However, what is most striking about recent customer experience interventions initiated by Transport for NSW is that they have studiously ignored or avoided questions of multiculture and racism. Instead, there has been a focus on specifying and promoting "customer courtesy" that has very little connection to any political questions of being together. In the wake of a customer survey conducted by the Customer Experience Division, Transport for NSW initiated two communications initiatives designed to specify and discourage different forms of "beastly behavior" on the transport network. The first 2011 "customer courtesy campaign" was "designed to encourage customers to consider their fellow passengers and be more courteous while travelling on our network."[6] The specified targets of this campaign were the blaster, the yeller, the shover, the groomer, the splutterer, the bumper, the blocker, the grubber, the hogger, and the rubbisher. Cartoon images of these beasts were developed and displayed on posters across the network (see Figure 8).

A second poster campaign, "Travelling Together," initiated in 2016, spelled out a similar set of rules of etiquette for riding public

FIGURE 8. *Images of the hogger and the yeller, two of the targets of Transport for NSW's "Beasts of Bad Behavior" customer courtesy campaign. (Source: Transport for NSW.)*

transport. These were communicated in a series of pictograms, once again postered across the network, that illustrated rules like "Blocking the way delays everyone's day," "Being noisy at night is just not right," "It may not be intended but people are offended," and "Taking up all the space is a disgrace" (see Figure 9).

These media initiatives seek to improve the experience of public transport by specifying and shaming various forms of "antisocial behavior" that might inhibit a trouble-free sharing of the intimate space of the carriage or bus. Two aspects of these initiatives are worth consideration here. The first is how the transport authority has sought to intervene in the intimate spaces of public transport encounters through *media* located in the space of the encounter. The posters make explicit a set of norms about using public transport that are often left unspoken. In doing so, they seek to govern public transport users at a distance through signage (Hermer and Hunt 1996), by both reminding passengers of their obligations and licensing passengers to enforce those rules when they are (perceived to be) breached by others. Given the impossibility of policing every train carriage or bus with uniformed police, there is an

FIGURE 9. *Poster from the Transport for NSW "Travelling Together" campaign, 2016. (Photograph: Kurt Iveson.)*[7]

Moving around the City in Sydney 151

implicit recognition here that passengers must govern their own behavior, and potentially the behavior of others with whom they share the service.

A second point concerns the outcomes that these media interventions seek to achieve. Undoubtedly, the forms of behavior that are identified in these posters may be a cause of annoyance to some (perhaps many) passengers. The attempt to curb these behaviors may emerge from a desire to improve the "experience" of public transport for all. But in conceptualizing the "public" of public transportation through the lens of a universalized and undifferentiated "customer," these initiatives make no reference at all to the forms of "bad behavior" (i.e., racism) that are regularly experienced by passengers from visible ethnic and religious minorities. The concern with the "customer experience" is not informed by an analysis of, or a concern with, any of the forms of difference and inequality that characterize the public transport experience in Sydney's heterogeneous multicultural public. Indeed, these campaigns are devoid of references to any forms of behavior that might contribute to identity-based or status-based exclusions, be they related to class, ethnicity, religion, gender, sexuality, age, or anything else. Nor do they articulate any vision or ideal of what might be a good way of being together on the network—much less one informed by any notion of equality or social justice. As a consequence, they have no meaningful connection to any political attempt to make the experience of using public transport a more equal one.

Indeed, not only do these customer courtesy initiatives fail to target racism and other forms of inequality, they actually have the potential to give license to some of the forms of racism reported by passengers in studies of everyday racism. Notions of "antisocial behavior" are frequently filtered through racist (or other) stereotypes—so, for instance, a conversation among a group of passengers speaking English may go unnoticed, where a conversation in a language other than English may be perceived as "noisy" or "loud." Posters shaming "loud talkers" take on a different, and potentially problematic, meaning in this context.

Interestingly, and perhaps unexpectedly, a different approach has been taken by Transdev, one of the privately owned bus companies providing services in some of the outer suburbs of Sydney.

Drivers on their buses, as well as passengers, have frequently been targets of racist abuse and violence. In 2014 the Transport Workers' Union conducted a survey of over three hundred bus drivers working for private operators, and 32 percent of those surveyed reported being the victim of racist abuse or violence (Transport Workers' Union of NSW 2014). Partly in response to this union campaign, and in distinction to the strategy adopted by Transport for NSW, Transdev developed a poster campaign with an explicit antiracist message. Their "This Bus Is for Everyone" poster campaign, which was developed in partnership with the broader "Racism—It Stops with Me" agenda of the Australian Human Rights Commission, informed passengers that racist discrimination and harassment on Transdev buses are not acceptable. The posters asked passengers to act if they witnessed harassment or discrimination by speaking up (if it is safe to do so), offering support to the person being harassed or discriminated against, notifying the driver, and/or calling police (see Figure 10).

FIGURE 10. *"This Bus Is for Everyone" poster. (Source: Transdev and Australian Human Rights Commission.)*

Unlike the customer courtesy campaigns of Transport for NSW, these Transdev posters do have an explicit orientation toward equality—the poster both establishes a claim about public transport being "for everyone" and names racism as a wrong that inhibits the realization of this ideal. And by partnering with the Australian Human Rights Commission and their "Racism—It Stops with Me" campaign, the posters also attempt to connect the space of the bus to a broader national discussion about racism and multiculture in Australia. This seems significant—as we noted earlier, sites like train carriages and buses are simultaneously local and national spaces, and the intimate time-spaces of an individual journey are profoundly shaped by the broader geography within which they are situated.

Of course, while it is possible to critically analyze the content of these different media interventions in the spaces of public transport, it is more difficult to analyze their impact. These poster campaigns seek to address the traveling public about the nature of their being together. They do so through a one-way assertion of public authority, rather than through any attempt to facilitate a public discussion. But we know that passengers are not simply passive readers of such communications. Messages are filtered through their diverse experiences and orientations, and/or potentially ignored altogether. And of course, passengers may also seek to address one another and the transport authorities about the nature of their being together in the space of public transportation. Indeed, passengers are increasingly themselves making use of new media technologies for this purpose, and their media interventions take quite a different form to those of the transport authorities discussed above.

"Racist Rants" and Social Media: Making Trains and Buses Public

Posters, stickers, and announcements are not the only media passengers encounter in their use of public transport. In Sydney, as in many cities around the world, passengers increasingly have their own mobile media devices to access music, games, news, videos, and the like. This has profound implications for the encounters and atmospheres of public transport journeys, and makes for an interesting comparison with the poster campaigns discussed above. In their use of these devices, passengers sometimes act not only as media consumers but also as media *producers*, initiating public discussions of the nature of their being together on public transport. In a number of recent high-profile cases in Sydney, such discussions have explicitly problematized the presence of, and response to, racism on trains and buses.

Since the first mobile media devices became commonplace, there have been concerns about their implications for encounters on public transport. In the physical site of encounter, our engagement with such devices can take the form of an "involvement shield" of the kind discussed by Goffman in his classic studies of public interaction (see Goffman 1961; Urry 2007). But such disconnections occur at the same time as new kinds of connections take shape with others in diverse media spaces. With the networking of mobile media devices, their users can be simultaneously "present" in the digital spaces of the internet and the physical spaces of the city, like public transport infrastructures. Certainly, as McFarlane (2016, 642) points out, the diffusion of these communications technologies has profound significance for the nature of urban encounters:

> The politics of the urban encounter debated in urban studies from Wirth and Mumford to Jacobs and Sennett is not just topographically *there* in the landscape, but is instead topologically made through combining physical proximate densities and spatially translocal e-densities. Indeed, this combination of digital and non-digital realms is increasingly vital to the experience, negotiation, and contestation of urban density.

The development and rapid uptake of smart phones with cameras and video recording capabilities has been particularly significant for the experience and atmosphere of public transport. In combination with new scenes of public address associated with digital

Moving around the City in Sydney 155

and social media platforms like Facebook, Twitter, Instagram, and YouTube, passengers have new means at their disposal for making the public transport experience more "public," by recording, sharing, and discussing events that take place during their travels.

In particular, personal media devices are now being used by some passengers to capture instances of racist abuse and violence on public transport, in Sydney and elsewhere. Captured video has been uploaded to open platforms such as YouTube, and footage and narrative accounts have been promoted via social media such as Facebook and Twitter. More and more often, videos or experiences shared by individual passengers on social media have subsequently been "re-mediated" via mainstream media outlets such as daily newspapers and nightly television news programs. This has certainly contributed to an ongoing public discussion about the norms and politics of togetherness on public transport. As video moves from social media to mainstream media, this stretches the time and space of the encounter and makes racism, and the "rules" of our being together on public transport, more public.

Consider the following examples of passengers using mobile and social media to circulate accounts of racist experiences and generate follow-up public discussions of racism on public transport and in Australian society more broadly.

In February 2013, Sydney-based newsreader Jeremy Fernandez tweeted a series of messages about one experience of racism on a Sydney bus:

> Just had my own Rosa Parks moment: Kept my seat on a #Sydney Bus after being called a black c**t & told to go back to my country.
>
> Anyone who says racism is dying is well and truly mistaken. Copped 15 mins of racial abuse. Bus driver said "your fault for not moving."
>
> Worst thing is—i had my 2yo daughter with me. She [the abuser] had her primary school aged kids with her. All heard every word of her racist rant.
>
> It's a sad thing when a coloured man in 2013 has to show his kid how to hold their nerve in the face of racist taunts.[8]

As a high-profile newsreader and person of color who migrated to Australia from Malaysia, Fernandez's tweets were widely circulated and then discussed in social and mainstream media, locally in Sydney as well as nationally and internationally. Fernandez also wrote his own reflections on the event for his employer, the Australian Broadcasting Corporation (ABC).[9] Various aspects of this episode were discussed in these re-mediated accounts—from the persistence of everyday racism in Australia to the actions of others on the bus, the presence and involvement of children in the event, and more.

While Fernandez captured some video of the abuse directed toward him on his smart phone, he did not share or circulate that video, choosing to write about it instead. Others have shot and shared video of similar incidents. For example, in one episode in September 2015, a young woman from a Chinese Australian background used her phone to record a ninety-second video of a fellow passenger shouting racist insults at her on a bus on Sydney's North Shore. The footage was uploaded to her Facebook page, and then picked up by mainstream media.[10] No fellow riders came to her aid as she was called a "fucking chink" as part of a prolonged verbal attack, nor did the driver eject her abuser from the bus when she asked for assistance. In December of the same year, another woman was abused for speaking Spanish on a train traveling through the CBD. In this instance, a fellow passenger is filmed intervening in the situation. When the abuser said, "It's not English. Why should we have to listen to her fucking rambling?" her fellow passenger replied, "Because we're a multicultural country." When this is contested, the victim replies "Yes we are, just look at the carriage." Again, this video was picked up by mainstream media and generated public discussion about everyday racism.[11]

Such episodes have also tended to generate discussion about the role of bystanders to racist abuse and violence—both fellow passengers and transit staff. In several high-profile cases, social and mainstream media reports have documented instances where bus drivers, train guards, and fellow passengers have come to the aid of people being racially abused on public transport. Indeed, the act of holding up a camera to an abuser has become a form of bystander intervention. For instance, in April 2015 a family of Pakistani back-

Moving around the City in Sydney 157

ground on a train to Sydney airport were verbally attacked and physically threatened by another passenger. Another passenger started filming the incident on her phone, and intervened in defense of the family in question. Here again, the footage uploaded on her Facebook page attracted thousands of views, hundreds of comments (many of which were from people outside of Sydney and Australia), and mainstream media coverage.[12]

In these interventions, and in many others like them, passengers themselves are mobilizing media devices both to intervene in the moment of an encounter and to initiate public discussion about the nature of their being together on public transport. In both its content and its form, the relatively open public discussion initiated by passengers is distinct from the unidirectional messaging of the customer courtesy posters discussed above. The passenger interventions make the experience of sharing space on public transport a matter of "public" interest and discussion, through which claims about equality and racism can be asserted and enacted.

Importantly, these passenger-initiated media interventions are also distinct from the surveillance conducted by transport operators through their own extensive surveillance camera network. Many thousands of these cameras are installed across the public transport network by operators—nearly all train stations and carriages now have them, as do all buses across Sydney and major bus stops. Notices informing passengers that they are under surveillance are displayed across the network—indeed, on inner-urban buses operated by the state-owned Sydney Buses, the surveillance camera feed is displayed in real-time on screens installed inside the bus for passengers to view. These notices and feeds are intended to shape passenger behavior in the moment of travel by emphasizing that their actions can be witnessed now and at a later date by authorities. But there is something distinct about the experience of being filmed by a camera-holding *passenger* in the moment of encounter. This very act is a direct intervention in a situation that can change its dynamics in a way that remote surveillance cannot—in part because of the possibility that such footage will not only be viewed by authorities, but by a broader public through its subsequent circulation.[13]

Media scholars McCosker and Johns, in their 2014 consideration of public media interventions on public transport and in other social spaces where racism is experienced, have discussed the significance of this public dimension of passenger media use. They argue that "the presence of the camera seems to alter the social context in which bystanders respond" (70), and even note a case in Melbourne in which passengers directly address a fellow passenger's camera. Further, they argue that the re-mediation of video footage on social media platforms has the potential to "provide an alternative public forum where obstacles are minimized and the role of bystander anti-racism is extended beyond the immediate scene."

> In these circumstances, social media play an important "witnessing" role, but they also open up a space for rejoinder, by encouraging a new public to form, to claim and assert rights, and to assume civic responsibility for these actions without fear for their personal safety. (70)

They conclude that social media sites

> [have an] evident capacity to support agonistic—that is, contested but inclusive and sustained—micro-publics from which productive expressions of cultural citizenship, solidarity and counter-racist practice can emerge (71).[14]

However, while McCosker and Johns suggest that participating in social media discussions of racism on public transport enables participants to "assume civic responsibility for these actions without fear for their personal safety," it is important to remember that the potential for social media platforms to extend the encounter beyond its immediate space-time is only possible thanks to the very *embodied* form of "civic responsibility" enacted by the person prepared to hold up a camera in a moment of racist abuse and/or violence. As Butler (2015) has pointed out in her account of political assemblies like the Occupy movement, while the presence of media can help to extend a scene across time and space, the body holding the camera is simultaneously part of the immediate scene of the encounter, with all that this entails:

> If they are transported in one way, they are surely left in
> place in another, holding the camera or the cell phone,
> face to face with those they oppose, unprotected, injurable,
> injured, persistent, if not insurgent. It matters that those
> bodies carry cell phones, relaying messages and images. (92)

To hold up a camera to racism, and/or to offer other forms of support as a bystander, is a form of care and responsibility-taking that enacts a kind of "being together in difference as equals" (see the discussion of care and the politics of equality in chapter 3).

So, the media activities of passengers both intervene in the atmospheres and the shared physical space of encounter, while also producing and inciting representations of those atmospheres and spaces. There is clearly an affective dimension to the nature of our being together on public transport. But the actions discussed above show that we can take collective responsibility for shaping the nature of our being together both "in the moment" and through representational means—we can also initiate and take part in public discussions that seek to focus our attention on the nature of encounter, and to verify in those debates that there should be no particular qualification—racialized or otherwise—to ride a bus or a train.

While we might rightly celebrate these documentations and contestations of racism emerging from the "grassroots" via digital and social media technologies, it is also important to note two limitations to the media interventions of passengers discussed above. First, we should remember that the experience of interpersonal racism on public transport is not confined to these more "spectacular" media-friendly incidents. As noted earlier in the chapter, some passengers may experience physical aversion and/or subtle hostility from others who dislike the color of their skin, their style of dress, or the language they speak. This can take a range of forms—from bags not removed from vacant seats, refusal of eye contact, or standing rather than sitting in a vacant seat next to someone. This may even take the form of hostile eye contact and looks that are not immediately obvious to other passengers (Australian Human Rights Commission 2015, 39).

Perhaps this is part of the significance of the public discussion launched by #illridewithyou, discussed in the introduction. Recall that the incident to which that sentiment responded was the observation of a woman removing her scarf on a crowded train in Brisbane, on the afternoon of the armed siege in Martin Place over a thousand kilometers away in Sydney. *Anticipations* of racist aggression and violence, and the need to develop strategies to deal with the ever-present possibility of such aggression and violence, are part of the embodied experience of public transport for many inhabitants of multicultural cities like Sydney. And of course, such experiences are themselves differentiated by other threats of aggression and violence, such as those based on gender, age, and class.

Second, we should note that racism on public transport should not be reduced to the interpersonal. As we noted earlier in this chapter, a politics of equality focuses our attention on the accessibility, as well as the atmospheres, of public transport infrastructure. Of course, racist atmospheres can contribute to inaccessibility when they prevent people from feeling safe on the network. But there are further dimensions of equality and inequality that demand our attention. Lentin (2016) worries that media focus on "racist rants" may actually focus public attention on instances of individual abuse that can be collectively shamed rather than structural questions that are even more challenging to identify and address. She argues that making such events "public" in the manner discussed above reduces racism to uncommon outbursts of aberrant behavior by "racist" or "uneducated" individuals rather than a societal condition that allocates privileges according to racialized logics and categories:

> The public nature of the event permits the recognition of an act as racist, but also a distancing from it as external both to modes of "acceptable" behavior and thus isolated and containable. This element of publicness, while providing formulaic examples of what racism looks like, allows for a further distanciation between this supposedly "real," and thus extreme and uncommon, racism and the hidden forms of "systemic" racism, which, by virtue of their very obscurity (in both senses of the word), are severed from understand-

Moving around the City in Sydney   161

ings of racism as both public (hence verifiable) and universalized, thus disconnected from what Song (2014) calls racism's "historical basis, severity and power." (37)

We now turn to consider such systemic forms of racialized inequality in our next case from Sydney.

Mobility with Dignity: Campaigning to Make Public Transport Accessible to People Seeking Asylum in Sydney

With this case, we shift our attention from the atmosphere of public transport to other structural determinants of accessibility, considering a campaign in Sydney to make public transport more accessible to a particular group of migrants—people seeking asylum—by reducing its cost. This campaign sought to address a form of inequality founded in the kind of "public racism" that Lentin (2016) identifies above—that is, one based on more "systemic" and institutional arrangements, rather than one based on interpersonal prejudice. As we will see, this campaign emerged in the context of a highly fraught national political context, in which both sides of mainstream politics have taken increasingly punitive approaches to border security that have explicitly targeted people seeking asylum. While "asylum seeker" is of course not inherently an ethnic or racial categorization, in Australian political life there has been a nationalist and racialized process of othering at work in which "asylum seekers" are frequently characterized as a security threat to be excluded from the national space (Dickson 2015; Hage 2016).

The setting of ticket prices for public transport in Sydney offers a powerful example of the ways in which institutions and processes operating at a range of scales "reach in" to the times and places of urban encounter (see chapter 1)—in this case, by determining who has affordable access to public transportation. Ticket prices for trains and buses in the Sydney metropolitan area are set by the NSW state government. In some recognition of the fact that not everyone has the same means to pay for transport, reduced or "concession" fares are made available for some journeys, and to some groups. Unsurprisingly, given its significance for the accessibility of public transport, the question of which journeys and people qualify for these concession fares has been a regular matter of contention in the city.

The NSW government offers concession travel to a range of groups—including people aged over 65, full-time school and university students, apprentices, the unemployed, and those on disability pensions and other forms of income support. In order to purchase these cheaper tickets, passengers are required to apply for, and travel with, a concession card documenting their entitlement. To apply for one of these concession cards, people need to prove their eligibility. The NSW government relies on welfare criteria established by the commonwealth government in granting access to concession cards. As a result, applicants for concession travel on public transport in Sydney are required to apply by providing proof of their eligibility that has been determined and documented by Centrelink, the income support agency of the commonwealth government.

During the 2000s, this complex and multiscalar system came to intersect with national border-control measures in ways that had profound effects for people seeking asylum (and other groups including international students) living in Sydney, whose rights to welfare and work are severely curtailed by migration legislation. By the early 2010s, anyone who arrived in Australia on a valid visa and then applied for humanitarian protection was issued with a bridging visa, which allowed them to remain in Australia to live "in community" while their application for refugee status was assessed.[15] In 2010, a further group of people seeking asylum who had arrived by sea were also released from detention and granted bridging visas to enable them to live in "community detention." For many people seeking asylum on such visas, there is no right to work.[16] Depending on their circumstances, people seeking asylum are entitled to some assistance through the Asylum Seekers Assistance Scheme (ASAS). In most cases, they are not entitled to this for six months after their application, and the support is capped at a maximum of 89 percent of the standard unemployment benefit—a payment well below the poverty line.[17] Many thousands of people have lived in these circumstances for several years while waiting for their applications for asylum to be processed. The harshness of this scheme is deliberate—it is part of a broader range of measures designed to discourage people from traveling to Australia in the hope of accessing humanitarian protection.

Among their many difficulties, those living on bridging visas in Sydney—estimated to be around thirteen thousand people[18]—had no right to reduced public transport fares. Because people seeking asylum living in the community are not entitled to any Centrelink payments, and because entitlement to such payments is the eligibility criteria for access to a transport concession card, the NSW government had no arrangement in place to offer them a concession. Worse still, those living in the community on bridging visas are subject to a punitive "code of conduct" that means any minor offenses—such as traveling on public transport without a ticket—can result in the cancellation of their visa, resulting in detention or even deportation.[19]

The requirement for people seeking asylum with extremely low incomes to pay full fares for public transport had the effect of locking them out of the network, and the basic mobility that it might afford. This lack of mobility significantly compounds the disadvantage they experience. As a Catholic priest who runs a support service for people seeking asylum and refugees in Sydney (and who was one of the leaders of the campaign we are about to describe) puts it:

> With no work rights and receiving less than 80% of the Newstart Allowance as their only income, most asylum seekers in Sydney are living below the poverty line. By the time they have paid for food and rent for shared and frequently overcrowded accommodation, there is nothing left over from their fortnightly entitlement payment of $412 for public transport in order to access the assistance they need.
>
> NGO services offering asylum seekers assistance, particularly with health and medical care, trauma rehabilitation, language classes and other vital services, are spread out across the city. But the cost of getting to each of these services and receiving the help they need made accessing these services extremely difficult and simply added to the stress of what are already traumatised people.[20]

For several years, community-based service providers working with asylum seekers and refugees actively and collectively lobbied the NSW government to provide concession transport for asylum seekers. Most of that lobbying was conducted behind closed doors, out of a concern that going public might only generate a negative reaction from politicians and decision-makers, given the extent of resentment toward people seeking asylum in mainstream media and political discourse in Australia. Given that much of this resentment was founded on (inaccurate) stories about the extent of entitlements and services provided to people seeking asylum, it was perceived that policy-makers would be fearful of being seen to side with them on the issue of transport concessions.

Some of the organizations involved in that advocacy work, such as Settlement Services International, Western Sydney Community Forum, and services aligned with the Catholic Church, were also involved in a broad-based urban coalition called the Sydney Alliance. The Sydney Alliance is a coalition of unions, faith-based groups, and community organizations that was launched publicly in 2011 (Tattersall 2015). In 2014, the Alliance also began to engage with the issue of transport concessions for people seeking asylum. But the Alliance engaged with the issue in a different manner, through community organizing as well as advocacy.

The Alliance was founded on the notion that different parts of civil society could establish common ground, and take collective action, through a slow process of relationship-building and dialogue that could identify and develop shared concerns, commitments, and resources. This particular approach to coalition building and organizing is promoted by the Industrial Areas Foundation, a network of broad-based coalitions primarily based in the United States with which the Sydney Alliance is affiliated (Tattersall 2015).

Two of the issues that emerged from the process of coalition building in Sydney were accessible public transport and improving the everyday lives of refugees and people seeking asylum. The transport work initially focused on developing, and organizing around, a set of principles for accessible public transport that included affordability (Iveson and Fincher 2014; Troy and Iveson 2014). The asylum seeker and refugee work initially focused on

Moving around the City in Sydney 165

"changing the conversation"—not through alternative representations of the plight of people seeking asylum in the media, but by organizing face-to-face meetings in which members of Sydney Alliance partner organizations—including synagogues, churches, schools, and unions—would hear the story of a person seeking asylum and be invited to participate in an open conversation about the issue of refugee policy in Australia. These encounters were carefully planned—people seeking asylum who told their story were trained and supported in doing so by Sydney Alliance organizers, and the meeting places were chosen carefully to disrupt the existing political fault lines on the issue. As the lead organizer of the Alliance put it:

> The aim was to reach beyond the "usual suspects" by going to communities rather than having the usual discussions with supporters. These sessions were very successful, with thousands participating in synagogues, schools, Catholic, Anglican, and Uniting churches, and unions across the city.[21]

Here, we see a kind of application of the "contact theory" in action, with the hope that encounters with people seeking asylum—so frequently demonized in the mainstream media—might lead to a change of attitude.

According to the organizer employed on the "changing the conversation" project, while feedback from the early meetings was very positive in general terms, there was a sense that "the sessions lacked a tangible action." As Wilson (2013, 81) has observed, efforts to change attitudes through managed encounters often confront the challenge of how they might become significant in the subsequent actions of participants. In order to give the encounters a political dimension, there was a sense that they had to do more than change people's attitudes—they had to "do something." This was the impetus for the bringing together of the transport and asylum seeker work of the Sydney Alliance. Alliance leaders began to engage with policy-makers (including the Transport Minister) directly on this issue. Meanwhile, participants in the "changing the conversation" meetings who felt inspired to do something after the meetings were asked to send a used transport ticket to the Transport Minister, with "Mobility with Dignity" handwritten on the ticket. By the end of 2014, thousands of these tickets had been sent to the Minister—and not only from the usual suspects who might be expected to support the issue: they were coming from students at expensive private schools, retirees, and well-to-do people from deeply conservative electorates.[22]

Interestingly, like the service providers who were already advocating on this issue, the Alliance chose not to pursue a media campaign alongside the face-to-face meetings and direct mail campaign. The horizon of publicity for the campaign was limited to the participating organizations within the Sydney Alliance, so as not to provoke a potential backlash. The campaigning also included a meeting between a Sydney Alliance delegation and the Minister for Transport in 2014. Through their relationships across different religious communities in the city, Alliance leaders were able to build a relationship with the Primate of the Armenian Apostolic Church—who also happened to have a close relationship with the Minister for Transport (his church is in her electorate, and she is the child of Armenian migrants). The Primate attended the meeting with the Minister at which this issue was discussed, alongside delegates from the Arab Council of Australia, a community organization based in the south of the city, and the National Tertiary Education Union.[23] In that meeting, the Primate reminded the Minister of the difficulties faced by newly arrived migrants, and the moral imperative for government to minimize such difficulties. While the Minister informed the Alliance representatives that there were technical difficulties to be overcome in extending concession transport to people seeking asylum, she promised that she would task her department to look into the issue.

Some months later in 2015, after the reelection of the same conservative government, the NSW premier gave a widely reported speech in which he broke with the bipartisan political consensus in order to argue that government should be doing more for people seeking asylum and refugees. The Asylum Seeker Interagency immediately followed this speech with a submission to the government on the issue of transport concessions, and began to hear promising noises through back channels. In the middle of the year, the premier announced the daily transport costs for any asylum seeker in Sydney on a bridging visa would be capped at $2.50, in a concession scheme to be administered by service providers.

Of course, in the wake of a political decision like this, it is always difficult to disentangle the extent to which any particular strategy or tactic is decisive. But it seems reasonable to conclude that in this case, the community organizing work of the Sydney Alliance had some effect—at the very least it gave ministers in a conservative government some confidence that they would not be upsetting their political base in offering more affordable transport to people seeking asylum. The Alliance campaign clearly demonstrated that concession transport for people seeking asylum was supported by people from different walks of life and different parts of the city, not only the vocal critics of Australia's migration policies. And from our perspective, an analysis of the Alliance campaign opens up some interesting perspectives on the politics of encounter and equality in urban multicultures.

The campaign to extend transport concessions to people seeking asylum and the bystander actions described above both insisted that public transport should be accessible to all, and that racist and racialized forms of exclusion should be contested. But there are also some important differences. In distinction to spontaneous bystander actions and media interventions that emerge from the moment of encounter in the intimate space of a train or bus, the encounters involved in the Sydney Alliance Mobility with Dignity campaign were carefully planned and primarily supported through *organizational* (rather than media) infrastructures. These encounters were also designed to facilitate "contact" of a particular kind—not a contact of the "rubbing shoulders" variety that occurs in the times and sites of transport itself, but a planned contact that involved a facilitated exchange of experiences and perspectives across difference. And ultimately, these planned encounters were not only designed to change attitudes and build solidarities, they also became vehicles for a form of collective action that had some degree of political impact.

As we noted in chapter 2, there are justified critiques of the "contact hypothesis," especially those variants of the hypothesis that assume that once people get to know "others" better, prejudices will break down. But in the community organizing approach taken in the Mobility with Dignity campaign, we see the potential for contact when it is part of an organized process of coalition building and solidarity. The shared commitments and concerns of the diverse participants in the Sydney Alliance put the participants in the "change the conversation" meetings on an equal footing—that is, they participate as equals in a broader process of coalition building across differences. Moreover, with the conscious addition of an "action"—even one as small as sending a used train ticket to a government minister—the encounter becomes not only about the transformation of individual consciousness and belief, but also about the transformation of the city more broadly.

Of course, while cheaper transport might make everyday life a little easier for people seeking asylum in Sydney, it does not fundamentally transform their circumstances, or the policies that generate these circumstances. But perhaps it does point to the ways in which urban inhabitants might forge multicultures based on solidarities across their differences that can surely be a resource in the struggle for that broader transformation.

Our focus on public transport in Sydney has given us another window onto the politics of equality and encounter in urban multicultures. Our three case studies—focusing on media interventions that seek to articulate and enact a concept of the "good rider" in Sydney; media interventions that seek to disrupt and discuss instances of racism on the network; and a community organizing campaign to make transport more affordable for people seeking asylum—speak to the dual significance of public transport in urban multicultures as both a site of encounters with difference and an enabler of participation in urban life more broadly. The possibilities for "being together in difference as equals" on public transport, then, are shaped by both the atmospheres and experience of public transport journeys, and by the distribution and configuration of public transport infrastructures across the city.

Reflecting across our three examples, we can see that the prospects for being together in difference on public transport *as equals* are only partly a function of the ways in which we share a bus or carriage or platform with strangers as we move through the city together. Of course, these fleeting moments of encounter, and their atmospheres, matter greatly. But we have seen that both the policing and the politicization of people's togetherness on public transport in Sydney involves making public transport *public* not only as a site of public encounter, and not only as a kind of property, but also as an object of public interest and significance through a process of publicization (Iveson 2007, 32–40; Terzi and Tonnelat 2017). In the process of publicization, the enactment of a politics of equality relating to public transport is therefore also dependent on people's ability to make the infrastructures, and their norms and rules of use, a matter of public discussion, contention, and accountability—both with each other, and also with the authorities who provide and regulate the network.

In the cases of passengers initiating discussions about racism on the network and the campaign for affordable travel for people seeking asylum, people have worked to transform the relationship between everyday copresence (being "in public"), temporary (dis)identification (being *together* "in public"), and political subjectification (being together *as a public*). In other words, on public transport, the politics of urban multiculture becomes a question of when and how the strangers who make up the "traveling public" might actually identify with one another as equal participants in that public, and whether they are able to transform their experience, either in the moment of copresence on the network or in the way the network is planned and regulated.

Across the cases, we have also seen that these processes of publicization and politicization involve a significant amount of care, labor, and sometimes risk. Interestingly, these efforts can also make use of quite distinct kinds of public and political infrastructures—from new mobile and social media technologies to much more "old school" institutions like churches, community organizations, and unions. Of course, the capacity of such media and organizational infrastructures to influence the institutions of state and market which provide, operate, and regulate the public transport infrastructure is by no mean guaranteed. But we do see in the examples of the Transdev antiracism posters, the mainstream media focus on racism, and the shift in policy on concession cards, some sense in which passenger (and worker) action can generate shifts in the ways that the accessibility and experience of public transport is governed—both in the moment of encounter and in the very provision of services. Each of these infrastructures of publicization have their particular affordances and limitations in efforts to enact an everyday politics of equality. In the next chapter, we will make the building of such political infrastructures our main focus, as we shift from "getting around" to "making publics."

[6]

Making Publics in Los Angeles

IN THE PREVIOUS THREE CHAPTERS, we have seen that enacting equality in difference often involves a process of making racism and inequality a public matter of discussion and debate. We have seen various examples of this, from the conversational discussion of differences in the shops of Dandenong in Melbourne, to the actions of Unite-HERE in the establishment and performances of a workers' choir in Toronto, to the use of social media and community organizing strategies for challenging racialized exclusion on public transport in Sydney. This chapter focuses on the process of making progressive publics in urban multicultures: how different individuals come together to create spaces of encounter that are designed to enact solidarities and equalities. We show that this enactment entails hard work, endurance, and commitment, also requiring an institutional infrastructure and rule system that is put in place to realize it.

The place through which we narrate these enactments is the Los Angeles metropolitan area, for the past fifty years a center of immigration of mostly nonwhite immigrants from across Asia and South America and a site of dramatic inequalities in wealth and well-being. The throwing together of migrants from different parts of the world in this place has prompted encounters with culturally and racially different Others, creating not only new divisions and violence, but also new conditions of possibility for destabilizing stereotypes and prejudices and for change and collaboration across racial and other lines of difference. For many of the new immigrants, but also established racialized minorities, shared lived experiences of discrimination, racism, and other forms of prejudice and exclusion from citizenship rights have been powerful triggers for joining forces and openly challenging them. Indeed, during the past twenty-five years, Los Angeles has become a focal point for social and spatial justice struggles. New immigrants, in alliance with labor unions, religious institutions, and community organizations, have been a driving force in organizing and creating new political and social spaces across racial/ethnic lines.

Our narrative focuses on two sites. The first is the Immigrant Workers Freedom Ride of 2003, the idea for which originated in Los Angeles and then spread like wildfire across cities in the United States.[1] Second are the political spaces of worker centers that have been emerging in Los Angeles during the past twenty-five years, and their multiracial campaigns, such as the Raise the Wage campaign or $15 minimum wage campaign. Both of these sites are examples of being together in difference as equals, or enacting everyday equalities. They respond to and challenge neoliberalism's promotion of the self-interested, individual, entrepreneurial subject and neoliberal policies reducing workers' rights on the one hand, and neoconservative discourses and policies reprimanding expressions of cultural difference and emphasizing assimilation to a racial hierarchy dominated by whites on the other.

We conceive of the construction of these spaces as acts of making progressive publics of everyday equality. This involves the coming together of individuals and institutions from different racial, cultural, and religious backgrounds to simultaneously fight against exploitation, racism, sexism, and homophobia and for an extension of citizenship rights to promote social justice and enact new forms of being together in difference as equals. Making progressive multiracial publics involves (1) creating new political spaces and institutions, which become the sites for enacting inclusive forms of governance and experimentation with new ways of organizing; (2) a sustained commitment to learning from each other and negotiating across racial and other lines of difference, creating spaces of encounter where such negotiations are possible and encouraged rather than foreclosed; (3) publicizing and making visible existing injustices and discrimination, and making demands on the state to rectify these. Last but not least, multiple spatialities, including macro- and microgeographic contexts, the construction and configuration of physical spaces, and extralocal connectivities and

Making Publics in Los Angeles 173

mobilities are crucial in shaping, even as they are shaped by, the construction of multiracial publics.

This chapter provides insights into challenges and possibilities of encounters with difference and enacting equality in spaces of the routine everyday and through organized collective action in contemporary urban multicultures. We highlight the strategies deployed and emphasize the hard work and emotional labor required to accomplish this. We demonstrate the role of the quasi-sovereign spaces of the Freedom Ride buses and the worker centers, mobilities, and extralocal networks in facilitating and mediating the making of multiracial publics, also drawing attention to the role of female leadership of worker centers in constructing and enacting new forms of order that enable being together in difference as equals.

Acts of Making Publics and the Politics of Equality

As Fraser (1990) has noted, especially within capitalist immigrant societies, there exists a multiplicity of (counter) publics that emerge as overt alternatives to the hegemonic public sphere. The presence of multiple publics transforms the public sphere into a "structured setting where cultural and ideological contest or negotiation among a variety of publics takes place" (Eley 1993, 306). Counterpublics constitute "parallel discursive arenas where members of subordinated social groups invent and circulate counterdiscourses" (Fraser 1990, 67). They allow individuals to come together to voice their grievances, needs, and desires within particular venues, and to develop skills and strategies to communicate them to a wider public. As Fraser puts it, "on the one hand, they function as spaces of withdrawal and regroupment; on the other hand, they function as bases and training grounds for agitational activities toward wider publics" (Fraser 1990, 68). "Members of subordinated social groups—women, workers, peoples of color, and gays and lesbians—have repeatedly found it advantageous to constitute alternative publics" (Fraser 1990, 67). They contest and publicize discrepancies between liberal democracy's claims to equality, freedom, and citizenship and the reality in which women, racialized groups, and sexual minorities are subject to discrimination, oppression, and exclusion.

Such counterpublics can challenge undemocratic forms of authority, seeking to enact what Rancière has called a method of equality. Following Rancière, equality is not an outcome to be achieved but is the presumption that each and every one already is equal and taken seriously as a valid partner, with no particular group of people seen as better able, or born, to rule (see chapter 2 in this book). Rancière is fundamentally concerned with working toward radical democracy through a theory of egalitarian political action. For him, democracy is never an achieved end-state but rather must be constantly reworked through demands for equality. Further, such demands are not merely for inclusion made on the part of the excluded, rather they are demands that they "be taken into account not as subordinates with a limited (or no) part to play in society, but as *equals*" (Davidson and Iveson 2014, 139).

An important element in the making of counterpublics is questioning and transgressing the boundary between the public and private spheres, reconceptualizing who participates in defining matters of "public" or "private." As Fraser (1990) argues, drawing a boundary separating the public and private spheres is already a political act, constraining which issues can be debated and what constitutes appropriate behavior in the public sphere (Sziarto and Leitner 2010). For example, in an era of neoliberal governance, with its focus on autonomous individuals responsible for their own well-being, notions of social responsibility and issues of social justice and care are increasingly banished from political and public debate, and from guidelines for shaping encounters with the Other. Challenging this banishment, counterpublics reinsert issues and behaviors that have been relegated to the private sphere back into publics, thereby repoliticizing them. As we illustrate below, through enacting a politics of equality, worker centers repoliticize social inequalities, social justice, and the recognition of sociocultural differences.

In contrast to much of the literature on publics and counterpublics (Warner 2002), we focus on acts of making publics. Examining such processual aspects reveals that they are not completely free of relations produced by the dominant power, nor are they simply in agonistic relationship with the hegemonic public sphere and the state. Rather we argue that the making of publics involves both the development of an oppositional, alternative politics and an engagement with the state and multiple publics.

We also highlight the existence of cultural and political differences within as well as between publics, as we demonstrate below. Radical democratic theorists such as Jacques Rancière, Ernesto Laclau, and Chantal Mouffe suggest that differences and disagreements and associated conflict should be welcome, seeing conflict and agonistic struggle among different positions as the very substance of democratic politics (Purcell 2014, 170). Yet we also contend that differences and disagreements constitute both strengths and vulnerabilities. Encounters among socially and culturally diverse publics provide opportunities to learn from each other, benefiting from the different backgrounds, experiences, and perspectives of their members. At the same time, social inequalities and sociocultural and ideological differences within groups pose challenges that necessitate acknowledging these differences openly, and devising ways for negotiating across them. Failure to do so may foreclose effective collective action and even lead to the demise of a public.

Research to date has not adequately examined the dynamic process by which relations across social differences are constructed, challenged, and negotiated. Scholars have shown that encounters between immigrants of different ethno-racial backgrounds, as well as white residents, are often confrontational because we tend to not welcome difference (Leitner 2012). Encounters with difference are always shot through with emotions of different kinds—most often fear, anger, anxiety—that are not simply individuals' embodied experiences, but also shape the construction and perception of collectivities. Further, racism, sexism, xenophobia, and religious intolerance constitute obstacles in the formation of multiracial publics and of relations among differently positioned individuals. Relatedly, Kun and Pulido's edited collection *Black and Brown in Los Angeles* (2014) reveals stereotypes and prejudices among people of color (e.g., the racialization of African Americans by Latina/os as lazy), examining their impact on relations between Latina/os and black Angelinos.

At the same time, encounters with difference also hold open the possibility for destabilizing and disorienting us from our stereotypes and prejudices, creating conditions of possibility for change and transformation. Yet, as Gordon Allport (1954) has argued, certain preconditions need to be met in order for an erosion of stereotypes to materialize, a key one being the absence of social hierarchies as in- and out-groups encounter one another. Everyday encounters are hardly free of hierarchies and asymmetric power relations, but as we shall see, worker centers have attempted to transcend such hierarchies through inclusive governance structures, care, and learning.

Further, the making of publics and the enactment of a politics of equality entails multiple spatialities. Drawing on sociospatial theory, we make visible how physical and virtual spaces, networks, and mobilities help shape and are shaped by the construction of multiracial publics and egalitarian political spaces (Leitner et al. 2008). As we have argued elsewhere, the process of making counterpublics has its own distinctive geography, reflecting the dual purposes of counterpublics in enabling both withdrawal and agitation (Sziarto and Leitner 2010; Iveson 2017). Fraser (1990) sees physical spaces—such as coffee shops, community centers, union halls, sports fields—as crucial sites for coming together, congregating and concealing counterpublics from surveillance. Our study confirms the importance of physical spaces—in our case the buses of the Immigrant Freedom Ride and the worker centers—in constructing egalitarian political spaces. We refer to these as *spaces of refuge*; spaces that provide protection from the hegemonic public sphere and state surveillance, as well as material and moral support and relative safety. Conversely, designated public spaces—streets, squares, public buildings—become sites from which to publicize existing injustices, make demands, and propose alternatives. Responding to increasing surveillance by the state and capital seeking to monitor and restrict political expression in public spaces, virtual public spaces have become an increasingly important means to gain publicity in recent decades (Clough and Vanderbeck 2006; Mitchell 2016). A further central spatiality in the construction of publics is the web of local and extralocal networks connecting them with other publics in other places. As we demonstrate below,

Making Publics in Los Angeles 177

such networks are important sources of information, inspiration, and support, operating through both face-to-face interaction and in virtual space through diverse communications technologies.

Rancière's conceptualization of a politics of equality draws attention to another aspect of the spatiotemporality of contentious politics. He argues that a politics of equality has no single, proper place and time, but remains open to the emergent spaces and times of politics in the city (Davidson and Iveson 2015). Politics does not emerge from particular places, but in practice: "What makes an action political is not its object or the place where it is carried out, but solely its form, the form in which confirmation of equality is inscribed in the setting up of a dispute" (Rancière 1999, 30). As we understand it, he is not arguing that politics is everywhere and always, but that any a priori privileging of certain sites as the proper space of politics is itself an act of ordering, one that presupposes what should count as progressive political action, and where. Avoiding such privileging implies that the spatiotemporalities of an egalitarian politics become a matter of empirical investigation. Before turning to such an investigation in the organizing of immigrant workers in Los Angeles, we outline some of the key dimensions of that city's contemporary multiculture.

Multicultural, Multiracial, Unequal LA: Between Violence and Cooperation

Los Angeles' ethnic and racial diversity has shaped its history and culture, as well as its economic dynamism. The origins of immigrants have changed and further diversified since the late 1960s, with immigrants from Mexico and Latin America and Asian immigrants from China, Korea, Vietnam, and Thailand dominating. Today, the Los Angeles metropolitan area[2] has one of the highest proportions of foreign-born residents in the United States (34 percent for Los Angeles County); with the majority (57 percent of the population) speaking a language other than English (mostly Spanish) at home (U.S. Census Bureau 2015).

The greatest concentration of immigrants and nonwhite populations can be found in the City of Los Angeles. In 2010 the Hispanic population made up the largest ethno-racial group, comprising 49 percent of the total population, followed by 29 percent white, 12.3 percent Asian, and 10 percent non-Hispanic black. About 80 percent of the Hispanic population is from Mexico, followed by immigrants from Central America (Brown University 2016a). Many neighborhoods have seen a growing ethno-racial diversity. Even Koreatown, one of its most ethnically identified neighborhoods due to the number of Korean businesses and signage in the Korean language, by 2008 was no longer dominated by Korean or even Asian immigrants, but by Latino immigrants: 54 percent Latinos, 32 percent Asians, 4.8 percent blacks, and 7.4 percent whites (*Los Angeles Times* 2008).

Ethno-racial diversity also rose substantially in the Los Angeles metropolitan area, with the Hispanic population increasing from 25 percent in 1980 to 45 percent in 2010 and the Asian population increasing from 5 percent to 16 percent over the same period. New immigration also has contributed to the further mixing of different ethno-racial groups in many cities and neighborhoods of the metropolitan area. Nevertheless, black-white, Hispanic-white, and black-Asian segregation continues at relatively high levels, with 2010 dissimilarity indices of 65 (black-white), 62 (Hispanic-white) and 64 (black-Asian) (Brown University 2016b).[3]

This racial and ethnic diversity intersects with dramatic and increasing inequalities in wealth, also manifest in distinct ethno-racial geographies. Whereas ethno-racial diversity has been increasing and segregation decreasing during the past two decades, income inequalities have been increasing. According to the Brookings Institute, the Los Angeles metropolitan area ranked seventh in income inequality in the nation in 2014, with falling incomes at the bottom helping drive inequality increases in its cities and metropolitan areas (Holmes and Berube 2016). For example, according to the *Los Angeles Times* (2008), median household incomes in 2014 (in 2008 dollars) ranged from $15,000 in East Los Angeles to $250,000 in Beverly Hills. Beverly Hills is 94 percent white, East LA is between 80 and 90 percent nonwhite (Latinos, Asians, and blacks). More generally, wealthy white and poor Latino residents live in the most segregated environments, occupying neighborhoods where they make up over 90 percent of the total population: Malibu, Pacific Palisades, Beverly Crest, almost 90 percent white;

Florence, Watts, Green Meadow, almost 100 percent nonwhite (City-Data.com 2014).

Los Angeles, like many other U.S. cities, is laden with ethnic, racial, class, and geographic divisions, but the classic narrative of Los Angeles dwells on its history of periodic eruptions of violent conflict among different ethno-racial groups. South Los Angeles in particular, with its growing populations of color (first African Americans and now Hispanics), has been the site of both blatant police brutality and resistance to it. In 1965 Watts exploded, triggered by a confrontation between a white police officer and black African American youth. As Pulido et al. (2012, 121) put it,

> This incident was simply the straw that broke the camel's back in terms of community/police tension.... The Watts Riot was the largest instance of urban unrest in US history up to that time, and it led to the almost complete out-migration of whites and abandonment of the area by corporate retail outlets.

The upshot of several days of violence, looting, and arson was thirty-five dead, over one thousand wounded, and four thousand arrested. The political unrest in the aftermath of the 1992 Rodney King beating further cemented the image of South LA as riven with urban pathologies—violence, crime, dilapidated housing—a dangerous and barren place to fear and stay away from.

Yet such experiences of state violence, discrimination, and deprivation not only triggered unrest, but also spawned visionary community organizations, an alternative press, and cross-cultural, cross-racial organizing. Throughout the twentieth century, there were moments when progressive activists—African Americans, Japanese Americans, Mexican Americans, and immigrants—came together to join forces, forging numerous links that Laura Pulido (2006), Daniel Widener (2008), Ed Soja (2010), and others have traced. These chroniclers have found that collaborations among communities of color are not only motivated by the multiracism experienced by people of color, but also are a response to institutional and everyday discrimination, police brutality, exploitation, and fear of deportation. These have been powerful triggers for

180   *Making Publics in Los Angeles*

collaboration among communities of color and immigrant rights activism (Brodkin 2007; Milkman 2006).

New forms of multiracial politics, new sites of struggles, and new alliances have been emerging across Los Angeles since the 1992 Rodney King uprising (Nicholls 2003, Widener 2008, Soja 2010). In the 1990s, unions, especially those that had turned to labor community coalitions and rank-and-file organizing to revitalize labor as a movement, found themselves organizing immigrant workers (Sherman and Voss 2000; Milkman 2000, 2006; Savage 1998). Immigrant workers formed the core of the successful Justice for Janitors organizing campaign waged by the Service Employees International Union (Waldinger et al. 1996). At the same time diverse assemblages of unions, community organizations, lawyers, and unorganized workers began setting up workers' centers (operating outside labor unions), and initiated collaborative multiracial alliances and campaigns, such as the successful 2015 $15 minimum wage campaign (to which we turn below). Notwithstanding the apparently single-issue nature of these campaigns, they have been undertaken by grassroots social justice organizations engaged in struggles ranging from living wages and benefits to wage theft to low-income housing, public health, transportation, police brutality, racism, and immigration reform.

The Immigrant Workers Freedom Ride

The idea of the 2003 Immigrant Workers Freedom Ride (IWFR) was instigated by a staff member of the Hotel Employees and Restaurant Employees Union (HERE) Local 11 in Los Angeles, which had a large immigrant membership. As indicated above, Los Angeles at that time, with its large immigrant labor force, had become an important center for organizing immigrants who were occupying low paid, insecure, mostly nonunion jobs, and also facing various forms of discrimination in the labor and housing markets and in accessing public services (Milkman 2000). Attempts by Local 11 to organize new immigrants of color often were confronted with hostility between Latino immigrants and African American workers. Thus one of the goals of the IWFR was to improve relations between these groups in order to build a movement addressing both immigrants' and workers' rights.

Organizers of the IWFR envisioned buses as "moving classrooms," where different ethno-racial groups would learn about others' histories and contemporary experiences. New immigrants would learn about the civil rights movement and its accomplishments and how the "movement was not the work of a few heroes, but of ordinary people [who showed] extraordinary courage" (IWFR 2003, cited in Sziarto and Leitner 2010, 385). African Americans would learn why Latino (and other) immigrants came to the United States, and how Latinos, too, face racial discrimination. Though the goals of the IWFR as listed in press releases do not address racism explicitly, internal documents, quotes from spokespeople and Riders (people who took part in the IWFR), and the popular education exercises introduced on the buses indicate that organizers intended that the IWFR would incorporate antiracist themes.

The conception of the IWFR as a journey by bus from multiple cities converging on Washington, D.C., made a symbolic and material connection with the Freedom Rides of the 1960s. The design of the route and the stops along it reinforced this connection through visiting civil rights movement memorial sites (for further details see Sziarto and Leitner 2010).

As the IWFR traveled across the United States (Figure 11), the buses became spaces of encounters with difference: spaces for storytelling, listening, singing, but also enacting solidarity. The practice of storytelling was critical. From the time participants boarded the buses, they were encouraged to tell one another who they were and how they came to be on the buses. Of course, there was initial reluctance to share personal histories, and many conversations were prompted by the IWFR organizers as part of their "mobile classroom" plan, but once Riders had been traveling together for a few days, they were moved to tell their stories. Indeed, some Riders were persuaded by organizers, and gained the courage, to tell their stories also at rallies at stops along the way. Storytelling in the space-time of the buses also involved attentive listening to other's stories. Suely, a Rider on the Washington State bus writing in the Washington State Riders' blog, described her experiences as follows:

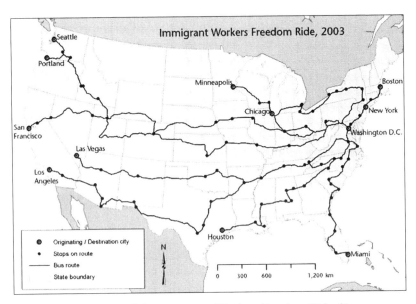

FIGURE 11. *Routes of the Immigrant Workers Freedom Ride. (Source: www.iwfr.org, reproduced by the Cartography Lab of the Department of Geography, University of Minnesota.)*

> This was a difficult day for me. As I become more comfortable on this ride I am overwhelmed with emotions. I am getting to know the other bus riders and their reasons for going on this ride. Every day I learn about families being separated, workers being abused, discrimination on the job due to race and religion, sexual discrimination amongst undocumented female workers and the list goes on and on and on. All of these things I have listed, I can put a face to each one. I am also replaying sad stories from my past over and over again. . . . And I shared it with the other freedom riders. And this was a good turning point for all of us. More and more people are able to express how they are feeling and cry. (Suely 2003, quoted in Sziarto and Leitner 2010, 387)

Here Suely describes how telling and listening to each others' stories unleashes emotions, finding this difficult, but good. Many Riders' journals and blogs recount similar experiences of feeling overwhelmed with emotions when listening to others' experiences, as they found themselves putting a face to each story and telling their own stories of sadness.

While Riders' personal and family histories diverged, common threads emerged. Repeated themes in oral histories, interviews, media reports, and blogs included pain and anger over separation from family, discrimination, and the denial of equal opportunity, oppressive working conditions, and detention upon suspicion of terrorism. Through these interactions, Riders developed emotional investments not merely in "immigrant justice" in the abstract, but in people they knew, sat next to, and sang songs with. A sense of collective identity as Riders emerged.

It was the hours together on the bus that enabled Riders to get to know one another, to learn from each others' life experiences and struggles, to build affective relationships, and to develop a sense of commonality of experience and perspective. As Briana, a student on the Minnesota bus, recalled: "The bus made all the difference, being packed on. . . . People really have to commit time, energy, focus" (2006 interview, cited in Sziarto and Leitner 2010, 387). The bus ride provided a space and time to get to know one another, to learn from each other, to connect with others in ways that otherwise would have been difficult, to develop relationships, and to understand their relationship with other participants in new ways.

The solidarity that developed on the buses was not only a matter of the practices of and interactions among Riders, but was also enabled by the absent presence of enemy Others. These included repressive state agents—from racist white sheriffs remembered from the 1960s to the racist police officers of today, paramilitaries in immigrants' home countries, U.S. immigration authorities, nativist groups such as the Minuteman, and exploitive and abusive employers. Riders on the IWFR buses prepared themselves for how to respond to possible encounters with some of these Others. Indeed, each bus had a plan in place in case they were stopped by Immigration and Customs Enforcement (ICE) and/or La Migra (the Border Patrol, in Latino/Chicano parlance). Immigrant rights' activists knew from experience that any gathering of brown-skinned people are most likely to be categorized as immigrants, most likely undocumented, rendering them vulnerable to detention by ICE.[4]

Since the IWFR buses advertised themselves as transporting immigrants, IWFR organizers had Riders practice what they would do when stopped by state agents. Riders taught each other the song "We Shall Overcome" from the civil rights movement. Riders performed being silent while organizers played the roles of Border Patrol agents. They stored their legal identifications in the buses' locked luggage compartments, and wore only their IWFR identification cards showing just a first name.

The Los Angeles Riders saw these preparations put to the test. On the fifth day on the road, the buses were stopped by the Border Patrol seventy miles outside El Paso, Texas. Agents boarded the bus and demanded identification from all the Riders of color, ignoring white Riders. The Riders sang "We Shall Overcome" and held out their IWFR badges, which read:

> I am a participant in the Immigrant Workers Freedom Ride, a peaceful campaign by citizens and immigrants in support for equal rights for all workers. I wish to exercise my right to remain silent. (Ehrenreich 2003, 19)

The Border Patrol ordered all Riders off the bus and into small detention cells in the buildings of the checkpoint station. One by one the Riders were taken out of the cells for questioning. They were threatened with arrest unless they revealed their names and citizenship. None of the Riders answered, and those in the cells kept on singing "We Shall Overcome."

This act of civil disobedience by the Los Angeles Riders was a performance of embodied solidarity, made possible by their encounters and engagement with each other on the buses. All Riders symbolically gave up their names and citizenship or immigration status; the privileged white citizens or immigrants with documents were for a brief time treated as potentially undocumented immigrants and detained. For about four hours, the Los Angeles Riders were neither immigrants nor citizens, but people without documents challenging the authority of the nation-state. By cell phone and email, word of the Los Angeles buses being stopped reached the other buses, whose Riders imagined themselves in the places of the LA Riders—an imaginative move that strengthened their resolve to stand together should they face detention.

Thus, on the buses, separated from their everyday lives and from the often naturalized and invisible power relations operating within them, the IWFR Riders were able to construct alternative social and political imaginaries and craft solidarity. These imaginaries were challenged as the buses arrived in Washington, D.C., and New York. Riders expressed frustration that the human rights discourse they had developed on the bus—No Human Being Is Illegal—was replaced at rallies in these centers of power by a discourse of "hardworking and tax-paying immigrants," and that immigrants' experiences and stories were drowned out by the voices and speeches of union leaders and politicians. In light of this, it is particularly noteworthy that Riders continued advocating on behalf of immigrant rights after they returned to their hometowns, and developed local civic organizations in support of immigrant and workers' rights.

In sum, the case of the Immigrant Workers Freedom Ride highlights some major ingredients for being together in difference as equals: the importance of spaces of refugee—in this case the bus—where learning from each other (through storytelling and listening) and negotiations across racial and other lines of difference are made possible and encouraged. In turn, engagements and encounters with the Other fostered trust among the Riders and advanced the enactment of solidarity across racial and other lines of difference. In terms of outcomes, the IWFR accomplished its goal of mobilizing highly diverse groups of individuals across the country. It also facilitated the expansion of an emerging local and national organizational infrastructure in support of immigrant and workers' rights, including worker centers. It is to these sites that we now turn.

Worker Centers: Working Toward Being Together in Difference as Equals

While worker centers did not originate in Los Angeles, that city has experienced some of the most rapid growth and greatest density in worker centers of all U.S. cities (from approximately 155 in 2007 to over 225 in 2016).[5] This dramatic upsurge reflects the presence of large documented and undocumented immigrant populations from Latin America and Asia with associated needs for assistance, support, and representation. Contemporary worker centers responding to these needs focus on three spheres of action, with each center deploying a unique combination of service, education, organizing, and advocacy (Fine 2006). First, most centers provide services such as legal assistance, job training, English as a second language (ESL) classes, or even affordable housing. Second, worker centers organize low-wage workers, mostly immigrants and minorities of color, for political mobilization, placing an emphasis on popular education and leadership training and development (Fine 2006, 13; Theodore 2015). Third, centers advocate for worker and immigrant rights through diverse strategies and tactics, including direct action, and engage in multiracial minimum wage, wage theft, and antiracism campaigns.

Worker centers in Los Angeles are organized around a particular industry (e.g., the Garment Worker Center, CLEAN Carwash Campaign, see Figure 12), ethnicity (e.g., the Black Worker Center, see Figure 13), or are place/community based (Korean Immigrant Worker Alliance [KIWA], see Figure 14). Yet the lines of difference between them are fluid. Particularly in Los Angeles, there is a significant commitment to multiracial organizing for antiracist action, both within and between organizations. Indeed, while they are *worker* centers, their actions and campaigns far exceed the sphere of production to focus on social reproduction issues such as

FIGURE 12. *CLEAN Carwash Campaign—Wash Away Injustice (Source: http://www.cleancarwashcampaign.org/.)*

FIGURE 13. *Black Worker Center—Stop Employment Discrimination* (Source: Lola Smallwood Cuevas, Black Worker Center, Los Angeles.)

FIGURE 14. *Koreatown Immigrant Workers Alliance—Stop Wage Theft* (Photograph: Helga Leitner.)

education, immigration reform, citizenship and immigrant rights, environmental justice, housing, and policing.

Whereas much of the scholarship on worker centers has focused on their role and importance in the American labor movement, we highlight their efforts in forging new political spaces that attempt to enact a particular form of being together in difference as equals. The physical spaces occupied by the worker centers, functioning also as spaces of encounter, have been crucial for the construction of these political spaces and new ways of doing things. They serve as spaces for withdrawal from the dominant public sphere, but also spaces of refuge, where popular education can happen, where new forms of governance and organizing can be experimented with, and where members can express themselves and their identities without fear, learning to negotiate across their differences and care for one another, as we demonstrate below.[6]

Spaces of Inclusive Governance

One of the stated goals of worker centers is to create democratic, inclusive governance that encourages and allows active participation and equal voice to members in defining agendas and service needs, as well as organizing, skill, and leadership development. As Alexandra Suh, the director of the Korean Immigrant Workers Alliance (KIWA), put it, this distinguishes them from the hierarchy and the guild system that characterizes unions. Worker center leaders expressed a strong commitment to democratic decision-making among staff and workers, which in their opinion is facilitated by their relatively small scale. As she notes, "I'd like to say that we are so democratic because we are so righteous, but if I had a staff of ten thousand, well there probably would be a lot more hierarchy. We probably wouldn't sit around building consensus with all ten thousand people."

Yet, as one worker center director pointed out, even small-scale decision-making processes in flat governance structures are difficult and lengthy, requiring patience and endurance. This is something to work through by facilitating decisions among workers through workshops, classes, and training. Embracing a flat governance structure also is in line with center ideals of popular education and leadership development, sometimes identifying explicitly with the pedagogy of Paulo Freire and other leaders of the popular education movement (Theodore 2015). The institutional infrastructure of worker centers facilitates this philosophy and pedagogy. For instance, meetings of the KIWA are simultaneously translated into Korean, Spanish, and English to allow for equal participation across their member base.

While worker centers embrace flat governance, rules governing behavior still exist. At the Instituto de Educacion Popular del Sur de California (IDEPSCA) worker center, for example, a verbal code of conduct prohibits discriminatory language in an effort to create a space of mutual respect for encounters with difference among the members. Maegan Ortiz, the director, recounts a situation in which such rules were enforced when a church donor spoke at the center:

> They were singing and then they started talking about how horrible gay marriage was, and how horrible the Supreme Court decision was, and I said, "You can't do that here. That's not what's allowed." [It was difficult] because some of the workers who do identify as evangelical Christians were kind of like, "Well, that's how I feel." I said, "That's great, but not here." You know we have rules, we have a code of ethics, and nondiscrimination and non-hateful language is a part of that. (Los Angeles, July 2015)

Here, formal rules—even if not written down—become crucial for negotiating social differences among worker center members, in this case enacting a politics of equality that does not reinforce heteronormativity.

Spaces of Care

While the worker's center movement in Los Angeles originally was male dominated, by 2015 women of color were spearheading their organizing campaigns, as well as overseeing day-to-day activities. Indeed, women of color were the majority of the leadership, most of them mothers. When asked what they see themselves as specifically bringing to organizing and the construction of progressive multiracial publics, center directors agreed that as women they are trying to construct spaces that encourage not only building community, but also building care that translates into action. Lengthy discussions sometimes ensued over the issue of women and care. Rosemarie Molina, a project manager of the CLEAN Carwash Campaign, was most adamant that care is one of the most distinct features that women bring to organizing and the creation of the political space of the worker center, which she locates in her other role as family caregiver.

> It was nurturing, it was caring, and I said that and my professor actually challenged me on that. But I said it because I have always been the mother figure in a lot of people's lives. Growing up, taking care of my brother, taking care of my dad now, he has a mental illness, and taking care of my brother's friends, who came to stay with us when I was younger, who are my brothers now. So I've always kind of had this mothering thing that was taught from my mom. I have a matriarchy, I come from a family where women run things because they've had to. So, you know, all of this stuff just gets passed down, so it was instilled in me to always assume that role. (Los Angeles, July 2015)

Maegan Ortiz echoes this sentiment, emphasizing specific needs due to the trauma experienced by communities of color:

> Yeah, I mean, for me . . . it comes down to—and this is very gendered, it's really interesting but I'm gonna say it. It's gendered, but it's also not—it comes down to caretaking, to caretaking the community, . . . the need to care for our communities so that certain things don't happen again, or so that for future generations we move forward from where we [people of color in the U.S.] were, to heal that collective trauma. Because I think there is a lot of collective trauma that we hold. (Los Angeles, July 2015)

Female directors also promote and emphasize worker centers as spaces of care through the design of their material spaces, for example by bringing elements of domestic space, such as a kitchen, into the public space of the worker center. This helps create an atmosphere of comfort and care, of being in the same space with different others. In terms of social space, female leaders strive to promote love and care among staff and members. They are used to

Making Publics in Los Angeles 191

doing this in their families, but it also is beneficial in creating an atmosphere that eases negotiations across social differences.

Through transferring care and care work associated with the private sphere of the family into the making of worker center publics, female leaders not only transgress the boundary between the private and public but also those of liberal democracy. Liberal democracy is primarily concerned with matters of justice, redistribution, and recognition of difference, excluding care from its maps of the political (Brown 2008). While the notion of justice is understood as universal and rational in mainstream political theory, care is considered "highly emotional and irrational. It is women's work: prepolitical and congruent to the private sphere" (Brown 2003, 835). Both female activists of color and feminist political theorists and geographers have challenged this bounding. As Iris Marion Young (2000, 487) put it:

> The public realm of politics can be so rational, noble, and universal only because the messy content of the body, meeting its needs, providing for production, caretaking, and attending to birth and death, are taken care of elsewhere.

We endorse this argument that it should not only be women who give care: we all give and receive care, which should be an important part of democratic politics. As Tronto (1994, 103) contends, care is "a species of activity that includes everything that we do to maintain, continue, and repair our 'world' so that we can live in it as well as possible. That world includes our bodies, our selves, and our environment, all of which we seek to interweave in a complex, life-sustaining web." Care has both an emotional and agentic orientation. "Care can be both emotion and labor, typically culturally signified. Its emotive and material facets mark it as a form of 'heart politics' in Peavy's (1996) eloquent words" (Brown 2003, 835).

Lawson (2007, 8) draws our attention to the need for a critical care ethics, which involves understanding not only how structures, institutions, and historical relationships are implicated in the construction of social difference, the various forms of oppression, and social and spatial inequalities and exclusion, but also the formation of "new forms of relationships, institutions, and action that enhance mutuality and well-being." An understanding of care as an ethic, emotion, and labor informs the relationships being constructed in worker centers, the governance of the worker centers, and more generally the politics of equality in difference practiced there.

Spaces of Learning and Negotiation

Worker centers are not only spaces of experimentation with inclusive forms of governance and care, but also spaces of learning and negotiating across differences that can contribute to overcoming racialized hierarchies and inequalities. They have become sites where difficult conversations about prejudice and stereotypes, racism, sexism, religious intolerance, and other isms are problematized and addressed head on, rather than avoided. There are numerous challenges in accomplishing this. As Maegan Ortiz commented, one such challenge is to begin naming and calling out individuals who engage in racist and/or sexist talk without shaming them.

> I think some of the biggest challenges we've had are just— there has not been a lot of discussion about the racism and anti-blackness coming from the immigrant workers themselves. And that's only just been something that we've started to talk about, especially in the midst of everything that's happened in the last few years. (Los Angeles, July 2015)

Describing how racial stereotypes, prejudice, and sexism were coming up in talk and practices, she went on to discuss how she felt compelled to make this visible and start conversations about where this was coming from, through organizing a popular education workshop on race and gender.

> I think [racist comments] are a good starting place for conversation. . . . I don't think people have ever named these things. . . . Or, it's said—I think a lot of the time what happens too—is it's said and ignored. Like "Oh, that's just how things are." And it's like "No, wait a minute. Why? Why'd you say that?" And *not in a way that shames*, not in a way

Making Publics in Los Angeles

that we're saying "how dare you?" because we're working together here. Just trying to break that down and understand why. So, I think for us, it's not the *end*, it's just the starting point, because these things have never been spoken about. Never. (Los Angeles, July 2015)

She notes that, rather than an end point, such conversations are a place from which to start the process of naming racism, sexism, homophobia, and inequalities. In terms we developed in chapter 2, gender and racial equality is a normative assumption from which to proceed—in this case, through conversation that disrupts prejudiced beliefs. She and other center directors identified conversations as the most important ingredient of how to move forward, often requiring extensive meetings and sustained efforts.

Lots of talking. Our meetings can be very long for that reason. . . . We really end up talking through a lot of it. . . . I think we throw all these terms around [queer, LGBTQ, for example] and we think everyone is on the same page about it. And we're not! So I think having lots of conversations and understanding that we may not always agree in the end, but at least in terms of our policies we have strict policies about nondiscrimination and respect, so we're not going to call names. (Los Angeles, July 2015)

Here, Maegan Ortiz hints at another very important aspect of negotiating across differences. It is not enough to have conversations about stereotypes, prejudice, and discrimination, learning about the Other. Rules are needed that spell out conduct with the Other—a nonnegotiable code of ethics—such as the banning of racist talk, religious intolerance, name-calling, use of derogatory terms, and harassment. While not necessarily specified in writing and made visible at worker centers, the day labor programs run by some worker centers post rules that are clearly visible to everyone entering this space. Posters spell out rules of conduct, participants' rights and responsibilities, and advice about personal appearance, in order to "build a healthy and safe environment, to promote transparency, justice and equality, to prevent conflict and promote friendship, and project an image of order and profession-alism to the community" (Pasadena Community Job Center 2016, courtesy of Nik Theodore).

To conclude, encounters with difference are shaped by how worker centers are governed and run, and by their intimate physical environment. Learning about life histories of the Other and sharing their individual experiences of discrimination and oppression facilitate negotiations across differences. At the same time their spatial proximity within worker centers, together with rules of conduct, requires them to acknowledge, come to terms with, and address their differences. These findings echo arguments developed by Pulido (2006, 110) that community organizing and popular education, while not necessarily generating solidarity, are important means for members of different racial groups to negotiate across their differences and "together help alleviate interethnic tensions among people of color by providing an alternative framework in which to view their differences."

Spaces of Publicity: Making Campaigns

If the space of the worker center is one of withdrawal and refuge, facilitating the formation of progressive publics and politics, then centers' campaigns for social justice represent their outward agitational dimension: spaces of publicity. These campaigns have ranged widely, from those primarily driven by a single center on a single issue to coalitions of multiple worker centers with other social justice organizations (e.g., Watts Labor Community Action Committee, the South Los Angeles Community Coalition), academic institutions (such as the UCLA Labor Center), and civil rights organizations including legal aid clinics (e.g., Asian Pacific American Legal Center), collaborating together on campaigns and making demands on the local or national state. Innovative campaigns include the Forever 21 campaign (an effort to organize garment workers) and the $15 minimum wage campaign. These campaigns have pushed the city of Los Angeles to pass new ordinances: Forever 21 triggered an ordinance in Los Angeles that established "(1) a sweat-free procurement policy for equipment,

Making Publics in Los Angeles

materials, goods, and supplies; and (2) compliance procedures for the City's Contractor Code of Conduct" (Narro, 2005, 479).

The most recent success story is the multiracial campaign that brought together worker centers and different actors and groups of the larger progressive community in the city of Los Angeles to trigger a $15 minimum wage ordinance. In May 2015, following precedents set by cities such as Seattle and San Francisco, Los Angeles became the largest city in the United States to pass a $15 minimum wage. Key to this success was the Raise the Wage campaign, spearheaded by a coalition of worker centers, day laborer centers, faith-based organizations, labor unions, and other advocacy and community organizations. The Raise the Wage campaign formed a steering committee of twenty organizations, whose representatives signed a memorandum of understanding (MOU) committing themselves to in-kind or monetary contributions to the campaign and to working toward a collaboratively developed set of demands. In addition to the $15 minimum wage, these demands included a city ordinance against wage theft and establishment of an office of enforcement within the city government. These eventually were approved by the city council alongside the $15 minimum wage ordinance.

Worker centers were instrumental for building momentum, especially for the wage theft and enforcement provisions (Figure 13). Wage theft, which is the practice of employers not paying workers their full wage by violating minimum wage laws, stealing tips, withholding overtime pay, and forcing workers to clock out and continue working, is a pervasive problem among the low-wage workers who participate in the worker centers, and is particularly prevalent in Los Angeles. Milkman et al. (2010) calculated that workers from low-wage industries lost more than US$26.2 million weekly in 2010, mostly from minimum wage violations. As Maegan Ortiz put it, "Everybody else can talk about where it [the wage theft ordinance] came from. It came from worker centers, and specifically it came from *day laborers*."

Like its origins, the success of this campaign was far from a simple matter. Paralleling how the space of worker centers is often one of encounter and negotiation across social difference, the solidarity required for a successful campaign could not be taken for granted.

As Pulido (2006, 144) writes, referencing earlier political coalitions in Los Angeles, "connections between various groups are not inevitable or automatic but must be articulated." It took extensive social and political work to bring together different groups and move forward, transcending the differences encountered between worker centers in how to approach a common goal and negotiating competing and conflicting claims for recognition. This is the work of upscaling from intra-center to inter-center encounters, of making a broader multiracial public.

For example, there was intense discussion among worker centers over the meaning of wage theft and the formulation of demands on the state. To the Black Worker Center, high levels of job discrimination against African Americans in Los Angeles—what center director Lola Smallwood Cuevas calls the "black jobs crisis"—constitute a form of wage theft. She explains:

> The minimum wage campaign . . . [is] a really good example of our coming to the table to fight for raising the floor for workers [while] educating that table about what's happening to black workers and how this policy can be improved to address . . . discrimination by saying . . . that discrimination is wage theft. And therefore we need to enforce and protect workers against discrimination as well as against wage violations. (Los Angeles, July 2015)

The campaign against wage theft thus became not only a moment for political action, but also a claim for equality. For the Black Worker Center, the political momentum behind the wage theft ordinance was an opportunity to fight discrimination against African American workers in the Los Angeles region, but crucially it also was a moment to force the progressive labor movement in Los Angeles to recognize the plight of black workers, a claim that brought its own set of issues. As Rosemarie Molina, project manager of CLEAN Carwash Campaign, which supports carwash employees, says:

> There was an issue when the Black Worker Center started participating in our space. There was a push to change our

Making Publics in Los Angeles 197

messaging to "being unemployed is the ultimate form of wage theft" And there was a lot of resistance against that because we were like "that might be true for your membership, but our membership—one person got $67,000 stolen from them. That's pretty significant." So for [our members], the ultimate form of wage theft is working for free. (Los Angeles, July 2015)

From the challenges of negotiating competing claims for recognition and understandings about what constitutes wage theft, Rosemary Molina describes how the Coalition Against Wage Theft sought resolution:

Honestly, it was a lot of meeting collectively, a lot of talking, challenging each other. . . . I think what we came to in the end was, . . . "this train is moving and we have every intention of getting that piece of the policy [wage theft] passed. So even if it's not in the forefront, you have to know and trust us, that in every place we can, we are inserting that antidiscrimination language." . . . And the Black Worker Center still came out to every single action. And we are lifting up the antidiscrimination policy. (Los Angeles, July 2015)

Here, she underlines the importance of learning and trust for moving past such differences toward a common goal, but also the collective commitment to the common objectives enshrined in the MOU among the leaders of the different organizations before the start of the campaign. The MOU, which made each organization on the steering committee accountable to work in good faith toward passing the full package agreed on, was itself the outcome of intense negotiations across differences, of course.

The $15 minimum wage campaign in Los Angeles erupted in moments of protest and high public visibility, but it was in no way limited to those spaces and times. Intralocal and extralocal networks of actors, ideas, and policies also provided a crucial foundation of inspiration, supporting worker centers and their campaigns for social justice. Locally, worker centers benefited from the formal and informal relationships between worker center leaders.

The leaders we spoke to discussed how their prior relationships of working collaboratively on campaigns and their personal connections enriched their organizing. Speaking of leadership in the Coalition Against Wage Theft, Rosemarie explains:

> With the women that I've worked with, we genuinely care about each other in more than just the work sense. And that's [the case] with . . . all of the worker centers. . . . Because we are trying to lift each other up, all at the same time. We all work with marginalized bases. We can't just build power for carwash workers and not think about the garment workers, not think about the black workers in South LA who are unemployed. And I think that since all of us in the higher positions feel that way, we're able to do that together. (Los Angeles, July 2015)

Rosemarie connects these informal relationships to a solidarity that extends across worker centers. She feels that the leaders' care for one another translates into the collective, in which one worker center cannot make claims for equality without the others. Aquilina Soriano, the executive director of the Pilipino Worker Center, also stresses that networking among worker center leaders enabled strong collaborations and collective action: "We've been able to develop pretty strong networks and collaboration with other worker centers, which it seems is not necessarily the case in other places" (Los Angeles, July 2015).

As Walter Nicholls (2003, 892) has argued, such formal and informal networks constitute a kind of organizational infrastructure that can "serve as the relational grounds for the elaboration of more institutionalized forms of coordinated interactions." Indeed, leaders of the worker centers have sought to institutionalize these relationships by developing a Los Angeles Federation of Worker Centers that will share resources, coordinate action, and build power within the regional labor movement for marginalized populations often considered "unorganizable" by labor unions (Fine 2006; Milkman 2006). With worker centers gaining more political clout and prominence through such victories as the $15 minimum wage and the wage theft ordinance, these types of "coordinated

Making Publics in Los Angeles

interactions" are expanding. The AFL-CIO now maintains a full-time worker center director position that coordinates between organized labor and worker centers,[7] and worker centers have begun to federate nationally (Fine 2016).

Such intra-urban networks also articulate with extralocal circulations of ideas and people. In their modalities of governance and campaign strategies, worker centers draw also on national and international progressive movements. Particularly for the $15 minimum wage campaign, worker centers leaders—and the coalitions in which they participated—learned from similar successful movements in Seattle and the San Francisco Bay Area. As worker centers begin to federate nationally, institutional support for the interlocal circulation of successful models and tactics will only grow. Indeed, the success of the Raise the Wage campaign in localities like Oakland and Los Angeles has been crucial in building momentum toward a California-wide campaign that seeks a raise in the minimum wage across the entire state.

Worker center networks and mobilities also circulate beyond national borders. For example, Aquilina Soriano describes how they drew on international organizing models for domestic workers, assembling different elements that would work in the Los Angeles context: "[We started studying] these more decentralized organizations, and pulling different elements from that, looking at domestic worker organizations abroad, . . . South Africa and other places, and pulling in different elements and seeing what would work" (Los Angeles, July 2015).

In this chapter we have examined acts of making progressive publics of everyday equality. These publics bring together people from different social groups who face similar challenges and are committed to fighting injustices and discrimination and enacting equality. Quasi-sovereign spaces like buses and worker centers have been crucial for making the publics we have considered: these spaces are experimented with to promote intimate encounters among members and incite and facilitate negotiations across differences. But this does not just happen in a vacuum; it is supported by an institutional infrastructure involving inclusive and caring governance that gives equal voice to members and promotes care as an ethic, emotion, and labor. This in turn shapes encounters with others and the relationships constructed in these egalitarian public spaces. While not free from conflict, we suggest that these types of environments, by promoting learning, negotiations, and shared practices across racial and cultural differences, help construct mutual respect, trust, and a sense of community.

The other crucial foundational factors in constructing publics of everyday equality are broader-scale connections—real and virtual—with similar publics, both locally and farther afield. These networks provide moral support for these publics, and also constitute important channels for the flow and exchange of ideas, information, and strategies for organizing and gaining publicity. Thus the Los Angeles worker centers' successful $15 minimum wage campaign benefited from both formal and informal relationships between their leaders and members of grassroots organizations, NGOs, and politicians within Los Angeles, the United States, and internationally. Further, it is through such networks that efforts on the ground in LA can influence conditions elsewhere, meaning that the enactments of equality in difference that we have discussed in this chapter reverberate beyond the locality in which they are located.

Psychologist Gordon Allport (1954) has suggested that prejudice against racial or cultural minorities can be reduced through face-to-face contact, because exposure to the Other enhances knowledge about him or her. Such contact is seen as helping people develop their ability to inhabit the Other's perspective, increasing the empathy they are capable of feeling toward the Othered subject (Pettigrew and Tropp 2000; for further details see Matjeskova and Leitner 2011). As Allport originally argued, however, such positive results will only materialize under certain preconditions, including equal status of those in contact, shared common goals, and lack of competition. Such preconditions are hardly present in contemporary urban societies and life; everyday contact between members of different social groups is always structurally mediated and embedded in historically and geographically contextualized unequal power relations both between and within social groups (Ahmed 2004; Leitner 2012). Such often deeply entrenched unequal power relations are not suspended during face-to-face con-

Making Publics in Los Angeles   201

tact, but always saturate and exceed it. Thus it requires particular effort to construct political spaces where hierarchies and unequal power relations can be transcended to create new forms of order characterized by equality.

This has been enabled in the worker centers by inclusive and empowering governance structures; by making them spaces of care and learning; and by designating them as places where racism, sexism, homophobia, and religious intolerance are addressed head on and banned through codes of conduct. In turn, these new forms of order, together with the worker centers' multiracial campaigns for social justice, have galvanized more positive types of encounter and progressive political outcomes. These examples also underline the importance of inclusive institutional infrastructures and rule systems, and not simply individual dispositions and good will, for living together in difference as equals.

{ Conclusion }

Toward a Praxis of Everyday Equalities

WE BEGAN THIS BOOK BY NOTING that we were writing from and about four centers of settler colonialism—cities occupying particular positions in time and space, founded on processes of dispossession and expropriation of indigenous people. Ever since, these cities have been centers of immigration from different parts of the globe, resulting in an ever-changing racial and cultural diversity that has been the target of varying forms of government intervention, from assimilation to multiculturalism. In our four cities, people with different ethnicities, histories, cultures, languages, religions, and more encounter one another as they make homes, as they go to work, as they move around for a wide range of reasons and activities, and as they participate in collective efforts to change their lives. Having considered these encounters in depth, in this final chapter we reflect on what we have learned about the challenges and potentials of enacting equality in urban multicultures. The chapter begins with some brief reflections on the changing dynamics of our four cities over the six years we have been working on this book. It then discusses what we have learned about encounter from the diverse range of encounters that we have considered. Finally, and most substantially, the chapter offers a series of propositions for a "praxis of equality in difference" that we have discerned across our case studies.

Our Changing Times and Places: The Political Prospects of Urban Multicultures in Settler Colonial Cities

Recently, our four cities have seen incidents of renewed right-wing populism, white nationalism, and overt racism. Even as we have written this book, our times and spaces seem to have changed. Claims are now being made publicly, from the heights of high public office to the depths of everyday hate speech, that have not been widely heard for decades. As nativist, anti-immigrant, and racist rhetoric heightens, local governments are scrambling to manage the fallout for their diverse populations. In the United States, some city governments are establishing policy frameworks to defend their vulnerable migrant populations against attacks from national and subnational levels of government. For example, the city and county of Los Angeles are putting together a ten-million-dollar legal fund to defend undocumented immigrants from federal immigration enforcement. Confronted with increasing numbers of hate crimes against Muslim Canadians and other minorities, Canadian cities are struggling to prevent acts of violence such as the murders of six Muslim men at prayer in a Quebec City mosque on January 29, 2017. Several of Canada's largest municipal governments endorsed a charter for inclusive communities proposed by the National Council of Muslim Canadians. In Australia, the rise in anti-Muslim rhetoric has left city governments struggling to balance their commitments to diversity with responsibility to prevent any repeat of the Sydney hostage crisis. Difficult though it is to say at a time of such apparently momentous change in the political disposition of the places from which we write, it is our contention that identifying circumstances in which people are making efforts to live and act together in difference as equals in these places is even more important now than it was a few short years ago.

Moving beyond the settler colonial cities of Los Angeles, Melbourne, Sydney, and Toronto, it is important also to investigate the manner in which being together in difference as equals may be happening elsewhere. While we have been writing from and about very particular places, the institutional stances, behaviors, problems, and forms of resistance we have described are not unique to them. This is in part because cities across the globe are now embedded in neoliberal nation-states and a neoliberal global marketplace in which a laissez faire approach to the economy, one that reveres individual choice and responsibility and tolerates great inequality, dominates. It is also a result of how information about protest and resistance strategies circulates more readily around the world than ever before. Accordingly, though national and global forces and policies may circumscribe actions at the local level, they do not determine people's everyday lives. One recent example comes from the resident and volunteer support provided on the Greek island of Lesbos for refugees fleeing war in Syria, Iraq, and Afghanistan during 2015 and the early part of 2016. Encouraged by reports and callouts on social media, many volunteers from western countries in Europe and elsewhere arrived and stayed to help at this time of crisis, forming effective, community-based organizations to do so. One report describes a young Dutch woman starting up a group to distribute baby slings to refugee women, a Dutch real estate executive bringing a food truck, and an Australian photographer establishing a laundry service to wash the clothes of refugees and launder the blankets donated by the UN (Smith 2016). Such volunteers have joined with residents of the island who had been offering support to refugees since 2015 (a year when 850,000 refugees are estimated to have arrived). The two groups (volunteers and residents) formed a social movement of local action that, through care, has resisted treating refugees as strangers and instead has engaged in a practice of equality.

Encounter as an Ontology, Epistemology, and Method for Studying Everyday Urbanism

Through our case studies, we have put the notion of encounter as an ontology, epistemology, and methodology to work. We have shown that encounter, ontologically, is an indispensable "motor" of everyday life in the city: social life in cities consists of encounters between people, material things, and nonhuman, living others. Second, we have deployed encounter as a means of making knowledge, an epistemological strategy, consistent with our ontological view of the role of encounter in forming, even being, everyday life in the city. We have focused our study on four spheres of everyday life in the city: making a home, being at work, using public transport, and making publics. We have narrated what happens in encounters with difference in these spheres—chronicling the challenges but purposefully highlighting successful negotiations across differences that are frequently overlooked in both academic and public discourses on urban multicultures. We contend the latter are made possible by a politics of equality resulting in new understandings of, and relations among, culturally and racially different Others. Third, and relatedly, our methodology has relied on extended case studies using qualitative and ethnographic methods, which we feel are best suited to uncover the dynamics of encounter in the urban everyday.

In implementing this ontology, epistemology, and method, we have sought to extend theorizations of encounters with difference in several fruitful directions. First, we have looked beyond the classic "public spaces" that have received so much attention by scholars studying urban encounters with difference, examining encounters across a range of spheres and sites of the urban everyday. In doing so we have uncovered encounters that take a remarkable variety of forms, each with its own possibilities and challenges for the participants. While we have certainly shown the ongoing significance of the kind of fleeting encounters associated with urban public spaces, the encounters that take place in the process of making a home, making a living, and making publics in particular have quite distinct dynamics. To extend Wilson's (2017) useful formulation, not only does urban life consist of encounters that both "make difference" and (have the potential to) "make a difference," they also *"exhibit difference"* across diverse spheres of everyday urban life. Looking across the encounters that are involved in making a home, making a living, getting around, and making publics, we have seen encounters that range from unpredictable to habitual, unplanned to organized, individual to collective, unmediated to mediated, unfocused to focused, and beyond. We have more to say below on the implications of this diversity for the politics of encounter in urban multicultures, but here we would point out that there remains great potential for further research to continue to diversify the spheres of everyday life that are studied for the purposes of understanding, and shaping, urban multicultures.

Second, we have looked beyond the moment of encounter with difference to examine the significance of institutions and ideologies of governance in shaping their dynamics and possibilities. We show the crucial role played by institutional actors and settings— from the more obvious significance of immigration policies and

Conclusion

policing, to the operation of housing markets, workplace regulation and organization, transport ticketing prices, and familial relationships and hierarchies. So while the dynamics of encounter at the supermarket checkout or on the train carriage are accessible to researchers who care to spend the time observing them or talking to their participants, such observations need to be contextualized and enriched through critical analysis of the institutions and powers that act to shape expectations about the kinds of people and practices that are in or out of place—expectations participants might conform to, evade, react against, or seek to transform.

Third, and we think most importantly, we have aligned the political potential of encounters with difference with a politics of everyday equality or *being together in difference as equals.* This implies being together with culturally and racially different Others in our daily life and in the collectivity of communities, without either losing our identities or having some identities privileged over others, premised on a political and practical commitment to equality that is vital for contemporary urban multicultures. We argue that the prioritization of equality in difference is preferable to implicit or explicit normative frames that frequently animate studies of encounter in urban multicultures—such as "social cohesion," "tolerance," "peaceful coexistence," and the like. None of these, we argue, is adequate for addressing the justice questions that arise in circumstances of racialized inequality.

In prioritizing equality, we have not simply applied a predefined, unchanging definition of equality to empirical reality, asking whether or not that reality "measures up." Rather, we have argued that equality comes to exist (and to be redefined and verified) through its enactments in time and space, and in response to the particular forms of inequality and hierarchy against which it is enacted. Thus, we have sought instead to understand *how* urban inhabitants struggle to enact equality across a range of situations and encounters in which they find themselves as they go about their everyday lives in our four cities.

We argue that even in urban contexts characterized by inequality, a commitment to equality is not only a hope for a future city, but also a way of being together in the present. However, as we have seen, the praxis of being together in difference as equals is neither easy nor free of conflict. As we suggested in chapter 2, ours is not a book oriented toward "making the shift from unhappy to happy diversity" through the management of encounters with difference (Ahmed 2007, 123). Emerging from our inquiries and observations of urban encounters with difference in different spheres of the urban everyday, we identified six interconnected propositions to enact a politics of equality.

Toward a Praxis of Being Together in Difference as Equals

> **Proposition 1:** Being together in difference as equals—or the enactment of equality in urban multicultures—involves resisting and struggling against dominant modes of conduct, through new practices that transgress those normalized ways of doing things.

All institutions, including governmental ones, have developed particular forms of policing, with monitoring, enforcement, and conflict-resolution mechanisms to manage difference. But we also see new practices emerging, many of them experiments of different kinds. Some transgress the normal way of doing things within long-standing institutions and organizations through acts of agitation, and others take shape outside them in new organizations that include new modes of governance. For example, membership in a Toronto choir of hotel workers and union members sensitized participants to their cultural differences (chapter 4). Choir members acknowledged religious differences among union members as they instituted practices to accommodate difference respectfully. This respectful stance toward difference stands in stark contrast to much divisive contemporary public rhetoric, and of course also illustrates Allport's (1954) contention that repeated interaction among equals encourages respectful understanding of difference. In the worker centers of Los Angeles, people have made deliberate and intentional efforts to enact a politics of equality (chapter 6). They have introduced a flat governance structure that provides equal voice in decision-making processes that are sensitive to the needs of workers and that establish rules of conduct that are re-

Conclusion

spectful of the Other. As center directors pointed out, this deliberative process has been facilitated by the small scale of the centers.

Transgressive behaviors associated with making a home (chapter 3) are evident in the practices of migrant students in Melbourne, and of second-generation Italian immigrants who resisted their parents' expectations of home-ownership and heterosexual marriage. Overseas students in the tiny apartments and buildings without communal spaces to which they have access have taken up socializing together in the food courts of nearby shopping malls, in a manner that conforms to, and yet also exceeds, their purpose as sites of individual consumption. Restricted by the cultural expectations of parents in the Italian diaspora in Melbourne, young people wanting same-sex relationships organized alternative housing responses to those expected of them in the "home rules" of their parents.

Chapter 5 documents the emergence of bystander antiracism on Sydney's public transportation, when travelers on buses and trains use their cameras or smartphones to capture video footage of racist abuse of their fellow passengers. Once posted on platforms like YouTube or Facebook, such footage can be taken up by the mainstream media and can circulate in wide public discussion. While the technology of personal media devices has certainly facilitated the visibility of these transgressive behaviors, the users of the technology make active and sometimes risky decisions to intervene in instances of racist abuse premised on the notion that public transport ought to be a site where passengers can "be together in difference as equals."

> **Proposition 2:** Much of the collective practice that emerges from experiences of marginalization and crisis is realized through enormous hard work, determination, learning, and ethical and political commitment on the part of participants.

There is much emotional labor and care work, combined with an openness to learning from each other and negotiating across differences, that goes into constructing environments that foster being together in difference as equals. The Sydney Alliance, described in chapter 5, is an organization learning from its affiliates in the United States and beyond that networking and forming partnerships with a wide range of groups across the city is required to build powerful campaigns for change in the city. Forming such partnerships is a long-term process of developing relationships with the members of partner organizations. In turn, learning of different kinds occurs among people who have experienced incidents of racism over prolonged periods on trains and buses, like the woman whose removal of her headscarf as she rode a bus far from Sydney prompted the #illridewithyou campaign. People adjust their behavior, adapting and enduring, in anticipation of racist taunts on public transportation.

Learning, hard work, care, adjustment, and endurance are evident in Italian immigrants' efforts to make homes in Melbourne over the last five decades (chapter 3). In its suburban streetscapes (particularly its northern suburbs), their houses are testimony to their blending of ways from their pasts with the ways of their present. Front gardens include Australian plants and lawns, while back gardens often have big vegetable gardens and paving; houses have been decorated to reference Italy somewhat in building materials and trims, while retaining the forms of their neighbors.

The same dedication combined with political commitment to being together in difference as equals is found in some workplaces. In the Los Angeles worker centers discussed in chapter 6, the commitment of administrators to democratic decision-making and equitable speech is time-consuming and emotionally taxing. They work hard to create spaces where people can be together in difference as equals. Their continuing efforts to inculcate change in individual speech and actions through education, regulation, and cajoling are rarely acknowledged and inadequately compensated.

The same pressures threaten the hotel union's efforts to promote the cultural contributions of its diverse membership in Toronto (chapter 4). Negotiators fight continuously for hotels' continued financial support for the union's cultural activities, as they also must convince some of their own members that cultural activities such as the choir contribute to the struggle for better pay and improved working conditions. Even with sufficient financial resources, the choir's existence is jeopardized by participants' precarious daily

Conclusion 211

lives. Earning little more than minimum wage, choir members must balance physically demanding shift work with their household responsibilities and the challenges of long commutes to free time for choir practices and performances.

Live-in caregivers demonstrate the same commitment. After long days of work, they attend meetings organized by nongovernmental organizations where they can meet other live-in caregivers while learning about their workplace rights and responsibilities. Their struggles to overcome the isolation associated with working alone in private houses that are also their residences contrasts with the lack of social interaction among Toronto grocery store cashiers. Part-time workers, the cashiers are isolated from each other by their jobs' temporary status as much as they are separated from each other by individual workstations and a demanding and inflexible labor process.

> **Proposition 3:** New organizational infrastructures promote and support practices that enact equality from the bottom up.

The enactment of equality from the bottom up at the urban scale does not emerge from thin air. Rather, the "being together in difference as equals" that we have observed has tended to depend on the existence—indeed, the production—of organizational infrastructures that are crucial to their emergence. In the current moment, in the cities and countries from which we write, there is little political appetite for resourcing new forms of practices and infrastructures to support being together in difference as equals. In the United States, as white nationalism is reappearing, the police apparatus of the state is being used to criminalize and expel those deemed strangers. Resisting such oppressive national policies, city governments are enacting Sanctuary City policies by which local governments commit to protecting immigrants (documented and undocumented) and refugees in their midst by preventing the use of local police or resources in the enforcement of national immigration law.

In Sydney, we see the emergence of an influential set of partnerships working for equality in mobility (chapter 5). The Sydney

Alliance, a coalition of unions, faith-based groups, and community organizations, works through community organizing as well as advocacy, seeking to establish common ground among its partners through a slow, dedicated process of relationship-building and dialogue in organized encounters in order to share knowledge and resources. Establishing the Alliance has involved both collective efforts to determine the ways in which partners will work together and the commitment of financial resources from partner organizations to sustain its infrastructure of staff and facilities. Since 2014, the Alliance has had some success in pushing the state government to allow transport concessions for asylum seekers so that they have the mobility to access services distributed throughout the city.

In Melbourne (chapter 3), concerned with making a home, new nongovernmental, community-built organizations formed through the work of immigrants themselves in the middle of the twentieth century. Some of these organizations remain to this day, having been influential in voicing immigrants' needs in national and urban policy. In the decades since their formation, they have benefited from new organizational directions initiated by their members and new rules for thinking about housing. And of course, in chapter 6 we examined the formation and operation of a particular kind of organizational infrastructure for enacting and advancing a politics of equality—the worker center.

In recent times, discussions of the politics of equality have questioned the significance of such organizational infrastructures. For example, Rancière, from whom we have taken some inspiration, finds that the question of organization is not of much interest: "As far as organization goes, it exists always and everywhere. No need to wear yourself out shouting about it from the rooftops. The only question is: what is being organized? Why? And, so, how?" (Rancière 2016, 122). Yet for those engaged in the practice of equality and for the feminist thinkers we discussed early in the book, organizational infrastructures are important in facilitating being together as equals—in particular, through their role in imbuing encounters with difference with political intent and content that seek to relate their dynamics to action on equality. Indeed, our engagement with the activities of people in building the migrant

Conclusion   213

associations, unions, churches, worker centers, and other organizational forms has shown that, while not necessarily political in themselves, infrastructures have been instrumental to the emergence of a politics of equality (see also Sparks 2016). Further premises below are in some ways an elaboration on the forms of work that establish the conditions in which experiments with equality might occur.

Proposition 4: Enacting equality requires the creation and observance of codes of conduct, especially prescriptions about respect and openness toward difference in speech, and about the way we talk about others in public, as well as in our written documents.

Across our cases we have seen that enacting equality through new practices has also involved the making of rules, the monitoring of their implementation, and the continued evaluation of their efficacy. Enacting equality at the level of the organization, however, is embedded in the larger context of government policies and laws. Social policies and laws, and the way we talk about Others in and beyond the city, have ramifications for whether societies can be more equal and just. Social policies and laws frequently entrench hierarchies, which is why they are commonly the target of resistance, but they may also work to reduce inequalities and hierarchies. Rules regulating hate speech, either formal or informal, are particularly important to being together in difference as equals, and govern encounters in all of the cases we have studied even as right-wing politicians seek to weaken them in some places.

On public transportation (chapter 5), our analysis highlights how the injustice of racist talk and racist aggression is recognized by both governments and fellow-travelers. While the "customer courtesy" campaign of the state government's transport authority emphasizes civil behavior on trains and buses, it is a private bus company, in their own signs on buses, that more explicitly targets racist abuse of passengers and drivers. In workplaces, legislation should prohibit racist, sexist, and homophobic vocabulary. But our investigations of three different workplaces (chapter 4) highlight Ahmed's (2012) conclusion that diversity policies often fail

214 *Conclusion*

to ensure working together in difference as equals. We note that even in the worker centers discussed in chapter 6, new organizations with a highly progressive agenda, it has been felt necessary to develop and enforce a code of conduct, such as banning racist, sexist, and homophobic talk, name-calling, use of derogatory terms, religious intolerance, and harassment. It is accepted that gaining compliance with such codes of conduct in everyday encounters requires hard and ongoing work: codes of conduct must be lived, rehearsed, and enforced if necessary—enacted in the everyday. The worker centers highlight the need for workplaces to reflect upon and amend themselves on an ongoing basis to achieve a politics of equality. Meanwhile, in chapter 3, we note the caring effects of everyday, inclusive, jocular speech in the marketplace of diverse Dandenong, and the language of negotiation in the words of young gay and lesbian second-generation Italian immigrants as they carve out a new housing pathway different from that expected of them by their parents.

The rules we have identified in efforts to enact equality go beyond forms of speech. Workplaces, discussed in chapter 4, are particularly interesting in this regard. In all four cities, formal legislation protects the rights of racialized and ethnic minorities, supposedly ensuring fair treatment with regard to hiring, earnings, promotion, and firing. Nevertheless, workers report discrimination in all these cities, particularly migrant workers. Our analysis from Toronto shows that employers, managers, and supervisors rely on stereotypes to justify pigeonholing workers from specific national origins in particular occupations, rarely considering them for promotion or training. In other cases, employers justify discrimination on the grounds of hiring reliable and qualified workers. Working against this, the analysis of worker centers in chapter 6 shows how the successful enactment of formal rights depends on the active policing of encounters within the centers, whose staff insist on respectful engagement with difference by all participants.

This focus on a kind of "policing" of equality might at first seem to sit uncomfortably within the framework we established in the opening chapters, where we drew upon Rancière's understanding of the tensions between politics and policing. We think, however,

Conclusion 215

that our work draws attention to the relation and interaction between politics and policing, a point that Rancière himself makes:

> If the distinction between politics and the police can be useful, it is not to allow us to say: politics is on this side, police is on the opposite side. It is to allow us to understand the form of their intertwinement. We rarely, if ever, face a situation where we can say: this is politics in its purity... we ceaselessly face situations where we have to discern how politics encroaches on the police and the police on matters of politics. (2009, 287)

Yet it is important to attend to the differences between different kinds of policing. Our work suggests that politics not only acts upon the police but also may generate its own forms of policing, which can be essential to its practice. In the LA worker centers, we see a commitment to rules that are both democratically established and open to renegotiation—rules for, and founded in, the equality of anyone to have a say in their development and enforcement.

Proposition 5: Enacting a politics of encounter that promotes being together in difference as equals entails distinct temporalities.

Establishing trust and a mutual recognition of equality with those who may at first appear to embody the stranger requires time and endurance. The fleetingness of many everyday face-to-face encounters with difference does not necessarily lend itself to such recognition and trust. Indeed, as scholars like Valentine (2008) have shown, fleeting encounters often reinforce deeply held preconceptions and stereotypes of, and prejudice toward, the Other. This is because present encounters always open up past encounters, such as past events of racial violence. Transgressing such reinscriptions of past encounters is a big challenge if being together in difference as equals is to occur, requiring struggle and resistance to old ways of doing and thinking (Proposition 1). Our examples show how awareness of the timescales involved in making changes of

216   *Conclusion*

different kinds often underpins the strategy of groups seeking and enacting equality.

In chapter 5, a range of temporalities is reported in encounters across difference on Sydney's public transportation, and in community organizing about it. On the one hand, the experience of being together with others as passengers on buses and trains is usually fleeting and unfocused; these are relatively brief encounters of copresent bodies. On the other hand, organizing undertaken by the Sydney Alliance to draw political attention to the injustice of high fares for asylum seekers has required years of effort devoted to building relationships among Alliance members. The social media activity of some passengers also extended moments of encounter across time, through capturing and circulating events that can then be discussed and debated over a longer period. It is also the case that the campaigns of the private bus company Transdev to publicize through signs on its buses the antiracist message that "This Bus Is for Everyone" is a long-term strategy—trying to influence behavior that will occur after repeated reading of the message by passengers.

The temporality of encounters in the Toronto workplaces examined in chapter 4 is equally varied. They range from brief and unfocused interactions to repeated and purposeful meetings devoted to training, supervision, and organizing for change in the workplace. No matter how often they are repeated, brief encounters between coworkers in grocery stores, supervisors and room attendants in Toronto hotels, and employers and caregivers seem to maintain inequality. On a more positive note, the choir of room attendants illustrates how repeated encounters over several years build awareness of difference and mutual trust that challenges unequal power relations in workplaces.

Making a home, as reported in chapter 3, involves fewer fleeting meetings with Others than other urban activities, especially travel on public transport. The encounters of home-making are repeated and occur over quite a long time—years, decades, and even generations—often involving the development of relations of care. In the diverse Melbourne suburb of Dandenong, the care of newcomer refugees has developed over many years as a practice of neighborly interactions, even exhibited in the activity of shop-

Conclusion   217

ping in the local market. In other suburbs, migrants have built or renovated houses over a long period, adapting their expectations of what a home should look like and how it should be used to fit with those in the dwellings and streetscapes around them.

As for those making publics in Los Angeles, described in chapter 6, the organizers of the Freedom Rides explicitly recognized the importance of the temporality of encounter. They conceived of their buses as mobile classrooms where workers would spend sufficient time to learn about the history of racism, sexism, and homophobia in American workplaces and workers' efforts to combat them. Interactions and understandings flourished as the buses traveled toward Washington, in part because of the long periods of time spent together. The directors of worker centers in Los Angeles also acknowledge the time demanded for effective inclusive and shared decision-making, extending the goals far beyond the single issue to be decided. Each decision-making process is an opportunity to deepen participants' familiarity with difference, and with principles of democratic decision-making that value each person's viewpoints and contributions. Among the many factors that limit the size of worker centers, the additional time required to build consensus as the number of participants increases is a crucial consideration.

Proposition 6: Spatialities and material infrastructures matter in facilitating being together in difference as equals.

People use, create, and appropriate spaces in order to enact a politics of equality. Physical spaces are important sites for coming together; in coffee shops, community centers, worker centers, and on sports fields, people congregate for any number of purposes, including the avoidance of surveillance. Designated public spaces—streets, squares, public buildings—are regularly appropriated to gain publicity for existing injustices, make demands, and propose alternatives. In response to increasing surveillance of public spaces in recent decades, virtual public spaces have become an increasingly important means to gain publicity. The virtual spaces facilitated through diverse communications technologies have also been crucial in enabling networking between people and groups within metropolitan areas, and also across national and international space. They are important sources of inspiration, information, and support.

The spatially and temporally contained buses of the Freedom Ride from Los Angeles to Washington, D.C., and the worker centers (chapter 6) illustrate the profound significance of space for learning about the Other and negotiating across differences. The proximity enforced by days of riding the bus and their shared commitment to an emancipatory project enabled Riders who entered as strangers to establish close relationships of trust among one another that were essential to the ride's success. The bus became a safe space where people could share their personal stories, knowing they would be encouraged rather than humiliated. This in turn enabled Riders to successfully challenge the dominant police order through embodied solidarity. Similarly, the material infrastructure of the worker centers has been crucial in facilitating the construction of alternative and emancipatory sets of norms and expectations consistent with Rancière's always emerging politics of equality.

Chapter 5 draws attention to how material things and their spatial distribution affect peoples' access to mobility in different parts of the city. Access to mobility will be uneven and unequal in the absence of an appropriate distribution of sidewalks, bicycle lanes, roads, railway lines, and other infrastructure. The "forest of artifacts" through which Molotch (2012) characterizes the subway system (in his case, in New York) includes the design of platforms, exits and entrances, announcements and instructions, staff members and security devices, as well as the carriages and the seating therein. These material aspects of public transportation can be influential settings shaping equality or inequality.

The material settings of work also influence struggles to achieve equality. The isolation of caregivers in suburban homes is matched by that of grocery cashiers whose workstations separate them from one another (chapter 4). For caregivers, emancipatory opportunities for social interaction arise only when they leave their workplaces for meetings organized by nongovernmental organizations or to spend time with fellow workers in close and intimate quarters. In contrast, hotel workers' jobs require various forms of collaboration, creating some opportunities for informal encounters.

The physical arrangement of housing influences social possibilities of interaction in urban spaces. The separation of public housing tenants from those occupying privately owned apartments into distinct buildings in Carlton's socially mixed housing (chapter 3), and the two group's differential access to common areas, such as the small garden in the development from which public housing tenants are banned, conveys the message that private property is superior to and should be differentiated from less desirable public housing nearby. Where the layout of student housing made encounter almost impossible, students appropriated nearby shopping center food courts for this purpose.

No doubt in response to how the policing of spaces—streets, buses, workplaces, and homes—actively seeks to prevent their appropriation and/or the emergence of political dissensus, we see instances where *new* spaces are produced for experiments with, and enactments of, equality in difference. The development of worker centers in Los Angeles (chapter 6) exemplifies not only the benefits of making such spaces, but also of the challenges of doing so. It requires the mobilization of a range of resources—from financial and environmental to human—that frequently are difficult to secure.

Through all these means, then, physical urban sites and spaces can be vital resources for the practice of equality in difference. In occupying and (re)making these spaces, they also come to serve as imaginary resources in the building of a democratic politics. Whether it be a suburb like Dandenong in Melbourne, a church hall like those in Toronto, a train carriage like those in Sydney, or a worker center in Los Angeles, such spaces can come to be invested with egalitarian identities—no matter who you are or where you are from, these spaces are meant to be for everyone across their multiple and intersecting social differences. In all these ways, urban inhabitants in the cities we write from have sought to transform an urban condition of "throwntogetherness" into one of "being together in difference as equals." This way of urban living faces many growing obstacles. In our present circumstances, it is too easy to dwell on those obstacles and the profound inequalities that characterize the urban condition in cities across the planet. Indeed, if equality is thought of as some perfect state, the end point of progressive politics, it can seem far away indeed. Yet in this book, we have shown ways in which equality need not be a distant goal but rather can be a resource for a politics in the here and now. Even in circumstances where political-economic processes persistently seem to generate racialized inequalities, urban inhabitants are showing us that change can happen when people act on the basis that they *are* equals across their differences, working together with others to trace out the consequences of that equality by reshaping their encounters in the home, the workplace, the street, the train platform, and beyond.

We are aware that the kinds of changes that we have documented across this book are not always systemic or revolutionary. Even in those instances where we can point to "success"—like the long-term production of a vibrant multiculture in the streets of suburban Dandenong, the granting of cheap travel to people seeking asylum in Sydney, or improvements in minimum wages and working conditions in Toronto and Los Angeles, such successes may seem inadequate in the face of structural, racialized inequalities. Yet we would argue that even apparently "micro"-scale changes to emerge from enactments of being together in difference as equals have transformative effects and potential. Once enacted, equalities can escape their confinement to apparently bounded situations and contexts through a range of relational sociospatial processes which themselves require further investigation. Across our cases, for instance, we see examples of a kind of horizontal translation and replication of initiatives, as well as cases of vertical "scaling up" of initiatives. The living wage campaign in the United States is a good example. Actors in Los Angeles worker centers and their allies were in part inspired by Raise the Wage campaigns in other West Coast cities, which they translated and developed to suit their particular circumstances. On the back of such successful city-based action, members of campaigns in Los Angeles, San Francisco, and across California successfully lobbied for a California-wide minimum wage increase. Likewise, the Sydney Alliance campaign on concession travel was itself a kind of extension of the solidarity established in a momentary church encounter to a campaign of a longer duration and wider geography. And its success then led to a more ambitious (and also successful) campaign to reduce fees for people seeking asylum to access state-based tech-

Conclusion

nical services and further education. And the circulation of people and stories of such successes (as well as failures) is part of a wider process of amplification through which equalities can travel. Our book is offered as a contribution to that amplification of egalitarian politics in which new meanings and practices of equality fit for our times and spaces are emerging.

We have seen in our case studies that such equality does not depend on conformity to ethno-nationalist or racialized identities, but rather can be premised on shared inhabitance and/or shared commitments and participation in urban routines and activities like making a home, working, moving around, or making publics. The conditions may be challenging, and the products of their labors fragile, but they are no less significant for that. As Raymond Williams (1989, 118) once put it: "To be truly radical is to make hope possible, rather than despair convincing." We do hope that this book contributes to this radical project, in our trying times.

Notes

Introduction

1. http://www.smh.com.au/nsw/martin-place-siege-illridewithyou-hashtag-goes-viral-20141216–127rm1.html.
2. https://twitter.com/sirtessa/status/544363242655449088.
3. This one came at 4:29 p.m., one minute after the earlier post.
4. https://www.smh.com.au/national/nsw/sydney-siege-aftermath-illridewithyou-shows-the-healing-power-of-the-hashtag-20141217-1294i2.html.

4. Working for a Living in Toronto

1. Without success, we sought to include a case study of animators to gain insight into the encounters among skilled workers in the creative industries. Like many other works in the creative industries (Leslie and Catungal 2012), animators work as independent contractors, often working alone and occasionally socializing for business purposes (Norcliffe and Rendace 2003). To take account of the emergence of work without fixed workplaces was beyond the scope of this analysis.

2. Scholars have commented that equity remains a major issue for trade unions as they try to respond to the increasing feminization of the workforce, and in the multicultures studied here, its increasing ethno-racial diversity (Colgan and Ledwith 2003).

3. The Toronto census metropolitan area (CMA) consists of the core municipality of Toronto and adjacent municipalities that have a high degree of integration with the core as measured by commuting flows (Statistics Canada 2017a). Currently, the CMA includes Toronto along with four adjacent regional municipalities—Halton, Peel, York, and Durham—and Orangeville, Mono, New Tecumseth, and Bradford West Gwillimbury in Dufferin.

4. In Canada, racialized minorities are identified officially as visible minorities, people who do not identify as white or Caucasian or as Aboriginal (Statistics Canada 2003, 2013).

5. Individual visible minority groups include the following: Chinese, South Asian, Black, Arab, West Asian, Filipino, Southeast Asian, Latin American, Japanese, and Korean (Statistics Canada 2017c).

224   *Notes*

6. Information about pay rates was taken from www.payscale.com/research/CA/Job=Hotel_Room_Service_Attendant/Hourly_Rate.

7. The requirement to live in the employer's home was removed by new regulations on November 30, 2014, that now require caregivers to have a temporary work permit and place strict annual limits on the number that may apply for permanent residence. With an estimated backlog of almost 60,000 applicants at the time of the policy change, the annual limit of 5,500 applications for permanent residence was seen immediately as problematic (Tungohan et al. 2015).

8. Researchers have considered encounters with difference in other multicultures such as London (McDowell 2011), Sydney, Australia (Wise 2016), and Minnesota (Leitner 2012), and for other occupations (Harris and Valentine 2016).

5. Moving around the City in Sydney

1. See http://www.latintimes.com/immigration-reform-news -california-issued-605000-drivers-licenses-undocumented-368771.

2. See https://www.theguardian.com/world/2013/jun/21/brazil -police-crowds-rio-protest.

3. See the data at https://www.westernsydney.edu.au/cws/gws_research.

4. These figures are from the NSW Bureau of Transport Statistic Household Travel Survey for 2014–15. See https://public.tableau.com/profile/bureau.of.transport.statistics#!/vizhome/HTSVisualisation2014 –15-Web/Welcome.

5. This comment was left online in the comments section under the following article: http://www.dailytelegraph.com.au/newslocal/northern -beaches/early-planning-under-way-for-possible-northern-beaches-rail -line/news-story/0a2d37a92bb0c1358de15b3ca2a2fa6c.

6. See the details at http://www.sydneytrains.info/travelling_with/trip_tips/customer_courtesy.

7. The rest of the images with accompanying text can be seen at http://www.transportnsw.info/en/travelling-with-us/using-public-transport/etiquette/anti-social-behaviour.page?&tnswsource=internal&tnswlocation= homepage&tnswtype=banner&tnswcontent=courtesy.

8. These tweets were posted in a series on February 8, 2013, immediately after the incident, by @JezNews; original spelling has been reproduced here.

9. See for example: "'Anyone Who Says Racism Is Dying Is Well and Truly Mistaken': ABC News Presenter Jeremy Fernandez Alleges Racial Abuse on Sydney Bus," *Sydney Morning Herald*, February 8, 2013, https://www.smh.com.au/national/nsw/anyone-who-says-racism-is-dying-is

Notes   225

-well-and-truly-mistaken-abc-news-presenter-jeremy-fernandez-alleges
-racial-abuse-on-sydney-bus-20130208-2e2fe.html; "ABC News Presenter
Jeremy Fernandez in Racist Attack on Sydney Bus," News.Com.Au, http://
www.news.com.au/entertainment/tv/abc-news-presenter-jeremy
-fernandez-in-racist-attack-on-sydney-bus/news-story/ec5014a2c4fb6b
dccd7ffd876e927b06; "Jeremy Fernandez: Children Were Watching,"
Mamamia, February 11, 2013, http://www.mamamia.com.au/racism
-jeremy-fernandez-jamila-rizvi/; "Bus Taunts That Sparked Australian
Racism Debate," BBC News online, February 16, 2013, http://www.bbc
.com/news/world-asia-21468892; Fernandez also wrote his own extended
reflection on the incident in "My Rosa Parks Moment in Sydney 2013,"
ABC News online, February 8, 2013, http://www.abc.net.au/news/2013
-02-08/fernandez-why-i-didnt-give-up-my-seat/4508686.

10. See http://www.smh.com.au/nsw/no-one-helped-me-racist-tirade
-on-sydney-bus-rattles-chineseaustralian-woman-20150924-gju6md.html.

11. http://www.smh.com.au/nsw/we-speak-english-in-this-country-woman
-films-racial-tirade-on-sydney-train-20151218-glr6kj.html.

12. http://www.smh.com.au/nsw/antiislamic-abuse-on-sydney-train
-victim-hafeez-ahmed-bhatti-thanks-stacey-eden-for-standing-up-for-him
-20150417-1mn138.html.

13. Of course, CCTV footage can be used to corroborate footage captured and circulated by passengers in follow-up prosecutions. But this
does not challenge the broader point that these two kinds of cameras
involve distinct forms of publicity.

14. Of course, social media has also been important in facilitating
and disseminating different forms of racism—see Dunn and Jakubowizc
(Australia Human Rights Commission 2015, 27–28). The point here is not
that such media are inherently antiracist, rather that they can help to
construct public discussion of antiracist action and solidarity.

15. Anyone who arrives in Australia without a valid visa and then
seeks asylum is detained while their application is processed—in the
case of maritime arrivals, in offshore detention centers, and in the case of
other arrivals, in detention centers on the mainland.

16. No statistics on this are available from the Australian government,
but recent reports estimate that over one-third of bridging visa holders
have no work rights. See https://www.theguardian.com/australia
-news/2016/apr/13/we-are-the-forgotten-people-the-anguish-of-australias
-invisible-asylum-seekers.

17. https://www.asrc.org.au/resources/fact-sheet/asylum-seeker
-financial-support/.

18. While no statistics are released by the commonwealth about the
location of people seeking asylum on bridging visas, services working

with people seeking asylum estimated that by the mid-2010s approximately thirteen thousand were living in Sydney.

19. See https://www.theguardian.com/australia-news/2016/apr/13/we-are-the-forgotten-people-the-anguish-of-australias-invisible-asylum-seekers.

20. See https://www.sydneycatholic.org/news/latest_news/2015/201571_1623.shtml.

21. Personal comment, 2016.

22. Personal comment, 2016.

23. Kurt Iveson was the NTEU representative at the meeting.

6. Making Publics in Los Angeles

1. The Immigrant Worker Freedom Ride discussed in this section draws closely on an article coauthored with Kristin Sziarto (Sziarto and Leitner 2010).

2. The Los Angeles metropolitan area extends across Orange and Los Angeles Counties, with the City of Los Angeles located within Los Angeles County.

3. The dissimilarity index has a range between 100 and 0, with 100 indicating a completely uneven and 0 a completely even spatial distribution of two different ethno-racial groups across all subareas of a city. A dissimilarity index of 65 between the black-white population means that 65 percent of whites (or blacks) would have to change the location of their residence to obtain an even distribution between black and white residents across all subareas of the city.

4. U.S. Immigration and Customs Enforcement (ICE) is part of the U.S. Department of Homeland Security (DHS). It is the largest investigative arm of the DHS, which "enforces federal laws governing border control, customs, trade, and immigration to promote homeland security and public safety." It "focuses on smart immigration enforcement, preventing terrorism and combating the illegal movement of people and trade" (ICE 2018). See Coleman (2007) on the spread to the interior of "border" enforcement practices.

5. The first wave of contemporary worker centers emerged in the American South during the late 1970s and 1980s in response to economic restructuring and the decline of manufacturing, but also racial and gender discrimination in union representation (Fine 2006, 11).

6. The research on worker centers is based on archival research and informal and formal interviews Helga Leitner and Sam Nowak conducted in summer 2015 with eight leaders in the Los Angeles worker center movement: Alexandra Suh, executive director of the Korean Immigrant

Workers Alliance (KIWA); Aquilina Soriano, executive director of the Pilipino Worker Center (PWC); Rosemarie Molina, project manager of CLEAN Carwash Campaign; Maegan Ortiz, executive director of Instituto de Educacion Popular del Sur de California (IDEPSCA); and at the Los Angeles Black Worker Center (BWC), Lola Smallwood Cuevas (founding director), Sherri Bell (organizer), Lanita Moris (project manager), and Loretta Stevens (co-executive director). Interviews were semi-structured and ranged from one to two hours. Each took place at the worker center.

7. For a detailed analysis of the relationship between organized labor unions and worker centers, see Fine (2007).

Bibliography

Ahmed, Sara. 1999. "Home and Away: Narratives of Migration and Estrangement." *International Journal of Cultural Studies* 2 (3): 329–47.

Ahmed, Sara. 2004. "Collective Feelings: Or, the Impressions Left by Others." *Theory, Culture & Society* 21 (2): 25–42.

Ahmed, Sara. 2007. "Multiculturalism and the Promise of Happiness." *New Formations* 63: 121–37.

Ahmed, Sara. 2012. *On Being Included: Racism and Diversity in Institutional Life*. Durham, N.C.: Duke University Press.

Ahonen, Pasi, Janne Tienari, Susan Merilainen, and Alison Pullen. 2014. "Hidden Contexts and Invisible Power Relations: A Foucauldian Reading of Diversity Research." *Human Relations* 67 (3): 263–86.

Allport, Gordon W. 1954. *The Nature of Prejudice*. Cambridge, Mass.: Addison-Wesley.

Amin, Ash. 2002. "Ethnicity and the Multicultural City: Living with Diversity." *Environment and Planning A: Economy and Space* 34 (6): 959–80.

Amin, Ash. 2012. *Land of Strangers*. Cambridge: Polity Press.

Amin, Ash. 2015. "Animated Space." *Public Culture* 27 (2): 239–58.

Amin, Ash, and Nigel Thrift. 2002. *Cities: Reimagining the Urban*. Cambridge, U.K.: Polity Press.

Anderson, Elijah J. 2011. *The Cosmopolitan Canopy: Race and Civility in Everyday Life*. New York: W. W. Norton.

Arat-Koc, Sedef. 1999. "NAC's Response to the Immigration Legislative Review Report 'Not Just Numbers: A Canadian Framework for Future Immigration.'" *Canadian Woman Studies* 19 (3): 18.

Arthurson, Kathy, Iris Levin, and Anna Ziersch. 2015. "What Is the Meaning of Social Mix? Shifting Perspectives in Planning and Implementing Public Housing Estate Redevelopment." *Australian Geographer* 46 (4): 491–505.

Askins, Kye. 2015. "Being Together: Everyday Geographies and the Quiet Politics of Belonging." *ACME: An International E-Journal for Critical Geographies* 14 (2): 470–78.

[229]

August, Martine. 2014. "Negotiating Social Mix in Toronto's First Public Housing Redevelopment: Power, Space and Social Control in Don Mount Court." *International Journal of Urban and Regional Research* 38 (4): 1160–80.

Australian Bureau of Statistics. 2011. *2011 Census of Population and Housing.* Canberra: ABS. www.abs.gov.au/census.

Australian Bureau of Statistics. 2014. "Percentage of Migrants in Melbourne by Suburb: 2011." *Australian Social Trends 2014.* Report 4102.0. Canberra: ABS. http://www.abs.gov.au/ausstats/abs@.nsf/Lookup/4102.0main+features102014.

Australian Bureau of Statistics. 2016. *2016 Census of Population and Housing.* Canberra: ABS. www.abs.gov.au/census.

Australian Human Rights Commission. 2015. *Freedom from Discrimination: Report on the 40th Anniversary of the Racial Discrimination Act.* Sydney: Australian Human Rights Commission.

Bakan, Abigail, and Audrey Kobayashi. 2007. "Affirmative Action and Employment Equity: Policy, Ideology, and Backlash in Canadian Context." *Studies in Political Economy* 79: 1145–66.

Balch, Alex. 2010. "Strike Continues for Toronto Hotel Workers." *Linchpin*, September 21, 2010.

Banerjee, Rupa. 2008. "An Examination of Factors Affecting Perception of Workplace Discrimination." *Journal of Labor Research* 29 (4): 380–401.

Bankston, Carl. 2014. *Immigrant Networks and Social Capital.* Malden, Mass.: Polity Press.

Banting, Keith, and Will Kymlicka. 2010. "Canadian Multiculturalism: Global Anxieties and Local Debates." *British Journal of Canadian Studies* 23 (1): 43–72.

Batnitzky, Adina, and Linda McDowell. 2013. "The Emergence of an 'Ethnic Economy'? The Spatial Relationships of Migrant Workers in London's Health and Hospitality Sectors." *Ethnic and Racial Studies* 36 (12): 1997–2015.

Bayat, Asef. 2010. *Life as Politics: How Ordinary People Change the Middle East.* 2nd ed. Stanford, Calif.: Stanford University Press.

Bernhardt, Annette, Michael W. Spiller, and Nik Theodore. 2013. "Employers Gone Rogue: Explaining Industry Variation in Violations of Workplace Laws." *Industrial & Labor Relations Review* 66 (4): 808–32.

Bissell, David. 2010. "Passenger Mobilities: Affective Atmospheres and the Sociality of Public Transport." *Environment and Planning D: Society and Space* 28: 270–89.

Blatman-Thomas, Naama, and Libby Porter. 2019. "Placing Property: Theorizing the Urban from Settler Colonial Cities." *International Journal of Urban and Regional Research* 43 (1): 30–45.

Bibliography

Bloemraad, Irene. 2011. "The Debate over Multiculturalism: Philosophy, Politics, and Policy." *Migration Information Source*, September 22, 2011. http://www.migrationpolicy.org/article/debate-over-multiculturalism-philosophy-politics-and-policy.

Blunt, Alison, and Robyn Dowling. 2006. *Home*. London: Routledge.

Bowen, Chris. 2011. "What Makes Multiculturalism Great Is Mutual Respect." *Sydney Morning Herald*, February 17, 2011.

Bridge, Gary, Tom Butler, and Loretta Lees, eds. 2012. *Mixed Communities: Gentrification by Stealth?* Bristol: Policy Press.

Briskin, Linda. 2003. "The Equity Project in Canadian Unions." In *Gender, Diversity and Trade Unions: International Perspectives*, edited by Fiona Colgan and Sue Ledwith, 28–47. New York: Routledge.

Broadway, Michael. 2007. "Meatpacking and the Transformation of Rural Communities: A Comparison of Brooks, Alberta, and Garden City, Kansas." *Rural Sociology* 72 (4): 560–82.

Brodkin, Karen. 2007. *Making Democracy Matter: Identity and Activism in Los Angeles*. New Brunswick, N.J.: Rutgers University Press.

Brown, Michael. 2003. Hospice and the Spatial Paradoxes of Terminal Care. *Environment and Planning A* 35 (5): 833–51.

Brown, Michael. 2008. "Working Political Geography through Social Movement Theory: The Case of Gay and Lesbian Seattle." In *SAGE Handbook of Political Geography*, edited by Kevin Cox, Murray Low, and Jennifer Robinson, 285–304. London: Sage.

Brown University. 2016a. *US 2010 Discover America in a New Century. Spatial Structures in the Social Sciences, American Communities Project*. http://www.s4.brown.edu/us2010/segregation2010/city.aspx?cityid=644000

Brown University. 2016b. *US 2010 Discover America in a New Century. Spatial Structures in the Social Sciences, American Communities Project*. http://www.s4.brown.edu/us2010/segregation2010/msa.aspx?metroid=31100

Burawoy, Michael, Joseph A. Blum, Sheba George, Zsuzsa Gille, and Millie Thayer. 2000. *Global Ethnography: Forces, Connections, and Imaginations in a Postmodern World*. Berkeley: University of California Press.

Butler, Judith. 1990. *Gender Trouble: Feminism and the Subversion of Identity*. New York: Routledge.

Butler, Judith. 2015. *Notes Toward a Performance Theory of Assembly*. Cambridge, Mass.: Harvard University Press.

Castles, Stephen, and Mark Miller. 1993. *The Age of Migration: International Population Movements in the Modern World*. New York: Guildford.

Citizenship and Immigration Canada. 2015. *Facts and Figures 2014.* http://www.cic.gc.ca/english/resources/statistics/facts2014.

City-Data.com. 2014. "Los Angeles, CA, Income Map, Earnings Map, and Wages Data." http://www.city-data.com/income/income-Los-Angeles -California.html.

Clough, Nathan L., and Robert. M. Vanderbeck. 2006. "Managing Politics and Consumption in Business Improvement Districts: The Geographies of Political Activism on Burlington, Vermont's, Church Street Marketplace." *Urban Studies* 43 (12): 2261–84.

Cockburn, Cynthia. 1998. *The Space Between Us: Negotiating Gender and National Identities in Conflict.* London: Zed Books.

Coleman, Mathew. 2007. "Immigration Geopolitics beyond the Mexico– U.S. Border." *Antipode* 39 (1): 54–76.

Colgan, Fiona, and Sue Ledwith, eds. 2003. *Gender, Diversity and Trade Unions: International Perspectives.* New York: Routledge.

Cook, Nicole, Aidan Davison, and Louise Crabtree, eds. 2016. *Housing and Home Unbound.* New York: Routledge.

Cope, Meghan. 2001. "Between Welfare and Work: The Roles of Social Service Organizations in the Social Regulation of Labor Markets and Regulation of the Poor." *Urban Geography* 22 (5): 391–406.

Crabtree, Louise. 2016. "Unbounding Home-Ownership in Australia." In *Housing and Home Unbound*, edited by Nicole Cook, Aidan Davison, and Louise Crabtree, 173–89. New York and London: Routledge.

Cranford, Cynthia. 2014. "Towards Particularism with Security: Immigration, Race and the Organization of Personal Support Services in Los Angeles." In *When Care Work Goes Global: Locating the Social Relations of Domestic Work*, edited by Mary Romero, Valerie Preston, and Wenona Giles, 203–26. New York: Routledge.

Creese, Gillian. 2011. *The New African Diaspora in Vancouver: Migration, Exclusion, and Belonging.* Toronto: University of Toronto Press.

Creese, Gillian, and Edith N. Kambere. 2003. "What Colour Is Your English?" *Canadian Review of Sociology/Revue canadienne de sociologie* 40 (5): 565–73.

Cresswell, Tim. 2010. "Towards a Politics of Mobility." *Environment and Planning D: Society and Space* 28:17–31.

Crosby, Emily. 2014. "Faux Feminism: France's Veil Ban as Orientalism." *International Women's Studies* 15 (2): 46–60.

Crouch, David, and Luke Desforges. 2003. "The Sensuous in the Tourist Encounter." *Tourist Studies* 3 (1): 5–22.

D'Addario, Silvia. 2012. "Finding Home: Geographical Links Between Paid and Unpaid Work for Transnational Care Workers in Toronto's Suburbs." PhD diss., York University.

Bibliography

Darling, Jonathon, and Helen F. Wilson, eds. 2016. *Encountering the City: Urban Encounters from Accra to New York*. London and New York: Routledge.

Das Gupta, Tania. 2009. *Real Nurses and Others, Racism in Nursing*. Black Point, Nova Scotia: Fernwood.

Datta, Kavita, Cathy McIlwaine, Joanna Herbert, Yara Evans, Jon May, and Jane Wills. 2012. "Global Workers for Global Cities: Low Paid Migrant Labour in London." In *International Handbook of Globalization and World Cities*, edited by Ben Derudder, Michael Hoyler, Peter J. Taylor, and Frank Whitlox, 390–97. Cheltenham, U.K.: Edward Elgar.

Davidson, Mark. 2010. "Love Thy Neighbour: Social Mixing in London's Gentrification Frontiers." *Environment and Planning A* 42 (3): 524–44.

Davidson, Mark, and Kurt Iveson. 2014. "Occupations, Mediations, Subjectifications: Fabricating Politics." *Space and Polity* 18 (2): 137–52.

Davidson, Mark, and Kurt Iveson. 2015. "Recovering the Politics of the City: From the 'Post-Political City' to a 'Method of Equality' for Critical Urban Geography." *Progress in Human Geography* 39 (5): 543–59.

Davison, Aidan. 2016. "Secure in the Privacy of Your Own Nature: Political Ecology, Urban Nature and Home Ownership in Australia." In *Housing and Home Unbound*, edited by Nicole Cook, Aidan Davison, and Louise Crabtree, 99–115. London: Routledge.

Davison, Graeme. 2009. "Carlton and the Campus: The University and Gentrification of Inner Melbourne 1958–75." *Urban Policy and Research* 27 (3): 253–64.

Dechief, Diane, and Philip Oreopoulos. 2012. *Why Do Some Employers Prefer to Interview Matthew But Not Samir? New Evidence from Toronto, Montreal and Vancouver*. Social Science Research Network (SSRN) e-Library: Elsevier. http://dx.doi.org/10.2139/ssrn.2018047.

Derouin, Jodey M. 2004. "Asians and Multiculturalism in Canada's Three Major Cities." *Diverse* 1:58–62.

DeVerteuil, Geoffrey. 2017. "Post-Welfare City at the Margins: Immigrant Precarity and the Mediating Third Sector in London." *Urban Geography* 38 (10): 1–17.

Dickson, Andonea. 2015. "Distancing Asylum Seekers from the State: Australia's Evolving Political Geography of Immigration and Border Control." *Australian Geographer* 46 (4): 437–54.

Dunn, Kevin M., and James Forrest. 2007. "Constructing Racism in Sydney, Australia's Largest EthniCity." *Urban Studies* 44 (4): 699–721.

Dunn, Kevin M., Bronwyn Hanna, and Susan Thompson. 2001. "The Local Politics of Difference: An Examination of Intercommunal Relations Policy in Australian Local Government." *Environment and Planning A* 33 (9): 1577–95.

Dunn, Kevin M., Therese E. Kenna, and Ian Burnley. 2007. "A Holistic Approach to Studying Segregation in Australian Cities." Papers of the 2007 State of Australian Cities conference, Adelaide. Available at: http://pandora.nia.gov.au/tep/40669.

Edgar, Barbara. 2014. "An Intergenerational Model of Spatial Assimilation in Sydney and Melbourne, Australia." *Journal of Ethnic and Migration Studies* 40 (3): 363–83.

Ehrenreich, Barbara. 2003. "Overcoming in Texas." *LA Weekly*, October 3, 2003, 19.

Eley, Geoffrey. 1993. "Nations, Publics, and Political Cultures: Placing Habermas in the Nineteenth Century." In *Habermas and the Public Sphere*, edited by Craig Calhoun, 289–339. Cambridge, Mass.: MIT Press.

Ellis, Mark, Richard Wright, and Virginia Parks. 2004. "Work Together, Live Apart? Geographies of Racial and Ethnic Segregation at Home and at Work." *Annals of the Association of American Geographers* 94 (3): 620–37.

Estlund, Cynthia. 2003. *Working Together: How Workplace Bonds Strengthen a Diverse Democracy*. Oxford: Oxford University Press.

Falzon, Mark-Anthony. 2009. *Multi-Sited Ethnography: Theory, Praxis and Locality in Contemporary Social Research*. Farnham, U.K.: Ashgate Publishing.

Falzon, Mark-Anthony. 2016. *Multi-Sited Ethnography: Theory, Praxis and Locality in Contemporary Social Research*. New York: Routledge.

Fincher, Ruth. 2011. "Cosmopolitan or Ethnically Identified Selves? Institutional Expectations and the Negotiated Identities of International Students." *Social & Cultural Geography* 12 (8): 905–27.

Fincher, Ruth, Paul Carter, Paolo Tombesi, Kate Shaw, and Andrew Martel. 2009. *Transnational and Temporary: Students, Community and Place-Making in Central Melbourne*. Final Report. University of Melbourne.

Fincher, Ruth, and Kurt Iveson. 2008. *Planning and Diversity in the City: Redistribution, Recognition and Encounter*. Basingstoke, U.K.: Palgrave Macmillan.

Fincher, Ruth, Kurt Iveson, Helga Leitner, and Valerie Preston. 2014. "Planning in the Multicultural City: Celebrating Diversity or Reinforcing Difference?" *Progress in Planning* 92:1–55.

Fincher, Ruth, and Kate Shaw. 2009. "The Unintended Segregation of Transnational Students in Central Melbourne." *Environment and Planning A* 41:1884–902.

Fincher, Ruth, and Kate Shaw. 2011. "Enacting Separate Social Worlds:

Bibliography

'International' and 'Local' Students in Public Space in Central Melbourne." *Geoforum* 42: 539–49.

Fine, Janice. 2006. *Worker Centers: Organizing Communities at the Edge of the Dream.* Ithaca, N.Y.: Cornell University Press.

Fine, Janice. 2007. "A Marriage Made in Heaven? Mismatches and Misunderstandings between Worker Centres and Unions." *British Journal of Industrial Relations* 45 (2): 335–60.

Fine, Janice. 2016. *Protecting the Immigrant Workers: New Strategies for Strengthening Labor Standards Enforcement.* Los Angeles: Institute for Research on Labor and Employment and UCLA (January 29, 2016).

Fish, Jennifer. 2014. "Organizing through State Transitions and Global Institutions: Crafting Domestic Labour Policy in South Africa." In Romero et al. 2014, 233–56.

Fleras, Augie. 2014. *Racisms in a Multicultural Canada: Paradoxes, Politics and Resistance.* Kitchener, Ontario: Wilfred Laurier University Press.

Forrest, James, and Kevin Dunn. 2010. "Attitudes to Multicultural Values in Diverse Spaces in Australia's Immigrant Cities, Sydney and Melbourne." *Space and Polity* 14 (1): 81–102.

Forrest, James, Michael Poulsen, and Ron Johnston. 2006. "A 'Multicultural Model' of the Spatial Assimilation of Ethnic Minority Groups in Australia's Major Immigrant-Receiving Cities." *Urban Geography* 27 (5): 441–63.

Fortier, Anne-Marie. 2000. *Migrant Belongings: Memory, Space, Identity.* Oxford: Berg.

Fraser, James, James De Filippis, and Joshua Bazuin. 2012. "Fourteen Hope VI: Calling for Modesty in Its Claims." In *Mixed Communities: Gentrification by Stealth?*, edited by Gary Bridge, Tim Butler, and Loretta Lees, 209–30. Bristol: Policy Press.

Fraser, Nancy. 1990. "Rethinking the Public Sphere: A Contribution to the Critique of Actually Existing Democracy." *Social Text* 25/26:56–80.

Fraser, Nancy. 1997a. *Justice Interruptus: Critical Reflections on the "Postsocialist" Condition.* New York: Routledge.

Fraser, Nancy. 1997b. "A Rejoinder to Iris Young." *New Left Review* 223:126–30.

Fraser, Nancy. 2008. *Scales of Justice: Reimagining Political Space in a Globalizing World.* Cambridge, U.K.: Polity Press.

Fuatai, Teuila. 2016. "Renaissance Hotel Workers' Inspired Fight for Right to Unionize." *Rabble,* July 29, 2016.

García, Robert, and Thomas A. Rubin. 2004. "Crossroad Blues: The MTA Consent Decree and Just Transportation." In *Running on Empty:*

Transport, Social Exclusion and Environmental Justice, edited by Karen Lucas, 221–56. Chicago: University of Chicago Press.

Gilroy, Paul. 2004. *After Empire: Melancholia or Convivial Culture?* London: Routledge.

Gilroy, Paul. 2005. "Multiculture, Double Consciousness and the 'War on Terror.'" *Patterns of Prejudice* 39 (4): 431–43.

Goffman, Erving. 1961. *Encounters: Two Studies in the Sociology of Interaction.* Indianapolis: Bobbs-Merrill.

Gow, Greg. 2005. "Rubbing Shoulders in the Global City: Refugees, Citizenship and Multicultural Alliances in Fairfield, Sydney." *Ethnicities* 5 (3): 386–405.

Graham, Steve, and Colin McFarlane. 2015. "Introduction." In *Infrastructural Lives: Urban Infrastructure in Context*, edited by Steve Graham and Colin McFarlane, 1–14. New York: Routledge.

Grosz, Elizabeth. 2004. *The Nick of Time.* Sydney: Allen & Unwin.

Hage, Ghassan. 1998. *White Nation: Fantasies of White Supremacy in a Multicultural Society.* Annandale, New South Wales: Pluto Press.

Hage, Ghassan. 2016. "Recalling Anti-Racism." *Ethnic and Racial Studies* 39 (1): 123–33.

Hall, Stuart. 2000. "The Multicultural Question." Political Economy Research Centre Annual Lecture, Firth Hall, Sheffield. http://red.pucp.edu.pe/wp-content/uploads/biblioteca/Stuart_Hall_The_multicultural_question.pdf.

Hall, Stuart. 2007. "Living with Difference: Stuart Hall in Conversation with Bill Schwarz." *Soundings* 37: 148–57.

Hall, Stuart. 2009. "Personally Speaking: A Long Conversation with Stuart Hall." Interview by Maya Jaggi. Northampton, Mass.: Media Education Foundation. http://www.mediaed.org/transcripts/Stuart-Hall-Personally-Speaking-Transcript.pdf.

Harris, Catherine, and Gill Valentine. 2016. "Encountering Difference in the Workplace: Superficial Contact, Underlying Tensions and Group Rights." *Tijdschrift voor economische en sociale geografie* 107 (5): 582–95.

Heckman, James J., and Tim Kautz. 2012. "Hard Evidence on Soft Skills." *Labour Economics* 19 (4): 451–64.

Henry, Frances, Tim Rees, and Carol Tator. 2010. *The Colour of Democracy: Racism in Canadian Society.* Toronto: Nelson Education.

Hermer, Joe, and Alan Hunt. 1996. "Official Graffiti of the Everyday." *Law and Society Review* 30 (3): 455–80.

Hewstone, Miles. 2003. "Intergroup Contact: Panacea for Prejudice?" *The Psychologist* 16:352–55.

Hinz, Bronwyn. 2010. "Ethnic Associations, Networks and the Construc-

Bibliography

tion of Australian Multiculturalism." Refereed paper presented at the Canadian Political Science Association Annual Conference, Montreal, June 2010.

Holmes, Natalie, and Alan Berube. 2016. *City and Metropolitan Inequality on the Rise, Driven by Declining Incomes.* Washington, D.C.: Brookings Institute. http://www.brookings.edu/research/papers/2016/01/14-income-inequality-cities-update-berube-holmes.

Howe, Renate. 2009. "New Residents, New City: The Role of Urban Activists in the Transformation of Inner City Melbourne." *Urban Policy and Research* 27 (3): 243–51.

Hsiung, Ping-Chun, and Katherine Nichol. 2010. "Policies on and Experiences of Foreign Domestic Workers in Canada." *Sociology Compass* 4 (9): 766–78.

Hugill, David. 2017. "What Is a Settler Colonial City?" *Geography Compass* 11 (5): 1–11.

ICE (United States Immigration and Customs Enforcement). 2018. https://www.ice.gov/.

Ilcan, Suzan, and Tanya Basok. 2004. "Community Government: Voluntary Agencies, Social Justice, and the Responsibilization of Citizens." *Citizenship Studies* 8 (2): 129–44.

Immigrant Workers Freedom Ride (IWFR). 2003. "Goals of the Freedom Ride." Internal document in possession of authors.

International Labour Organization. 2015. *ILO Global Estimates of Migrant Workers and Migrant Domestic Workers: Results and Methodology.* Geneva: International Labour Organization. http://www.ilo.org/wcmsp5/groups/public/—-dgreports/-dcomm/documents/publication/wcms_436343.pdf.

Iveson, Kurt. 2007. *Publics and the City.* Oxford: Blackwell.

Iveson, Kurt. 2017. "'Making Space Public' through Occupation: The Aboriginal Tent Embassy, Canberra." *Environment and Planning A: Economy and Space* 49 (3): 537–54.

Iveson, Kurt, and Ruth Fincher. 2014. "The Public City and Diversity: Rethinking the 'Public Interest.'" In *The Public City: Essays in Honour of Paul Mees*, edited by Brendan Gleeson and Beau B. Beza, 42–53. Carlton: University of Melbourne Press.

Jacobs, Jane. 1961. *The Death and Life of Great American Cities.* New York: Random House.

Jacobs, Jane M. 2012. "Urban Geographies I: Still Thinking Cities Relationally." *Progress in Human Geography* 36 (3): 412–22.

Jacobs, Jane M., and Susan Smith. 2008. "Living Room: Rematerializing Home." *Environment and Planning A* 40 (3): 515–19.

Jarzabkowski, Paula, Rebecca Bednarek, and Laura Cabantous. 2014.

"Conducting Global Team-Based Ethnography: Methodological Challenges and Practical Methods." *Human Relations* 68 (1): 3–33.

Jupp, James. 2002. *From White Australia to Woomera: The Story of Australian Immigration.* Cambridge, U.K.: Cambridge University Press.

Jureidini, Ray. 2014. "The Use and Abuse of Domestic Workers: Case Studies in Lebanon and Egypt." In *When Care Work Goes Global: Locating the Social Relations of Domestic Work,* edited by Mary Romero, Valerie Preston, and Wenona Giles, 95–116. New York: Routledge.

Kainer, Jan. 2002. *Cashing In on Pay Equity? Supermarket Restructuring and Gender Equality.* Toronto: Sumach Press.

Keung, Nicholas. 2015. "Toronto Police Urged to Stop Immigration 'Status Checks.'" *Toronto Star,* November 24. https://www.thestar.com/news/ investigations/2015/11/24/toronto-police-urged-to-stop-immigration -status-checks.html.

Khan, Rimi. 2014. "New Communities, New Attachments: Planning for Diversity in Melbourne's Outer Suburbs." *Journal of Intercultural Studies* 35 (3): 295–309.

Kobayashi, Audrey, and Valerie Preston. 2015. "International Migration and Immigration: Remaking the Multicultural Canadian City." In *Canadian Cities in Transition, Fifth Edition, Perspectives for an Urban Age,* edited by Pierre Filion, Markus Moo, Tara Vinoodrai, and Ryan Walker, 129–50. Toronto: Oxford University Press Canada.

Kokkonen, Andrej, Peter Esaiasson, and Mikael Gilljam. 2015. "Diverse Workplaces and Interethnic Friendship Formation: A Multilevel Comparison Across 21 OECD Countries." *Journal of Ethnic and Migration Studies* 41 (2): 284–305.

Koopmans, Ruud. 2013. "Multiculturalism and Immigration: A Contested Field in Cross-National Comparison." *Annual Review of Sociology* 39:147–69.

Kopun, Francine. 2015. "Behind the Doors of Room 1509." *Toronto Star,* May 1, 2015.

Kun, Josh, and Laura Pulido, eds. 2014. *Black and Brown in Los Angeles: Beyond Conflict and Cooperation.* Berkeley: University of California Press.

Lawson, Victoria. 2007. "Geographies of Care and Responsibility." *Annals of the Association of American Geographers* 97 (1): 1–11.

Lefebvre, Henri. (1991) 2001. *The Critique of Everyday Life.* London: Verso.

Leitner, Helga. 2012. "Spaces of Encounters: Immigration, Race, Class, and the Politics of Belonging in Small-Town America." *Annals of the Association of American Geographers* 102 (4): 828–46.

Leitner, Helga, and Sam Nowak. 2018. "Making Multi-Racial Counterpublics: Towards Egalitarian Spaces in Urban Politics." In *The International Handbook on Spaces of Urban Politics*, edited by A. Jonas, B. Miller, K. Ward, and D. Wilson, 451–64. London: Routledge.

Leitner, Helga, and Valerie Preston. 2012. "Going Local: Canadian and American Immigration Policy in the New Century." In *Immigrant Geographies of North American Cities*, edited by Carlos Teixeira, Audrey Kobayashi, and Wei Li, 2–21. Toronto: Oxford University Press.

Leitner, Helga, and Eric Sheppard. 2016. Provincializing Critical Urban Theory: Extending the Ecosystem of Possibilities. *International Journal of Urban and Regional Research* 40 (1): 228–35.

Leitner, Helga, Eric S. Sheppard, and Kristin Sziarto. 2008. "The Spatialities of Contentious Politics." *Transactions of the Institute of British Geographers*, n.s., 33 (2): 157–72.

Lentin, Alana. 2016. "Racism in Public or Public Racism: Doing Anti-Racism in 'Post-Racial' Times." *Ethnic and Racial Studies* 39 (1): 33–48.

Leslie, Deborah, and David Butz. 1998. "'GM Suicide': Flexibility, Space, and the Injured Body." *Economic Geography* 74 (4): 360–78.

Leslie, Deborah, and John Paul Catungal. 2012. "Social Justice and the Creative City: Class, Gender and Racial Inequalities." *Geography Compass* 6 (3): 111–22.

Levin, Iris. 2010. "Migrants' Houses: The Importance of Housing Form in Migrants' Settlement." PhD diss., University of Melbourne.

Levin, Iris. 2016. *Migration, Settlement, and the Concepts of House and Home*. New York: Routledge.

Lobo, Michele. 2009. *Reimagining Citizenship in Suburban Australia*. Cologne: Lambert Academic Publishing.

Lobo, Michele. 2014. "Everyday Multiculturalism: Catching the Bus in Darwin, Australia." *Social and Cultural Geography* 15 (7): 714–29.

Los Angeles Almanac (website). n.d. "'Sanctuary' Cities in Los Angeles County." Accessed January 10, 2016. http://www.laalmanac.com/immigration/imo4c.php.

Los Angeles Times. 2008. "Mapping LA Neighborhoods." http://maps.latimes.com/neighborhoods.

Manaugh, Kevin, Madhav G. Badami, and Ahmed M. El-Geneidy. 2015. "Integrating Social Equity into Urban Transportation Planning: A Critical Evaluation of Equity Objectives and Measures in Transportation Plans in North America." *Transport Policy* 37 (1): 167–76.

Marotta, Vince P. 2011. "Home, Mobility and the Encounter with Otherness." In *Migration, Citizenship and Intercultural Relations*, edited by F. Mansouri and M. Lobo, 193–208. Farnham, U.K.: Ashgate.

Massey, Doreen. 2005. *For Space*. London: Sage Publications.

Matjeskova, Tatiana, and Helga Leitner. 2011. "Urban Encounters with Difference: The Contact Hypothesis and Immigrant Integration Projects in Berlin." *Social & Cultural Geography* 12 (7): 717–41.

McCosker, Anthony, and Amelia Johns. 2014. "Contested Publics: Racist Rants, Bystander Action and Social Media Acts of Citizenship." *Media Australia International* 151:66–72.

McDowell, Linda. 2011. *Capital Culture: Gender at Work in the City.* Hoboken, N.J.: John Wiley.

McDowell, Linda, Adina Batnitzky, and Sarah Dyer. 2007. "Division, Segmentation, and Interpellation: The Embodied Labors of Migrant Workers in a Greater London Hotel." *Economic Geography* 83 (1): 1–25.

McFarlane, Colin. 2011. *Learning the City: Knowledge and Translocal Assemblage.* Oxford: Wiley-Blackwell.

McFarlane, Colin. 2016. "The Geographies of Urban Density: Topology, Politics and the City." *Progress in Human Geography* 40 (5): 629–48.

McLaren, Lauren M. 2003. "Anti-Immigrant Prejudice in Europe: Contact, Threat Perception, and Preferences for the Exclusion of Immigrants." *Social Forces* 81:909–36.

Meintel, Deirdre, Sylvie Fortin, and Madeleine Cognet. 2014. "On the Road and on Their Own: Autonomy and Giving in Home Health Care in Quebec." In *When Care Work Goes Global: Locating the Social Relations of Domestic Work,* edited by Mary Romero, Valerie Preston, and Wenona Giles, 159–76. New York: Routledge.

Merrifield, Andy. 2013. *The Politics of the Encounter: Urban Theory and Protest Under Planetary Urbanization.* Athens: University of Georgia Press.

Milkman, Ruth. 2000. "Introduction." In *Organizing Immigrants: The Challenge for Unions in Contemporary California,* edited by Ruth Milkman, 1–24. Ithaca, N.Y.: ILR Press.

Milkman, Ruth. 2006. *L.A. Story: Immigrant Workers and the Future of the U.S. Labor Movement.* New York: Sage.

Milkman, Ruth, Ana Luz González, Victor Narro, Annette Bernhardt, Nik Theodore, Douglas Heckathorn, Mirabai Auer, James DeFilippis, Jason Perelshteyn, Diana Polson, and Michael Spiller. 2010. *Wage Theft and Workplace Violations in Los Angeles: The Failure of Employment and Labor Law for Low-Wage Workers.* Los Angeles: UCLA Institute for Research on Labor and Employment. https://escholarship.org/uc/item/5jt7n9gx.

Mitchell, Don. 2016. "The Liberalization of Free Speech: Or, How Protest in Public Space Is Silenced." In *Spaces of Contention—Spatialities and*

Social Movements, edited by W. Nicholls, B. Miller, and J. Beaumont, 47–68. London: Routledge.

Mitchell, Kathryne. 2001. "Transnationalism, Neo-Liberalism, and the Rise of the Shadow State." *Economy and Society* 30 (2): 165–89.

Mojtehedzadeh, Sara. 2015. "New Workforce Training Program Doesn't Just Provide Jobs, It Builds Careers." *Toronto Star*, March 27, 2015.

Molotch, Harvey. 2012. *Against Security: How We Go Wrong at Airports, Subways, and Other Sites of Ambiguous Danger*. Princeton, N.J.: Princeton University Press.

Morihovitis, Kathy. 1998. "Ergonomics and Women's Work in the City of Toronto: A Case Study of Cashiers." MA thesis, York University.

Moss, Philip, and Chris Tilly. 1996. "'Soft' Skills and Race: An Investigation of Black Men's Employment Problems." *Work and Occupations* 23 (3): 252–76.

Murdie, Robert A. 2008. *Diversity and Concentration in Canadian Immigration: Trends in Toronto, Montréal and Vancouver, 1971–2006*. Toronto: Centre for Urban & Community Studies.

Murdolo, Adele. 2014. "Safe Homes for Immigrant and Refugee Women: Narrating Alternative Histories of the Women's Refuge Movement in Australia." *Frontiers: A Journal of Women's Studies* 35 (3): 126–53.

Nagel, Caroline R., and Lynn Staeheli. 2004. "Citizenship, Identity, and Transnational Migration: Arab Immigrants to the United States." *Space and Polity* 8 (1): 3–23.

Nagel, Caroline R., and Lynn Staeheli. 2008. "Integration and the Negotiation of 'Here' and 'There': The Case of British Arab Activists." *Social and Cultural Geography* 9 (4): 415–30.

Narro, Victor. 2005. "Impacting Next Wave Organizing: Creative Campaign Strategies of the Los Angeles Worker Centers." *New York Law School Review* 50:465–513.

Nash, Catherine. 2000. "Performativity in Practice: Some Recent Work in Cultural Geography." *Progress in Human Geography* 24 (4): 653–64.

Nayak, A. 2010. "Race, Affect, and Emotion: Young People, Racism and Graffiti in the Postcolonial English Suburb." *Environment and Planning A* 42:2370–92.

Naylor, Bronwyn. 2010. "L-Plates, Logbooks and Losing-Out: Regulating for Safety—Or Creating New Criminals?" *Alternative Law Journal* 35 (2): 94–98.

NCCS (National Center for Charitable Statistics). 2013. "Quick Facts about Non-Profits." http://nccs.urban.org/data-statistics/quick-facts -about-nonprofits.

Neal, Sarah, and Carol Vincent. 2013. "Multiculture, Middle Class

Competencies and Friendship Practices in Super-Diverse Geographies." *Social and Cultural Geography* 14 (8): 909–29.

New South Wales Bureau of Transport Statistics Household Travel Survey. 2014/15. https://www.transport.nsw.gov.au/data-and-research/passenger-travel/surveys/household-travel-survey-hts.

Nicholls, Walter 2003. "Forging a 'New' Organizational Infrastructure for Los Angeles' Progressive Community." *International Journal of Urban and Regional Research* 27 (4): 881–96.

Noble, Greg. 2009. "Everyday Cosmopolitanism and the Labour of Intercultural Community." In *Everyday Multiculturalism*, edited by Amanda Wise and Selvaraj Velayutham, 46–65. Basingstoke, U.K.: Palgrave Macmillan.

Noble, Greg, ed. 2009. *Lines in the Sand: The Cronulla Riots, Multiculturalism and National Belonging*. Sydney: Institute of Criminology Press.

Noble, Greg, and Scott Poynting. 2010. "White Lines: The Intercultural Politics of Everyday Movement in Social Spaces." *Journal of Intercultural Studies* 31 (5): 489–505.

Norcliffe, Glen, and Olivero Rendace. 2003. "New Geographies of Comic Book Production in North America: The New Artisan, Distancing, and the Periodic Social Economy." *Economic Geography* 79 (3): 241–63.

Ocejo, Richard E., and Stéphane Tonnelat. 2014. "Subway Diaries: How People Experience and Practice Riding the Train." *Ethnography* 15 (4): 493–515.

Ontario Ministry of Citizenship and Immigration. 2016. *A Career Map for Internationally Educated Engineers*. August, 2016. http://www.ontarioimmigration.ca/prodconsum/groups/csc/@oipp/documents/document/oi_en_eng_cm.pdf.

Parks, Virginia, and Dorian T. Warren. 2012. "Contesting the Racial Division of Labor from Below." *Du Bois Review* 9 (2): 395.

Pasadena Community Job Center. 2016. *Internal Rules*. Pasadena, Calif.

Peavy, Fran. 1996. *Heart Politics*. Montreal: Black Rose Books.

Peck, Jamie. 2009. "Neoliberal Hurricane: Who Framed New Orleans?" *Socialist Register* 43:102–9.

Peck, Jamie, and Adam Tickell. 2002. "Neoliberalizing Space." *Antipode* 34 (3): 380–404.

Pendakur, Krishna, and Ravi Pendakur. 2015. "The Colour of Money Redux: Immigrant/Ethnic Earnings Disparity in Canada 1991–2006." In *The Housing and Economic Experiences of Immigrants in US and Canadian Cities*, edited by C. Teixeira and W. Li, 227–60. Toronto: University of Toronto Press.

Pettigrew, Thomas. F., and Linda R. Tropp. 2000. "Does Inter-Group Contact Reduce Prejudice: Recent Meta-Analytic Findings." In *Reducing*

Prejudice and Discrimination: The Claremont Symposium on Applied Social Psychology, edited by Stuart Oskamp, 93–114. Mahwah, N.J.: Erlbaum.

Poynting, Scott, Greg Noble, Paul Tabar, and Jock Collins. 2004. *Bin Laden in the Suburbs: Criminalising the Arab Other*. Sydney: Institute of Criminology.

Pratt, Geraldine. 2004. *Working Feminism*. Philadelphia: Temple University Press.

Pred, Alan. 2000. *Even in Sweden: Racism, Racialized Spaces, and the Popular Geographical Imagination*. Berkeley: University of California Press.

Pulido, Laura. 2006. *Black, Brown, Yellow, and Left: Radical Activism in Los Angeles*. Berkeley: University of California Press.

Pulido, Laura, L. Barraclough, and W. Cheng. 2012. *A People's Guide to Los Angeles*. Berkeley: University of California Press.

Pulvirenti, Mariastella. 1996. "Casa Mia: Home Ownership, Identity and Post-War Italian Migration." PhD diss., University of Melbourne.

Purcell, Mark. 2014. "Rancière and Revolution." *Space and Polity* 18 (2): 168–81.

Rancière, Jacques. 1999. *Disagreement: Politics and Philosophy*. Minneapolis: University of Minnesota Press.

Rancière, Jacques. 2006. *Hatred of Democracy*. London: Verso.

Rancière, Jacques. 2009. "Afterword: The Method of Equality, An Answer to Some Questions." In *Jacques Rancière: History, Politics, Aesthetics*, edited by Gabriel Rockhill and Philip Watts, 273–88. Durham, N.C.: Duke University Press.

Rancière, Jacques. 2016. *The Method of Equality: Interviews with Laurent Jeanpierre and Dork Zabunyan*. London: Policy.

Randolph, Bill, and Robert Freestone. 2012. "Housing Differentiation and Renewal in Middle-Ring Suburbs: The Experience of Sydney, Australia." *Urban Studies* 49 (12): 2557–75.

Ray, Brian, and Valerie Preston. 2014. "Working with Diversity: A Geographical Analysis of Ethno-Racial Discrimination in Toronto." *Urban Studies* 52 (8): 1505–22.

Ray, Brian, and Valerie Preston. 2015. "Altérité, inconfort et discrimination: le multiculturalisme au quotidian et les lieux de travail à Toronto." In *Travailler et Cohabiter, L'Immigration au-delà de l'Intégration*, edited by Sébastien Arcand and Annick Germain, 195–226. Quebec City: Presses de l'Université Laval.

Reid-Musson, Emily. 2017. "Grown Close to Home™: Migrant Farmworker (Im)mobilities and Unfreedom on Canadian Family Farms." *Annals of the American Association of Geographers* 107 (3): 716–30.

Roberts, David J., and Minelle Mahtani. 2010. "Neoliberalizing Race,

Racing Neoliberalism: Placing 'Race' in Neoliberal Discourses." *Antipode* 42 (2): 248–57.

Robinson, Jennifer. 2006. *Ordinary Cities: Between Modernity and Development*. London: Routledge.

Robinson, Jennifer. 2013. "The Urban Now: Theorising Cities Beyond the New." *European Journal of Cultural Studies* 16:659–77.

Rogers, Dallas. 2016. "Uploading Real Estate: Home as a Digital, Global Commodity." In *Housing and Home Unbound*, edited by Nicole Cook, Aidan Davison, and Louise Crabtree, 23–28. London: Routledge.

Romero, Mary. 2011. *The Maid's Daughter: Living Inside and Outside the American Dream*. New York: NYU Press.

Romero, Mary, Valerie Preston, and Wenona Giles, eds. 2014. *When Care Work Goes Global: Locating the Social Relations of Domestic Work*. New York: Routledge.

Rosenbaum, Susanna. 2014. "Domestic Disturbances: Immigrant Workers, Middle Class Employers and the American Dream." In *When Care Work Goes Global: Locating the Social Relations of Domestic Work*, edited by Mary Romero, Valerie Preston, and Wenona Giles, 129–38. New York: Routledge.

Roy, Ananya. 2009. "The 21st-Century Metropolis: New Geographies of Theory." *Regional Studies* 43 (6): 819–30.

Salamon, Lester M. 1995. *Partners in Public Service: Government-Nonprofit Relations in the Modern Welfare State*. Baltimore: Johns Hopkins University Press.

Sandercock, Leonie. 1998. *Towards Cosmopolis*. Chichester, U.K.: John Wiley & Sons.

Sandercock, Leonie. 2003. *Cosmopolis II: Mongrel Cities in the 21st Century*. London: Continuum.

Sandercock, Leonie, and Giovanni Attili. 2009. *Where Strangers Become Neighbours: Integrating Immigrants in Vancouver, Canada*. London: Springer.

Savage, Lydia. 1998. "Justice for Janitors: Geographies of Organizing." In *Organizing the Landscape: Geographical Perspectives on Labor Unionism*, edited by Andrew Herod, 225–52. Minneapolis: University of Minnesota Press.

Savage, Lydia. 2006. "Justice for Janitors: Scales of Organizing and Representing Workers." *Antipode* 38 (3): 645–66.

Seager, Joni. 2006. "Noticing Gender (or Not) in Disasters." *Geoforum* 37 (1): 2–3.

Sennett, Richard. 1994. *Flesh and Stone: The Body and the City in Western Civilization*. London: Faber and Faber.

Shaw, Kate. 2012. "Beware the Trojan Horse: Social Mix Constructions in

Melbourne." In *Mixed Communities: Gentrification by Stealth?*, edited by Gary Bridge, Tim Butler, and Loretta Lees, 133–48. Bristol: Policy Press.

Sheppard, Eric, Helga Leitner, and Anant Maringanti. 2013. "Provincializing Global Urbanism: A Manifesto." *Urban Geography* 34 (7): 893–900.

Sherman, Rachel, and Kim Voss. 2000. "'Organize or Die': Labor's New Tactics and Immigrant Workers." In *Organizing Immigrants: The Challenge for Unions in Contemporary California*, edited by Ruth Milkman, 81–108. Ithaca, N.Y.: ILR Press.

Sidhu, Jasmeet. 2010. "Martin Sheen Joins Hotel Workers on Royal York Hotel Picket Line." *Toronto Star*, September 10, 2010.

Simmel, Georg. 1903. "The Metropolis and Mental Life." In *The Sociology of Georg Simmel*, translated and edited by Kurt H. Wulff. New York: Free Press.

Simone, AbdouMaliq. 2006. "Pirate Towns: Reworking Social and Symbolic Infrastructures in Johannesburg and Douala." *Urban Studies* 43 (2): 357–70.

Smith, Helena. 2016. "The Idealists of Lesbos: Volunteers at the Heart of the Refugee Crisis." *Guardian*, April 15, 2016. https://www.theguardian.com/world/2016/apr/15/idealists-of-lesbos-volunteers-refugee-crisis-pope-francis.

Smith, Susan. 2008. "Owner-Occupation: At Home with a Hybrid of Money and Materials." *Environment and Planning A* 40 (3): 520–35.

Snelgrove, Corey, Rita Kaur Dhamoom, and Jeff Corntassel. 2014. "Unsettling Settler Colonialism: The Discourse and Politics of Settlers, and Solidarity with Indigenous Nations." *Decolonization: Indigeneity, Education and Society* 3 (2): 1–32.

Soja, Edward W. 2000. *Postmetropolis: Critical Studies of Cities and Regions.* Oxford: Blackwell Publishing.

Soja, Edward W. 2010. *Seeking Spatial Justice.* Minneapolis: University of Minnesota Press.

Song, Miri. 2014. "Challenging a Culture of Racial Equivalence." *British Journal of Sociology* 65 (1): 107–29.

Soss, Joe, Richard C. Fording, and Sanford Schram. 2011. *Disciplining the Poor: Neoliberal Paternalism and the Persistent Power of Race.* Chicago: University of Chicago Press.

Sparks, Holloway. 2016. "Quarreling with Rancière: Race, Gender, and the Politics of Democratic Disruption." *Philosophy and Rhetoric* 49 (4): 420–37.

Spearritt, Peter. 1999. *Sydney's Century: A History.* Sydney: UNSW Press.

Staeheli, Lynn A., Patricia Ehrkamp, Helga Leitner, and Caroline R. Nagel. 2012. "Dreaming the Ordinary: Daily Life and the Complex

Geographies of Citizenship." *Progress in Human Geography* 36 (5): 628–44.

Stasiulis, Daiva, and Abigail Bakan. 2005. *Negotiating Citizenship: Migrant Women in Canada and the Global System.* Toronto: University of Toronto Press.

Statistics Canada. 2003. *Ethnic Diversity Survey: Portrait of a Multicultural Society.* Ottawa: Statistics Canada, Ministry of Industry. http://www.statcan.gc.ca/pub/89-593-x/89-593-x2003001-eng.pdf.

Statistics Canada. 2013. *Immigration and Ethnocultural Diversity in Canada.* Ottawa: Statistics Canada, Ministry of Industry. http://www12.statcan.gc.ca/nhs-enm/2011/as-sa/99-010-x/99-010-x2011001-eng.p.

Statistics Canada. 2015. "The Underground Economy in Canada, 2012." *The Daily*, April 29, 2015, 1–3.

Statistics Canada. 2017a. *Census Metropolitan Area (CMA) and Census Agglomeration (CA).* Statistics Canada catalogue no. 92-195-x. Released November 15, 2017. ww150.statcan.gc.ca/n1/pub/92-195-x/2016001/geo/cma-rmr/cma-rmr-eng.htm.

Statistics Canada. 2017b. *Census of Population.* Statistics Canada catalogue no. 98-400-X2016210. Released October 25, 2017. https://www150.statcan.gc.ca/n1/en/catalogue/98-400-X2016210.

Statistics Canada. 2017c. *Toronto Census Metropolitan Area, Census Profile, 2016 Census.* Statistics Canada catalogue no. 98-316-X2016001. Released November 29, 2017. http://www12.statcan.gc.ca/census-recensement/2016/dp-pd/prof/index.cfm?Lang=E.

Sundari, Anitha, Ruth Pearson, and Linda McDowell. 2012. "Striking Lives: Multiple Narratives of South Asian Women's Employment, Identity and Protest in the UK." *Ethnicities* 12 (6): 754–75.

Supski, Sian. 2006. "'It Was Another Skin': The Kitchen as Home for Australian Post-War Immigrant Women." *Gender, Place and Culture* 13 (2): 133–41.

Sziarto, Kristin, and Helga Leitner. 2010. "Immigrants Riding for Justice: Space-time and Emotions in the Construction of a Counter Public." *Political Geography* 29 (7): 381–91.

Tattersall, Amanda. 2015. "The Global Spread of Community Organizing: How 'Alinsky-Style' Community Organizing Travelled to Australia and What We Learnt." *Community Development Journal* 50 (3): 380–96.

Terzi, Cédric, and Stéphane Tonnelat. 2017. "The Publicization of Public Space." *Environment and Planning A* 49 (3): 519–36.

Theodore, Nik. 2015. "Generative Work: Day Labourers' Freirean Praxis." *Urban Studies* 52 (11): 2035–50.

Theodore, Nik. 2016. "Worlds of Work: Changing Landscapes of Production and the New Geographies of Opportunity." *Geography Compass* 10 (4): 179–89.

Thomas, Ward F., and Paul M. Ong. 2006. "Race and Space: Hiring Practices of Los Angeles Electronics Firms." *Journal of Urban Affairs* 28 (5): 511–26.

Thompson, Susan. 2003. "Planning and Multiculturalism: A Reflection on Australian Local Practice." *Planning Theory & Practice* 4 (3): 275–93.

Toronto Foundation. 2016. "Toronto's Vital Signs, 2016 Report." Toronto: Toronto Foundation. http://torontosvitalsigns.ca/wp-content/uploads/2016/10/WEB-OP-TorontosVitalSignsReport2016FINAL.pdf.

Transport for New South Wales. 2011. *Connections: 2012–17 Corporate Plan*. Sydney: New South Wales Government.

Transport Workers' Union of New South Wales. 2014. "Building a Better Bus Industry." *TWU News* (Winter): 8–9.

Triandafyllidou, Anna, Tariq Modood, and Nasar Meer. 2012. *European Multiculturalisms: Cultural, Religious, and Ethnic Challenges*. Edinburgh: Edinburgh University Press.

Tronto, Joan. 1994. *Moral Boundaries: A Political Argument for an Ethic of Care*. New York: Routledge.

Tronto, Joan. 2003. "Time's Place." *Feminist Theory* 4 (2): 119–38.

Tronto, Joan. 2013. *Caring Democracy: Markets, Equality, and Justice*. New York: New York University Press.

Troy, Laurence, and Kurt Iveson. 2014. "Featured Graphic: A Community-Led Critique of Accessibility of Sydney's Public Transport Network." *Environment and Planning A* 46: 2273–75.

Troy, Patrick N. 2012. *Accommodating Australians: Commonwealth Government Involvement in Housing*. Sydney: Federation Press.

Trudeau, Dan. 2008. "Towards a Relational View of the Shadow State." *Political Geography* 27 (6): 669–90.

Tufts, Steve. 2003. "A Contemporary Labour Geography of Hotel Workers in Toronto, Ontario, Canada." PhD diss., York University.

Tufts, Steve. 2006. "'We Make It Work': The Cultural Transformation of Hotel Workers in the City." *Antipode* 38 (2): 350–73.

Tungohan, Ethel, Rupa Banerjee, Wayne Chu, Petronila Cleto, Conely de Leon, Mila Garcia, Philip Kelly, Marco Luciano, Cynthia Palmaria, and Christopher Sorio. 2015. "After the Live-In Caregiver Program: Filipina Caregivers' Experiences of Graduated and Uneven Citizenship." *Canadian Ethnic Studies* 47 (1): 87–105.

United States Census Bureau. 2015. *Quick Facts Los Angeles County*. https://www.census.gov/quickfacts/table/PST045215/06037,00.

Urry, John. 2007. *Mobilities*. Cambridge, U.K.: Polity Press.

Valentine, Gill. 2008. "Living with Difference: Reflections on Geographies of Encounter." *Progress in Human Geography* 32 (3): 323–37.

Valentine, Gill, and Joanna Sadgrove. 2012. "Negotiating Difference through Everyday Encounters: The Case of Sexual Orientation and Religion and Belief." *Antipode* 44 (9): 474–92.

Vertovec, Steven, and Susanne Wessendorf. 2010. *The Multiculturalism Backlash: European Discourses, Policies and Practices.* London: Routledge.

Visser, M. Anne, Nik Theodore, Edwin J. Melendez, and Abel Valenzuela Jr. 2016. "From Economic Integration to Socioeconomic Inclusion: Day Labor Worker Centers as Social Intermediaries." *Urban Geography* 38 (2): 243–65.

Vosko, Leah F. 2010. *Managing the Margins: Gender, Citizenship, and the International Regulation of Precarious Employment.* Toronto: Oxford University Press.

Vosko, Leah F., Andrea M. Noack, and Mark P. Thomas. 2016. "How Far Does the Employment Standards Act, 2000, Extend and What Are the Gaps in Coverage? An Empirical Analysis of Archival and Statistical Data." https://cirhr.library.utoronto.ca/sites/cirhr.library.utoronto.ca/files/research-projects/Vosko.

Wacquant, Loic. 2008. *Urban Outcasts: A Comparative Sociology of Advanced Marginality.* Cambridge, U.K.: Polity Press.

Waldinger, Roger, Chris Erickson, Ruth Milkman, Daniel J. B. Mitchell, Abel Valenzuela, Kent Wong, and Maurice Zeitlin. 1996. *Helots No More: A Case Study of the Justice for Janitors Campaign in Los Angeles.* Lewis Center for Regional Policy Studies, Working Paper Series #15. http://escholarship.org/uc/item/15z8f64h#page-1.

Walks, R. Alan, Mihaela Dinca-Panaitescu, and Dylan Simone. 2016. "Income Inequality and Polarization in the City of Toronto and York Region." Research Paper 238. Toronto: University of Toronto, Neighbourhood Change Research Partnership. http://neighbourhoodchange.ca/documents/2016/05/walks-etal-2016-income-inequality-toronto-york-rp-238.pdf.

Warner, Michael. 2002. "Publics and Counterpublics." *Public Culture* 14 (1): 49–90.

Wasser, Judith Davidson, and Liora Bressler. 1996. "Working in the Interpretive Zone: Conceptualizing Collaboration in Qualitative Research Teams." *Educational Researcher* 25 (5): 5–15.

Wessel, Terje. 2009. "Does Diversity in Urban Space Enhance Intergroup Contact and Tolerance?" *Geografiska Annaler: Series B, Human Geography* 91 (1): 5–17.

Widener, Daniel. 2008. "Another City Is Possible: Interethnic Organizing in Contemporary Los Angeles." *Race/Ethnicity: Multidisciplinary Global Contexts* 1 (2): 189–219.

Williams, Raymond. 1989. *Resources of Hope: Culture, Democracy, Socialism*. London: Verso.

Wills, Jane, Kavita Datta, Yara Evans, Johanna Herbert, Jon May, and Cathy McIlwaine. 2010. *Global Cities at Work: New Migrant Divisions of Labour*. London: Pluto Press.

Wilson, Helen F. 2011. "Passing Propinquities in the Multicultural City: The Everyday Encounters of Bus Passengering." *Environment and Planning A* 43 (3): 634–49.

Wilson, Helen F. 2013. "Learning to Think Differently: Diversity Training and the 'Good Encounter.'" *Geoforum* 45 (1): 73–82.

Wilson, Helen F. 2017. "On Geography and Encounter: Bodies, Borders, and Difference." *Progress in Human Geography* 41 (4): 451–71.

Wilson, Helen F., and Jonathon Darling. 2016. "The Possibilities of Encounter." In *Encountering the City: Urban Encounters from Accra to New York*, edited by Helen F. Wilson and Jonathon Darling, 1–24. New York: Routledge.

Wirth, Louis. 1938. "Urbanism as a Way of Life." *American Journal of Sociology* 44 (1): 1–24.

Wise, Amanda. 2009. "Everyday Multiculturalism: Transversal Crossings and Working Class Cosmopolitans." In *Everyday Multiculturalism*, edited by Amanda Wise and Selvaraj Velayutham, 21–45. Basingstoke, U.K.: Palgrave Macmillan.

Wise, Amanda. 2010. "Sensuous Multiculturalism: Emotional Landscapes of Inter-Ethnic Living in Australian Suburbia." *Journal of Ethnic and Migration Studies* 36 (6): 917–37.

Wise, Amanda. 2016. "Becoming Cosmopolitan: Encountering Difference in a City of Mobile Labour." *Journal of Ethnic and Migration Studies* 42 (14): 2289–308.

Wise, Amanda, and Greg Noble. 2016. "Convivialities: An Orientation." *Journal of Intercultural Studies* 37 (5): 423–31.

Wise, Amanda, and Selvaraj Velayutham, eds. 2009. *Everyday Multiculturalism*. Basingstoke, U.K.: Palgrave Macmillan.

Wolch, Jennifer. 1990. *The Shadow State: Government and Voluntary Sector in Transition*. New York: Foundation Center.

Wright, Matthew, and Irene Bloemraad. 2012. "Is There a Trade-Off Between Multiculturalism and Socio-Political Integration? Policy Regimes and Immigrant Incorporation in Comparative Perspective." *Perspectives on Politics* 10 (1): 77–95.

Young, Iris Marion. 1990. *Justice and the Politics of Difference*. Princeton, N.J.: Princeton University Press.

Young, Iris Marion. 1997. "Unruly Categories: A Critique of Nancy Fraser's Dual Systems Theory." *New Left Review* 222: 147–60.

Young, Iris Marion. 2000. *Justice and the Politics of Difference.* Princeton, N.J.: Princeton University Press.

Youth Justice Coalition of NSW, Western Sydney Juvenile Justice Interest Group, and Youth Action and Policy Association of NSW, compiled by Adrian Pisarski. 1994. *Nobody Listens.* Sydney: Youth Justice Coalition of New South Wales.

Yuval-Davis, Nira. 1999. "What Is 'Transversal Politics?'" *Soundings* 12 (Summer): 94–98.

Index

abuse, 4, 96, 122, 138, 147, 160, 182, 213; racist, 5, 16, 133–34, 139, 152, 155–56, 209. *See also* racism

accessibility, 207; of communal spaces, 73, 77, 79–80, 90, 209, 219; employment, 104, 105, 146; housing, 56–57, 68; mobility infrastructures, 135, 218; public space, 45, 46; public transport, 15, 24, 63, 77, 125, 133, 134–36, 140, 143–44, 147–48, 159–68, 170, 212; of services, 146, 162–63, 180, 212, 220. *See also* atmospheres

activism, 6, 9, 38, 71, 179, 180, 191, 197, 199, 205; housing, 57, 63, 67, 72; multiracial publics through, 5, 16, 172–74, 189; talking/listening, 5, 70, 84, 113, 131–32, 165, 168, 171, 181–83, 185, 192–94, 218. *See also* campaigns; racism: documenting

African Americans, 28, 110, 175, 178–79, 180–81, 187, 196–97

African Australians, 67, 73

Against Wage Theft, 5, 195–98

agitation, 50, 51, 134, 173, 176, 194, 208

Ahmed, Sara, 22, 49, 58, 70, 213

Allport, Gordon, 35, 36, 98, 176, 200, 208

Amin, Ash, 20, 42, 50

antiracism, 20, 38; bystander, 158, 209; campaigns, 169, 181, 186, 216. *See also* inequality: racialized; racism

apartments. *See* high-rise apartments

Arab citizens, 28, 99, 102–3, 144, 166

Arthurson, Kathy, 71, 73–74, 75

Asian: immigrant communities in Canada, 99, 100, 102, 103, 107–8, 117; immigrant communities in Los Angeles, 177–78; international students in Melbourne, 2, 79. *See also* Chinese

assimilation, 6, 25, 29, 32, 34, 51, 52, 172, 203; geographies of, 61–62

asylum seekers, 16, 67, 134, 161–69, 212, 216, 220

atmospheres, 28; of care, 190–91; public transport, 137–40, 147–48, 154, 159, 160, 168–69

Australian Human Rights Commission, 146, 152–53

Bayat, Asef, 45–46

being together in difference as equals, 6–7, 16, 47–52; defining,

[251]

13, 33–34, 44, 207; toward a praxis of, 17, 208–20
belonging, 44, 56, 59, 70–71, 79, 89, 95, 147. *See also* home-making
Bissell, David, 137–38, 139
Black Canadians, 93, 99, 103, 110, 118
border controls, 6, 161, 162, 226n4
Border Patrol, 183–84
buses: being together on, 4, 16, 21, 133–34, 136–53, 168, 216, 219; drivers of, 97, 152, 155–56, 213; encounters at depots/stops for, 24, 96, 131, 133. *See also* accessibility; Immigrant Workers Freedom Ride; public transport
Butler, Judith, 32, 158

campaigns: public transport, 15–16, 133–34, 148–53, 161, 163–69, 209–10, 216, 220–21; workers' rights, 3, 5, 16, 108–9, 111–15, 129, 172, 189, 194–201, 218, 220. *See also individual campaigns*
care: developing an ethic of, 50, 191–92, 199; in difference as equals, 7, 34, 47, 50–51, 53, 93, 134, 159, 169, 205, 209–10; neighborly, 68–71, 89, 216; relationships of, 59, 188; spaces of, 5, 16, 48, 79, 126, 131, 189–92, 198, 201. *See also* caregiver(s); spaces: of refuge
caregiver(s), 95, 122–29, 131–32, 190, 211, 216, 218
care work, 121–29, 191, 209. *See also* care; caregiver(s)
Caribbean immigrants (Canada), 93, 111–12, 113–14, 131. *See also* hotel workers

Carlton estate (Melbourne). *See* public housing; social mix
central business district (CBD), 3, 53, 62, 76, 100, 104, 141
Centrelink (Australia), 162, 163
Chinese: Australians, 67, 85, 87–89, 145, 156; Canadians, 99, 100, 103, 109
choir (Toronto). *See under* hotel workers
citizenship, 46, 105, 158, 173, 184, 187; equality in, 36, 50, 104; rights, 171–72
class, 5, 8, 24, 27, 48, 126, 129, 143, 151, 160, 179; hierarchies, 26, 33, 109; middle, 28, 65, 67, 68, 85, 88
CLEAN Carwash Campaign (LA), 186, 189, 196
Coalition Against Wage Theft (LA), 197–98
codes of conduct, 17, 201, 213–14
collective, 42, 49, 50, 190, 206; action, 16, 164, 167, 173, 175, 197–98; bargaining, 105, 111; communities as, 33, 207; efforts, 46, 80, 171–72, 203, 209, 212; identities, 21, 137, 183; responsibility, 30, 139; spaces, 6, 58
colonialism. *See* setter colonialism
communities of color, 5, 179–80, 190
community, 34, 42, 44, 66, 162–63, 186, 189, 200; centers, 21, 36, 176, 217; collectivity, 33, 48, 59, 67, 71, 73, 207; groups/associations, 9, 15, 16, 57, 131, 180, 195, 205; organizing, 6, 16, 31, 134, 164, 167–68, 171–72, 179–80, 194, 198, 212, 216; unionism, 111–12

Index

253

conflict, 58, 175, 193, 196; difference and, 2, 7, 34, 50, 59, 71, 200, 208; ethno-racial, 5, 26, 144, 179
connectivity, 136, 140; local/extralocal, 10, 16, 172. *See also* mobile/mobilities
contact, 22, 35–37, 47, 51, 110–11, 119, 137, 159, 167–68, 200
contact hypothesis, 35–36, 165, 167, 200
copresence: passive, 23, 139; on public transport, 5, 22, 133, 136–37, 146, 169
counterpublics, 173–74, 176. *See also* publics
Cronulla riots (Sydney), 142, 144
customer courtesy campaign (Sydney), 149–51, 157, 213

D'Addario, Silvia, 95, 122, 125–27
Das Gupta, Tania, 118
democracy, 14; care in, 50, 191; and decision making, 188, 210, 215, 217; equality and, 39–41, 134, 219; negotiating/reworking, 51, 105, 173–75
demonstration. *See* protest
difference, 206–7; governing encounters with, 24–25; migrant encounters across, 14–15, 53–55, 57–59, 68–71, 75, 79–81, 83–84, 85, 88–91; politics of, 32, 39, 42, 44, 133, 135, 142, 147; social, 2, 8, 16, 26, 175, 189, 191, 195, 219. *See also under* negotiation
discrimination, 172, 174, 179, 199; non-, 189, 193; racial, 5, 152, 171, 180–81, 196–97, 226n5; sharing experiences of, 182–83, 194; workplace, 104, 106–7, 214

diversity (ethno-racial and cultural): celebrating, 6, 25, 27, 29, 51, 105, 111, 204; cities of, 1, 14, 28, 45, 62, 67, 141–42, 177, 203, 206, 214; encounters in, 21, 23–24, 59, 70, 138; geographies of, 143, 178; of workforces, 26, 95–96, 103–4, 107, 117, 120. *See also* religiosity: diversity and domestic workers, 94, 98, 121–27, 129–31, 199. *See also* caregiver(s)

Edgar, Barbara, 61–62
embodied: solidarity, 184, 218; urban encounter, 5, 9, 48–49, 158, 160, 175, 215
emotion(s): as care, 191–92, 199, 209; in encounter, 48–49, 89, 137, 148, 175; in making a home, 56, 70, 91; through sharing experiences, 182–83
emotional labor, 48, 121, 173, 191–92, 200, 209–10
encounter(s): everyday urban, 2, 6, 8, 23, 42–43, 44–47, 71, 176, 214; spatialities of, 10, 12, 15, 20–21, 24, 31–32, 34, 53, 58, 91, 96, 131, 150, 155, 158–59, 171–72, 181, 183, 218; temporalities of, 10, 12, 15, 21–24, 31–32, 53, 90–91, 94, 96, 131, 155, 158, 215–17, 218. *See also* interactions
encounters with difference: as multisited, 11, 20, 23, 24; ontology, epistemology, and methodology of, 8–12, 205–6; political potential of, 8, 10, 12, 15, 19, 32, 33–37, 46–47, 52, 207; rationalities shaping, 12, 19, 26–27, 30; stereotypes and,

31–32, 35–36, 93, 130, 171, 176, 215. *See also* inequality
English: learning, 3, 186; speaking/not speaking, 70, 109–10, 124–25, 151, 156
equality: claims, 121, 157, 173–74, 196, 198; enacting, 8, 13, 15–16, 50–52, 171, 173, 199–201, 203, 208, 211, 212–13, 216; politics of, 7, 12, 15, 33–44, 91, 93, 95, 107, 133–37, 147, 160, 167–70, 174, 176–77, 189, 191–92, 199, 206, 207–8, 212–14, 217–18; practice of, 6, 11, 39, 52, 153, 193, 205, 212, 219; social relations of, 59, 69, 71, 84. *See also* being together in difference as equals; everyday equalities; inequality
equals, 3, 6–8, 10, 13, 30, 32, 33–34, 36–37, 40–44, 47–52, 204, 207–20; in home-making, 14, 53–55, 61, 68, 74, 76, 79–81, 84, 88–91; new forms of being together as, 16–17, 185, 187–88, 201; on public transport, 16, 133–34, 141, 147, 159, 168, 172–74; workers as, 15, 93–96, 98–99, 105, 108, 114, 121–27, 130. *See also* codes of conduct
equal status, 36, 200
Ethnic Diversity Survey (Canada), 106
ethnographic: observation, 23–24; research, 7, 11, 13, 17, 20, 206
European immigrants (Canada), 99, 100, 102, 104, 106
everyday equalities, 2, 5, 11, 13, 17, 19, 33–34, 44, 52, 68, 71, 88, 130, 133, 137, 147; hard work of, 7, 16, 47–48, 53, 93, 134, 171, 173, 209–10; publics of, 172, 199–200

everyday urbanism, 7–13, 16, 19–20, 24, 30–32, 42–47, 49, 52, 205–8
exclusion, 45, 151, 174, 191; in housing, 57, 74; racialized, 2, 3, 94, 99, 107, 114, 146–47, 167, 171

Facebook. *See* social media
fear, 179; of difference, 1, 22, 35, 49, 175; spaces without, 158, 188
fêng shui, 88
festivals, 21, 45, 89, 105, 141
Filipino: Australians, 67; Canadians, 99, 103, 109, 123–25, 126–27, 129, 131
Forever 21 (LA), 194
Fraser, Nancy, 37–41, 42, 173–74, 176
Freedom Ride. *See* Immigrant Workers Freedom Ride
friendship, 47, 70, 85, 110, 117, 194; student migrants and, 3, 76, 78–80, 90

gardens, 72; household, 56, 60, 84–85, 87–88, 91, 210; private public, 73, 90, 219
gender, 8, 42, 110, 160, 190, 192, 193; identity, 32, 129, 151; inequality, 98, 102, 104–5, 146, 151, 226n5
gentrification, 27, 61, 63–64, 68, 72, 74, 76, 86, 100, 103
Gilroy, Paul, 1–2
global: ethnography, 10–11; forces, 57, 204–5
Goffman, Erving, 21, 23, 89, 137, 154
governance: flat, 188–89, 208; inclusive, 5, 16, 172, 176, 188, 192,

199, 201; institutional ideologies of, 1, 28, 31, 174, 206
Gow, Greg, 75
grassroots: activism, 21, 159; organizations, 6, 140, 180, 200
grocery store cashiers (Toronto), 15, 94–95, 115–20, 129–31, 211, 218

Hall, Stuart, 1–2, 37, 42, 51
heteronormativity, 54–55, 81–83, 90, 189, 209
heterosexuality. *See* sexuality
hierarchies: assimilation or status, 34, 52, 71, 74, 130, 134, 172; constructing, 8, 26, 30, 33, 55, 109, 111, 119, 139, 207, 213; destabilizing, 20, 31–32, 43, 108–9, 127, 147, 176, 192; in housing tenures, 90, 91; transcending, 6, 48, 188, 192, 201; at work, 15, 93, 95, 98, 108–9, 111, 114, 119, 127, 130. *See also* equality: politics of; inequality
high-rise apartments: private, 6, 57, 62, 66, 68, 76, 100; public, 63, 72
Hispanic community (LA), 177–79
home-making: encounters, 9, 14–15, 21, 53–59, 60, 69, 70–71, 79, 81, 94, 216; and heteronormativity, 54–55, 81–83, 90, 209; material forms of, 84–89, 91, 210, 217, 219; temporalities, 10, 14, 53, 89, 91, 94, 216. *See also* migrant home-making; neighborhood(s)
home-ownership, 14, 54, 56–58, 63, 64–65, 68, 71–75, 81–83, 90, 209. *See also* housing; renting a home
home rules, 59, 81, 91, 209

homophobia, 38, 172, 193, 201, 217
hope, 86, 221; for change, 35, 36, 37, 71, 165; for urban futures, 1, 5, 34, 52, 69, 207. *See also* being together in difference as equals
Hotel Employees and Restaurant Employees Union (HERE), 180
hotel workers (Toronto), 3, 15, 94–95, 107–11, 129, 208, 218; choir, 3, 5, 111–14, 130–31, 216. *See also* Unite-HERE
housing (Melbourne), 14, 29, 56, 61–68; private developers of, 6, 54, 66, 67, 71, 73, 75, 90; unequal access to, 57, 61. *See also* high-rise apartments; institutions: shaping housing encounters
Human Rights Code, Ontario, 104–5
Hurricane Katrina, 28

identity, 76, 105, 138, 151; attributes, 33, 129; belonging and, 59, 89, 95; ethno-racial, 85–88, 107, 127; as membership/collective, 21, 48, 183
#illridewithyou, 4, 160, 210. *See also* public transport
Immigrant Workers Freedom Ride (LA), 16, 172, 173, 176, 180–85, 217, 218
immigration, 33, 42; cities as centers of, 63, 67, 141, 171, 178, 203; defending, 204; policies/regimes, 6, 24, 25, 29, 62, 99–100, 131, 162, 206, 211; reform, 180, 187; services, 29, 109, 127; shared experiences of, 123, 126, 131, 183; status, 95, 123, 129, 184

256   *Index*

Immigration and Customs Enforcement, 183

inclusion, 39–40, 45, 48, 50, 69–70, 89, 147, 174; social, 34, 73–74, 75

income, 95, 116, 121; accessibility of public transport across, 142–43, 145, 162, 163; racialized inequality in, 94, 102, 103, 105, 107, 178; residential geographies by, 72–74, 75, 101–7

indigenous: dispossession, 2, 14, 140, 203; sovereignty, 25

Industrial Areas Foundation, 164

inequality, 16, 28, 31, 41, 50–51, 140, 146, 160, 171, 174–77, 193, 213; economic, 37, 38, 39; gender, 98, 102, 104–5, 146, 151, 226n5; in housing, 14, 57, 59, 61, 71, 74, 91; racialized, 3, 6–7, 13, 19, 25–26, 32, 33, 43–44, 47, 50, 52, 84, 105, 133, 136, 151, 161, 192, 207, 220; spatial, 134–35, 191, 218; urban, 1–2, 5, 8, 24, 34, 52, 204, 219; in work and income, 93–94, 98–99, 102–3, 107, 111, 115, 125, 178, 216. *See also* hierarchies; neoliberalism

infrastructure: institutional, 50, 54, 59, 171, 188, 199, 201, 212; organizational, 7, 17, 30, 167, 169, 185, 198, 211, 212–13; of publicization, 169–70; spatialities and material, 217, 218; transport/mobility, 15, 63, 133–35, 136–40, 142–47, 154, 160, 168–69, 218

injustice, 37, 39, 42, 50, 172, 176, 199, 213, 216, 217

institutions, 8, 39–40, 169, 179, 204; constructing social difference, 35, 42, 139, 147, 191–92; inclusive, 130, 171–72, 188, 191, 198–99, 201; interventions of, 147, 161, 208; mediating encounters with difference, 8, 9, 12, 19, 24–31, 43–44, 46–47, 49–52, 132, 134, 206–7; regulating work encounters, 93–98, 100, 105–6, 114, 120, 129; shaping housing encounters, 14, 56–57, 60, 68, 71–75, 77, 80–81, 90–91, 212. *See also* governance; hierarchies; neoconservatism; neoliberalism; state, the

Instituto de Educacion Popular del Sur de California (IDEPSCA), 189

interactions, 154, 177, 183, 198–99, 217; with difference, 1, 9, 15, 35, 48, 208; focused/unfocused, 22–23, 46, 89, 96, 137, 216; in home-making, 53–56, 59–61, 68–69, 71–72, 81; as limited, 15, 27, 49, 111, 119–21, 130–31, 211; urban, 11, 31, 19, 21, 44, 137–39, 147, 148, 219; among workers, 93–98, 107, 115, 117, 122–23, 218. *See also* encounter(s)

Intercede: Toronto Organization for Domestic Workers' Rights, 129

Italian: Australians, 54, 58, 63, 81–88, 90–91, 209, 210, 214; Canadians, 117, 118

IWFR. *See* Immigrant Workers Freedom Ride

Jacobs, Jane M., 56, 60

Johns, Amelia, 158

justice. *See* social justice

Justice for Janitors (US), 108, 180

Index

King, Rodney, 5, 179, 180
Korean community (LA), 103, 177–78, 186–87
Korean Immigrant Workers Alliance (KIWA), 186, 188

labor, 21, 105, 122, 117, 187; of creating equality, 47–48, 51, 169, 221; day, 193, 195; forces, 100, 104, 115; markets, 94, 97, 132, 140, 180; movement/unions, 172, 180, 195–96, 198–99; processes, 94–96, 115, 120–21, 130, 211. *See also* caregiver(s); emotional labor; hotel workers; political labor; unions
Labour Relations Act (Canada), 105
La Migra. *See* Border Patrol
Latin Americans (Toronto), 99, 103
Latinos (LA), 175, 177–78, 180–81, 186
learning: from each other, 12, 59, 71, 84, 172, 185, 209–10; to live as equals, 17, 34, 47, 51, 53, 176, 200; to negotiate differences, 49, 93, 141, 188, 193–94, 197; spaces of, 5, 16, 192, 201, 218
Lefebvre, Henri, 43
Lentin, Alana, 160–61
Levin, Iris, 54, 55, 71, 84–88
libraries, public, 21, 22, 50, 55, 57
live-in caregiver(s). *See* caregiver(s)
Lobo, Michele, 54, 59, 69–71, 91
local government, 60, 80–81, 105, 204, 211; celebrating diversity, 29, 105, 141; resisting national policies, 29, 211
Los Angeles, 5, 13–14, 28–29, 52, 204, 219–20; urban multi-

culture, 6, 171, 177–80. *See also* Against Wage Theft; Immigrant Workers Freedom Ride; minimum wage, $15

Massey, Doreen, 9, 21
McCosker, Anthony, 158
McDowell, Linda, 107
McFarlane, Colin, 49, 154
media, 169, 205; interventions on public transport, 147–53, 157–59, 167–68; remediation of, 4, 155–58, 160, 209; representations, 6, 22, 46, 138, 160, 164–65, 183; social, 5, 16, 133, 154–55, 216. *See also* social media
Melbourne, 2–3, 13–14, 28–29, 52, 204, 219–20; Dandenong, 54, 58–59, 67–71, 89, 171, 214, 216; urban multiculture, 60–68
Merrifield, Andy, 43
micro-publics, 21, 46, 114, 158
migrant home-making (Melbourne), 60–68, 90–91; in diverse neighborhoods, 68–71; social relations of, 54, 58, 63, 209, 210, 214; of students in apartments, 2–3, 6, 54, 62, 68, 76–81, 209, 219; in suburban streetscapes, 55, 81–89
migrants/immigrants: host communities and, 21, 22, 26, 29, 36, 49, 144, 175; housing/home pathways, 14–15, 53–55, 58–71, 76–91, 143, 209, 210, 214, 217; and mobility, 135, 142, 161, 166; organizing, 108, 172, 177, 179–85, 186, 212; racism against, 1, 6–7, 26–28, 171, 179, 183, 214; undocumented, 135,

182, 183, 184, 186, 204, 211;
urban destinations for, 2, 61,
67, 99–101, 141, 171, 177–78;
in workplaces, 93, 98, 99–101,
106–14, 118, 122–23, 131, 180,
185
minimum wage, $15 (LA), 5, 172,
180, 194–95, 197, 198–99, 200
minorities: racialized, 25, 27–28,
73, 93, 98–100, 171, 174, 186,
200, 214, 223n4; visible, 139,
146, 151
mobile/mobilities: classrooms,
181, 217; geographies of connectivity and, 16, 135, 140, 173,
176, 199; media, 16, 133, 147,
153–55, 169; sites of copresence, 133, 136, 144
Mobility with Dignity (Sydney),
166–68
Molotch, Harvey, 138, 218
Morihovitis, Ekaterina, 95, 115,
117–18
multiculturalism, 1, 21, 25–26, 27,
31, 35, 51, 203
multicultures, urban, 1–2, 12–15,
17, 20, 30–31, 141–42, 220;
based on solidarity, 168, 171,
173; difference in, 8, 10, 26, 47,
49, 52, 59, 99, 107, 138, 141,
169; encounter in, 37, 96, 98,
133, 206; equality in, 7, 42, 44,
134–35, 137, 167, 203, 207, 208;
politics of, 10, 133, 137, 144,
169; racism and, 149, 153
multiracial publics, 16, 172–73,
176, 189
Muslim community: violence
against, 4, 27–28, 146, 204

Neal, Sarah, 47, 49
negotiation: of difference, 5, 8,

12, 15, 16, 34, 48, 51, 55, 59,
81–84, 88–89, 91, 124, 130, 138,
172, 175, 185, 188–89, 191–97,
199–200, 205, 209, 214, 218;
working conditions, 118, 119,
124, 130, 210. *See also* democracy: negotiating/reworking
neighborhood(s): diverse, 26, 88,
103, 178; encounter in, 9, 21,
31, 36, 48, 50; home at the scale
of, 34, 53, 54, 55–56, 57, 59–60,
68–71, 80, 85, 89; networks,
44–45, 68; segregated, 102. *See
also* home-making
neoconservatism, 26–29, 30, 31,
172
neoliberalism, 3, 11, 26–27, 28–31,
64, 95, 102, 172, 174, 204
networks, 6, 60; intralocal and
extralocal, 173, 176, 197–98,
199; of media devices, 154, 157;
of organizers, 5, 164, 199–200,
210, 217; passive, 45–46; social,
3, 4, 27, 44, 80, 110; transport,
16, 133, 135, 137, 139–40,
142–44, 146–51, 157, 160, 163,
168–69

Occupy movement, 158
Ocejo, Richard, 137, 139
oppression, 34, 40, 42, 104, 174,
183, 194, 211; forms of, 10, 33,
37, 38, 47, 191; political interventions in, 20, 32, 33–34, 44
Other, the, 35, 51, 174, 185, 193–94,
200, 209, 215, 218

Philippine Women Centre
(Toronto), 129
Pilipino Worker Center (LA), 198
place. *See individual cities*
police/policing, 6, 29, 187, 207,

208, 218, 219; national immigration, 211; order, 41, 50, 214–15; public transport, 24, 147, 150, 152, 169; and racism, 105, 139, 179–80, 183

political labor, 6, 16. *See also* everyday equalities: hard work of politics, 10, 43–47, 155, 180, 219–20; of difference, 2, 5, 32, 37–42, 133, 135, 142, 147; encounter in, 14–15, 22, 37, 48, 96, 98, 133, 154, 167–68, 206, 215; of equality, 12, 32, 36, 37–42, 71, 91, 93, 95, 107, 133–37, 147, 160, 167–70, 174, 176–77, 189, 191–92, 199, 203, 206, 207–8, 212–14, 217–18

poverty, 72, 88, 103, 162

power: differentials at work, 93, 98, 105, 111, 112, 121, 123–25, 130; relations, 31, 36, 43, 46, 48, 174, 200, 207; transcending/challenging, 176, 198, 201, 216

prejudice, 49, 161, 175, 192–93, 185; breaking down, 5, 31, 35, 49, 167, 171, 176, 200; entrenching, 35–36, 49, 130, 215. *See also* stereotypes

protest, 6, 72, 128, 197, 204. *See also* activism; campaigns

public housing, 63–66, 67, 71; in Carlton, Melbourne, 14, 54, 57, 72–75, 219

publics, 9, 13, 23, 42, 52, 173–75, 191, 205–6, 217, 221; micro-, 21, 46, 114, 158; multiple spatialities in, 16, 172–73, 176; progressive, 171, 172, 189, 194, 199–200

public space, 79, 134, 176, 200, 206; encounters in, 9, 20–21, 25, 45–46, 70–71; political ex-

pression in, 142, 147, 176, 217; regulating, 73, 74–75

public transport, 4–5, 9, 16, 21, 219; fleeting encounters on, 8, 10, 15, 22–23, 89, 134, 169, 216; infrastructure, 133–35, 136–37, 140, 141–49, 105, 161, 167–70, 218; racism on, 139, 144, 146, 154, 156, 156–57, 159–60, 209–10, 213; regulating/policing, 24, 147–53, 157, 213. *See also* buses; trains

Pulido, Laura, 175, 179, 194, 196

Pulvirenti, Mariastella, 54, 63, 81–83

quiet encroachment of the ordinary, 46

racial profiling, 27, 139

racism, 20, 49, 50, 118, 142, 144, 175, 179–80, 183, 186, 203; addressing, 5, 35, 114, 167, 168–69, 172, 181, 192–93, 201, 213–14, 217; documenting, 16, 133, 155–60, 209; everyday, 3, 15–16, 33, 105, 134, 139, 146–49, 151–55, 160–61, 210; against immigrants, 1, 6, 7, 22, 26–28, 171, 204. *See also* antiracism; inequality: racialized

Racism—It Stops with Me (Sydney), 152–53

Raise the Wage, 172, 195, 199, 220

Rancière, Jacques, 32, 40–42, 44, 108, 174, 175, 177, 212, 218; politics and policing, 41, 50, 214–15

recognition, 23, 50, 160, 215; claims for, 196–97; of difference, 39, 174, 191

refugee(s), 59, 63, 64–65, 73, 75, 90, 162, 211; advocacy with,

164–65, 166, 205, 216; services, 63, 67, 163

religion, 8, 33, 43, 94, 106, 151, 182, 203

religiosity: in communities, 22, 80, 82, 126, 166; diversity and, 4, 14, 26, 47, 144, 208; in institutions, 164, 165, 169, 172, 213; intolerance of, 1, 5, 27, 175, 192–93, 201, 214; minorities and, 146, 151; superiority (ideologies of), 33, 37

renting a home, 54, 57–58, 63–66, 71–75, 81–82. *See also* housing

Riders (LA). *See* Immigrant Workers Freedom Ride

room attendants. *See* hotel workers

scale(s): of enacting equality, 188, 200, 211, 215, 220; of governance, 19, 24–25, 29–30, 162, 209; spatial (home/neighborhood), 53, 54, 55, 59–60, 68, 71, 85, 89; up, 35–36, 47, 196, 220; of urban encounter, 11, 24, 61, 138, 141, 147, 161

Service Employees International Union, 180

settler colonialism, 1–2, 10–11, 13–14, 25, 42, 93, 99, 140–41, 203

sexism, 5, 38, 50, 172, 175, 192–93, 201, 217

sexuality, 8, 42, 151; hetero-, 54–55, 81–84, 90, 91, 209; minority/queer, 83, 91, 173–74, 189, 193, 214

shopping malls, 3, 21, 76, 77–79, 90, 209

Simmel, Georg, 136

Smith, Susan, 55, 56, 59–60, 75, 81, 90

social cohesion, 34, 51, 207

social justice, 7, 38–40, 108, 151, 172, 174, 180, 193, 194, 197, 201, 207; redistribution, 39, 191. *See also* equality; injustice

social media, 4–5, 138, 169, 205, 216; documenting racism, 5, 16, 133, 155–60, 171, 209

social mix, 54, 57, 71–72, 74–75, 89–90. *See also* housing

solidarity, 43; absence of, 118, 123; building, 130, 158, 181, 183; creating change, 132, 168, 184, 198, 218, 220; across difference, 15, 75, 185, 194, 195. *See also* counterpublics; equality

spaces: of care, 5, 16, 48, 126, 131, 189–92, 198, 201; communal, 58, 76–77, 79–80, 90, 209; of encounter, 21, 36, 171–72, 181, 188; learning, 5, 16, 192, 201, 218; of publicity, 16, 45, 166, 194, 217, 225n13; of refuge, 5, 58, 131–32, 176, 185, 188, 194; quasi-sovereign, 16, 173, 199; solidarity, 181–85, 198–99, 218

spatiality: in creation of publics, 16, 171, 172–73, 176; of encounter, 10, 12, 15, 25, 31–32, 158–59, 161; of homes and housing, 53–54, 56, 58, 61–63, 68–69, 72, 91; of (in)equalities, 7, 12, 17, 40–41, 52, 134, 172, 177, 191, 197, 207, 217–18; 220; of mobility, 181, 183, 150, 154–55, 218; urban everyday, 11, 19, 20–24, 34; of urban multicultures, 2, 13–14; of work, 15, 96, 103, 115, 131, 194. *See also* public space; scale(s)

Index

261

state, the: active engagement with, 172, 175, 184, 194, 212, 220; and housing, 14, 54, 57, 63–66, 67, 71–75, 76, 80, 90, 219; multiple geographic scales of, 19, 25, 29, 50; non-, 15, 30–31, 50; policy/regulatory frameworks, 24–31, 35, 51, 141–42, 204, 211; regulation, 93, 96–98, 105, 114; transport and, 24, 143, 148, 157, 161, 169, 213; violence and surveillance, 5, 176, 179, 183. *See also* hierarchies; local government

stereotypes, 49, 71, 192; destabilizing/reinforcing, 31–32, 35–36, 93, 108, 130, 171, 176, 215; racialized, 35, 97, 110, 118, 124, 146, 151, 175, 214; talking about, 5, 192–93

storytelling, 165, 181–83, 185

strangers, 14, 42, 137, 169, 205, 211, 215, 218; being together of, 1–2, 7, 20, 22, 23, 31, 43, 45, 48, 137, 139, 168–69

students. *See under* Asian; friendship; migrant home-making

surveillance, 157, 176, 217

Sydney, 3–4, 13–14, 28–29, 52, 204, 219–20; urban multiculture, 140–47; Western, 75, 141–42, 143, 144, 164. *See also* #illridewithyou; Racism–It Stops with Me; This Bus Is For Everyone

Sydney Alliance, 164–68, 209, 212, 216, 220

temporality: of encounter, 8, 10, 12, 15, 32, 91, 215–17, 218; of equalities, 6–7, 12, 17, 33, 40–41, 177, 197, 207; of

home-making, 10, 14, 53, 59, 61, 89, 90–91, 94, 216; of mobility, 147, 153, 155, 158, 161, 167, 181, 183; urban everyday, 19, 21–24, 31; of urban multicultures, 2, 13–14; of workplace encounters, 15, 94, 96, 131, 216

terrorism, 1, 4, 183

This Bus Is for Everyone (Sydney), 152, 216

throwntogetherness, 9, 13, 219

time-space, 2, 10, 14, 33, 147, 153

togetherness, 42, 50, 155, 169; across difference, 5, 44, 88, 134

tolerance, 25, 34, 37, 51, 207

Tonnelat, Stéphane, 137, 139

Toronto, 3, 13–14, 28–29, 52, 204, 219–20; urban multiculture, 99–103, 105–7

trains, 24, 145, 153, 156, 157, 161, 209–10, 213; enabling mobility, 135, 136, 140, 143–45, 159–60, 218; encounters on, 4–5, 9, 16, 23, 133–34, 137, 139, 146–47, 148, 154, 167, 216, 219–20. *See also* public transport

Transdev (Sydney), 151–53, 169, 216

Transport for NSW, 148–49, 150, 152–53

Transport Workers' Union, 152

transversality, 48, 141

trauma, 163, 190

Tronto, Joan, 50, 191

trust, 12, 48, 197, 200, 215, 216; amongst neighbors, 70, 107, 218; amongst Riders, 185

Tufts, Steve, 95, 108–12

Twitter. *See* social media

unemployment, 105, 162, 197, 198

unions, 6, 15, 119–20, 166, 169, 176, 188, 195, 198; accom-

modating difference, 208, 210; campaigns of, 3, 95, 108, 111–14, 130, 131, 140, 152; in coalitions, 164, 165, 172, 180, 195, 212, 213; and immigrant workers, 180, 185; regulation of workplaces, 97, 104–5
United Food and Commercial Workers, 119
Unite-HERE (Toronto), 108, 111, 119, 129, 130, 171
urban everyday, 9, 11, 19, 24, 31, 32, 49, 52, 206, 208. *See also* everyday urbanism
Urry, John, 136, 140

Valentine, Gill, 35–36, 215
Vincent, Carol, 47, 49
violence: on public transport, 16, 133, 134, 139, 147, 152, 155–56, 158, 160; racial, 1, 5, 6, 14, 142, 171, 179, 204, 215. *See also* racism
visa: bridging (Australia), 162–63, 167; in Canada, 100, 122, 125

Watts Labor Community Action Committee (LA), 194
Watts Riots (LA), 5, 179
White Australia policy, 141
whiteness, 91, 142, 144, 172, 184; and encounter with difference, 21, 22, 35, 49, 69, 106, 142, 175; and nationalism, 99, 141, 203, 211. *See also* racism; settler colonialism
Wills, Jane, 107, 108
Wilson, Helen F., 138, 165, 206
Wise, Amanda, 21, 48, 49, 96, 97, 130

women: alternative spaces for, 5, 58, 112–14, 126–28, 131–32, 173–74; discrimination against, 182; and leadership, 5, 16, 173, 189–91, 198; stereotyping, 107–8, 110, 146, 191; vulnerability of, 28, 63, 98, 122, 129, 132, 205; in the workplace, 98, 102, 109–10, 115–19, 122. *See also* care; caregivers; gender
worker centers (LA): campaigns, 194–99, 220; enacting equality, 212–13, 214–15, 217, 218, 219; as progressive spaces, 16, 172–73, 185–89, 192–94, 199, 201, 208–9, 210; as spaces of care, 189–92, 214; as spaces of refuge, 5, 176, 188, 194. *See also* campaigns; care
working conditions: barriers to changing, 118, 119, 120, 122; campaigns to improve, 3, 5, 15, 16, 108, 129, 130–31, 172, 180, 186, 194–200, 210–11, 220; exploitative, 95, 98, 102, 116, 117, 183; regulation of , 15, 93–94, 96–98, 104–6, 114, 121, 129, 132, 207. *See also* inequality; multiracial publics; solidarity; state, the; unions
workplaces, 3, 15, 25, 45, 93–99, 102–32, 207, 210, 211, 213–14, 216, 217, 218, 219, 220. *See also* encounter(s)

Young, Iris Marion, 38–41, 42, 44–46, 48, 191
Yuval-Davis, Nira, 48, 49

Ruth Fincher is distinguished professor emerita of geography at the University of Melbourne.

Kurt Iveson is associate professor of urban geography at the University of Sydney.

Helga Leitner is distinguished professor of geography at the University of California, Los Angeles.

Valerie Preston is professor of geography at York University and director of York Research Data Centre.